Virgilio Vercelloni

European Gardens
an historical atlas

RIZZOLI
NEW YORK

First published in the United States of America in 1990 by
RIZZOLI INTERNATIONAL PUBLICATIONS, INC.
300 Park Avenue South, New York NY 10010

Copyright © 1990
Editoriale Jaca Book spa, Milan, Italy

Original title
Atlante Storico dell'Idea di Giardino Europeo

Translated from the Italian by
Vanessa Vesey

Library of Congress Cataloging-in-Publication Data

Vercelloni, Virgilio.
  [Atlas giardini, English]
  European gardens: an historical atlas / Virgilio Vercelloni.
      p.   cm.
  Translation of: Atlas giardini.
  ISBN 0-8478-1294-4
  1. Gardens—Europe—Design—History. 2. Gardens, European—
—History. 3. Gardens—Europe—Pictorial work. 4. Gardens,
European—Pictorial work.   I. Title.
  SB466.E9V4713   90-53155
  712.094—dc20   CIP

Printed and bound in Italy
by Amilcare Pizzi, S.P.A. - Arti Grafiche, Cinisello B. (Milano)

Table of contents

Foreword

Once I had accepted the thesis of developing a historical atlas on the concept of the European garden, the choice of how to draw relationships between the images and text was multifaceted. A study of history involves the construction of infinite interdependences of and incursions into consolidated disciplines, whereas a garden, from an academic point of view, is a fluctuating concept, a borderland or frontier that changes with time. Gardens are therefore a specific phenomenon of a complex culture that can only be governed by a logic of open systems that are always mutually dependent, and certainly not within the preconceived limits of any closed system. A historical atlas of the idea of the garden seemed to me to be the most effective instrument to prove this point. Here its emphasis is the history of this idea as it applies in Europe. This book, therefore, is not a mere history of the European garden.

Of all man-made constructions, the garden is, by nature, one of the most capable of expressing symbolic forms. The widespread exoticism evident in gardens is not dealt with here apart from a few brief comments. This specific aspect has been left to other iconological studies. Here, deliberately, the actual garden tells its own story, narrating the roundabout development of the idea that sustains it. It may seem odd, for example, that an alchemic image was studied not to reveal its complex mysteries but to read it as it was actually presented. I felt, however, that this was in line with the purpose of the book. The illustrations are contemporary with the subjects of each page because I am convinced this makes them more eloquent and meaningful. For example, a photograph prepared and taken by a gardener to document a work of his done in the twenties, possesses a unity that a photographer today could never achieve—at the most he could give his own present-day interpretation of that garden. This is true, logically, of any other kind of illustration. Therefore the criterion for selecting the one hundred and ninety-two pictures in this book (which could be substituted by infinite numbers of other ones) is based, first and foremost, on the need to find semantically complete illustrations related to the historical idea of the European garden, and not on the idea of forming, with these pictures alone, an exhaustive account and documentation of the history of the European garden.

By the way, passionate devotion to gardens means (as the book reveals and we hope will be true for all) living to a ripe old age. Humphry Repton lived until he was 83 years old, William Robinson to 97 and Gertrude Jekyll to 89.

During the course of writing this book, I discussed many of subjects with my friends Franco Giorgetta and Ippolito Pizzetti. Pizzetti is one of these few non-English gardeners and landscape gardeners who works in Italy. He patiently read the manuscript of this book and gave me considerable precious advice for its final draft. I was given invaluable organizational assistance from Paola Gallo especially concerning the infinito bibliographical congruities, while Riccardo Bianchi gave it an erudite revision. My young publisher friend, Sante Bagnoli, has chosen to share with me the adventure of this new atlas.

The short individual pieces which constitute, with their relative pictures, the book, contain bibliographical references in the text or notes useful for researching a significant moment of the historical idea of the garden. Other books of a more general nature but necessary to that history have been listed in a further bibliography. It is certainly not complete, but offers readers a useful list that complements the one in the text. The first editions of the books have been quoted as they are fundamental for a history of ideas, and also because I am sure that many of these classic works, translated into various languages, are available today both in reproductions of the original editions or in new ones.

Nature changes itself and its landscape over time. These two reconstructions of Linguadoc elaborated by Josette Renault-Miskovsky in 1972 show three landscapes during the Würm II, about one hundred thousand years ago. Ever since prehistory, man has modified the planet's botanical scenery with his presence and his various activities. Today the plant world has been totally subjected to human modifications.

The origins of the human landscape go back to prehistorical times, when man began to devastate the environment by provoking forest fires while hunting and deserts due to the intensive grazing of domestic animals. He set in motion a process of transformation which was marked later on by the transport and cultivation of exotic plants. This altered the whole European environment, its forests, woods, agriculture, and gardens. In an essay published in 1940, Lucien Febvre, one of the masters of the *Annales* school in Paris, wrote: "Imagine old Herodotus sailing around the Eastern Mediterranean again today. He would be amazed! These golden fruits, on these dark green trees, which are said to be 'characteristic of the whole Mediterranean area,' orange, lemon, mandarin trees: he doesn't re-

member ever having seen them in his life... By Jove! They are from the Far East, imported by the Arabs. These weird plants with unusual shapes, spines, flowering lances, strange names, cactus, agave, aloe; how they have spread! He had never seen them at all in his lifetime... By Jove! They are American. These great trees with pale leaves, and yet they have a Greek name, eucalyptus: he's never seen anything like them, in the known world, the Father of History... By Jove! They are Australian. And these palms? Herodotus had seen them in the past, in oases, in Egypt; but never on the European shores of the Mediterranean? Never, nor the cypresses, these Persians." But in the agricultural world these exotic botanical surprises would have been even more numerous.

PLATE 1

This Sumerian drawing is an accurate picture of a garden, with a tree planted in the center of a triangular enclosure. The idea of a garden as a place for cultivating plants, not to feed men or animals but for aesthetic requirements, for visual pleasure and aromas, came to Europe from the Middle East. The early writings of European peoples recount the legends of the wonderful gardens of the East.

The Hanging Gardens of Babylon, it is said, were the reconstruction of the environment of the native land of Nebuchadnezzar's wife, who was homesick for the countryside of Media. Those gardens, which are believed to have existed in the seventh century B.C., were described with all their charms in numerous texts from the fourth century B.C. onwards. It was a legend that undoubtedly had deep roots in the history of that country. In the British Museum, for example, there is a clay tablet inscribed with cuneiform characters coming from Babylonia, which lists the plants cultivated in the garden of Merodach Baladan. The tablet has been dated as belonging to the eighth century B.C., but it is believed to be a copy of a much older text. A bas-relief of the seventh century shows that King Ashurbanipal planted cedars and boxwood "the like of which none of the kings my forefathers ever planted." The *idea of the garden*, obviously, was conceived and developed in those societies that first could allow themselves a form of consumption which was not just for survival. In these societies a part of the income of the governing class could be used for embellishing the city, its temples, and great houses with gardens. When this was going on, the European peoples —the Greeks, the Italic tribes, the Celts and Teutons—had moved beyond simple agrarian utility. There was a religious tie: a glade in the forest formed the *sacred wood*, the symbol of the primeval relationship between man and nature. The interconnections between the Greek classical world and the Middle East brought the *idea of the garden* to Europe, which, with the advent of the Hellenistic Age, then started in a new historical direction.

PLATE 2

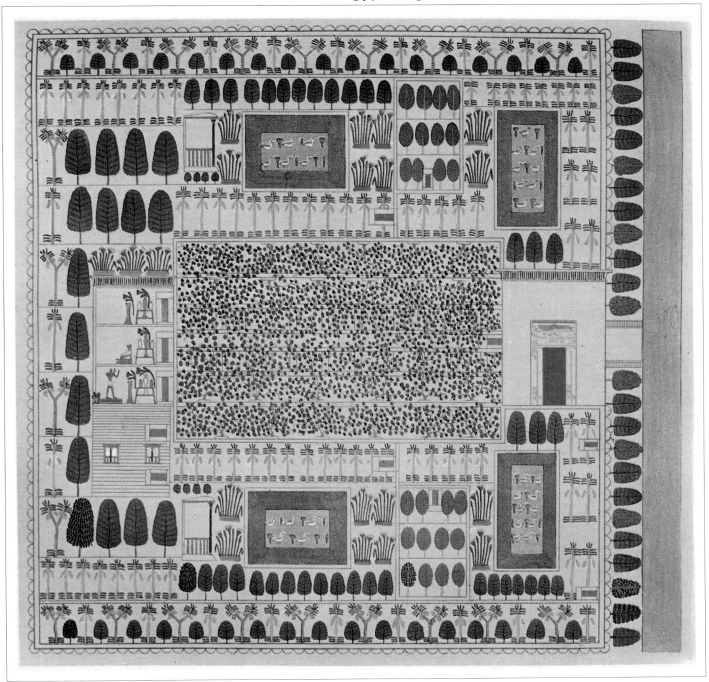

Thirty-five centuries ago in Egypt, a high official had his future tomb in Thebes frescoed to convey the images and significance of his garden. It has become a document illustrating how the *modern garden* was part of the human environment in that society. Hellenistic culture was grafted on to this tradition as on to other oriental ones, and offered the whole of Europe a specific *idea of the garden* based on the principle of the aesthetic domestication of nature for man's own pleasure.

This extraordinary painting showing the ordered rows of tall trees, orchards, palm groves, and the central vineyard, as well as pools with birds and the architectural pavilions, includes all the elements comprising gardens of all times, and, perhaps, in every civilization. No *idea of progress* can be applied at this historical point in time because the anthropological and cultural acme has already been reached. Today we can relive the pleasure of the owner as he walked in his ancient garden. It is a pleasure that we, too, feel in our own gardens, fully conscious of our privilege in comparison to those who do not have this possibility. This model held true for all future gardens, even for those of the Persian kings after the occupation of Egypt in the sixth century B.C., and for the European garden in particular, which assimilated it as a kind of achievement of humanity, a precious gift to be conserved and copied. Obviously it was not a formal model. Here the geometrical organization of nature (for systematic as well as aesthetic-conceptual ends) contrasts, humanistically, with both the practical management of the agricultural landscape and with the natural plant scenery. Cultivation and the selective arrangement of nature demonstrate perfect programmatic domination by man. This will be the relationship between man and nature in his garden for thousands of years. It will be the founding principle for every European garden from classical antiquity up to the eighteenth-century crisis of the French formal garden, during which European man learned that he could develop a relationship with an individual plant, as had always been the case in the Far East, rather than just with its serial repetition.

PLATE 3

There is no word either in Greek or Latin for garden: the Greek term *kepos* and the Latin *hortus* mean the enclosure for protecting a cultivated plot. Concepts of enclosure for the special domestication of animals and cultivation of plants can be found in more general terms in early Indo-European languages, but not with reference to the *garden* taken semantically as a place of pleasure for its sight and scents.

The Corinthian capital shown here in a neoclassical drawing first appeared in about the fifth century B.C. With the petrification of its leaves, the acanthus became the first European architectural plant. At the end of the eighth century B.C., the Odyssey describes marvelous gardens which were *merely* very fertile and masterfully irrigated vegetable gardens, orchards, and vineyards. It was probably Alexandrian culture that brought the ancient idea of Egyptian and oriental gardens to Greece, and then from there to Rome and to the whole of Europe. When seventy wise Hebrews had to translate the biblical *gan'eden* into Greek in the third century B.C., they used the oldest neologism in that language, *paradeisos,* a term of Persian origin invented by Xenophon a century earlier to describe the large eastern gardens and parks he had seen during the Persian wars. The Stoics made ironical comments about those who followed the fashion in the third century B.C., imported from the new capitals of culture and taste, of creating oriental gardens in Greece. It was Theophrastus, Aristotle's successor at the Athens Academy, who wrote, sometime between the fourth and third century B.C., the first book *On the History of Plants* in nine volumes, and also the work called *The Causes of Plants,* earning himself the name *founder of botanical science* in European culture. *On Medicinal Matter,* the work written by Dioscorides, the military physician, was a contribution to this tradition. His herbal was the most famous book on European botany from the first century A.D. to the Renaissance. Botanical science, including its therapeutic uses, and the garden thus established a fertile and continuous relationship in Europe.

PLATE 4

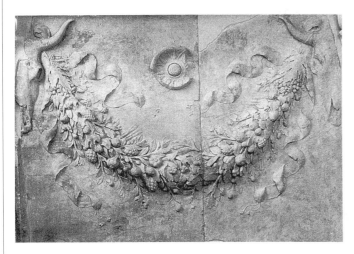

Greek and Roman garland makers formed a special, productive category dedicated to the cultivation of flowers and their twining together for the needs of diverse religious and secular festivals. A garland is a plant ornament, a kind of portable flower garden capable of embellishing both people and places. Sometimes it appears in a petrified form as an architectonic decorative theme. Various species of plants had symbolic meanings: oaks for strength, laurels for fame.

The festoon on the Ara Pacis Augustea, first century B.C., is a type of cornucopia, indicating every kind of abundance. The garland, a detail in Andrea Mantegna's painting of St. George, is the Renaissance version of a continuity in pictorial representation which has its roots in classical Rome. The drawing of cupids who wreathe garlands is a copy of a Pompeian fresco. Flowers had great significance in Rome and were the main feature of Hellenistic Roman gardens. The worship of Flora, the goddess of flowers and trees who governs all that blossoms, had its origins with Sabines but was soon absorbed by Hellenistic culture and spread to Rome and to the whole Roman world. At the same time there was a move from the worship of nature to the consumption, in aesthetic terms too, of the plant world, and a change in the relationship between man and nature from sanctuary in the sacred wood to cultivation of urban gardens. To illustrate the extent to which this was carried, Roman law regulated the problem of overshadowing proximity so that the planting of trees on roofs did not take the light away from neighboring buildings. It also referred to the construction of hothouses (*tepidaria*; the poet Martial wrote of "the little plot that never froze - that's always green even in January"). For the *otium* of citizens there were the public gardens near the *thermae* (Martial again wrote of "red paths decked with garlands of roses"), but the rich had large gardens in their suburban villas. The link with Hellenistic culture, with Alexandrian civilization, and with the eastern world was at the root of the *idea of the garden* in ancient Rome.

PLATE 5

This photograph illustrates the spectacular reconstruction in California of the Villa of the Papyri in Herculaneum, which was completed in 1974. The garden and huge peristyle are shown here. J. Paul Getty commissioned it as an expression of his cultural criticism of contemporary architecture. The geometrical organization of the oleanders, ivy, box hedges, laurels, myrtles, roses, and vine-clad pergolas forms the botanical scenery of this much-debated reconstruction of a Roman urban garden.

Next to the main peristyle is the herb garden for culinary and medicinal use, and the orchard with mint, dill, coriander, marjoram, sweet marjoram, camomile, thyme, fennel, garlic, and peas, and apple, pear, peach, fig, and citron trees. A kind of Disneylandish didacticism governed this reconstruction, which was, however, philological and based on very careful archaeological research. The scientific analysis of carbonized plant remains has made it possible to achieve a general reconstruction of the quality and quantity of the gardens of Pompeii and Herculaneum which, after J. Paul Getty's reconstruction, were amply confirmed by the research work of Wilhemina F. Jashemski. This scene is historically credible, as if it was a diorama capable of representing every environment of the past. The reconstruction of a historical garden is a debatable activity which needs more practical ex-

periments. Geoffrey Jellicoe has designed the reconstruction of all earthly paradises in a large garden comprehending the history of all gardens for the Moody Foundation at Galveston, Texas. From primordial forests with savage beasts to the Egyptian garden, from the Roman classical garden to the medieval, from the Islamic garden to the Mogul, from the Renaissance garden to the formal seventeenth-century, from the eighteenth-century English garden to the nineteenth-century one, from the Chinese garden to the Japanese, it is a crowded historical and cultural itinerary that visitors will assimilate while they travel on automatic boats along the waterway that winds through the large park.

Wilhelmina F. Jashemski, The Gardens of Pompeii, Herculaneum and the Villas Destroyed by Vesuvius, New York 1979; The J. Paul Getty Museum, Guide to the Villa and its Gardens, Malibu 1988; Geoffrey Jellicoe, The Landscape of Civilisation, Created for the Moody Historical Gardens, Northiam 1989.

PLATE 6

The Roman idea of the garden has been handed down to us by trompe l'oeil frescoes that create the illusion of the perspective of a garden on the walls of a room. These two details of frescoes show us the significance of those gardens. They were excessively pampered and enclosed gardens where the botanical cultivation of even exotic plants was undertaken for their pleasure to the eye and for their fragrance. The gardens are evidently the product of aesthetic values.

Above, there is the floral *cubiculum* of the *Casa del Frutteto* in Pompeii which offers a double illusion. The lower part of the wall is painted as if it was the exhaustive representation of a wall with trompe l'oeil frescoes picturing a garden. Inside the room, the viewer has the sensation of being inside an architectural treillage with precious urns on top of it and a niche containing a sculptured fountain. Tall trees can be seen behind, in the garden. But this wainscot, which is already self-sufficient in its representation and illusion, has been designed to be perceived as a simple decorative picture that simulates the balustrade of an elegant gallery, because above it there is a second illusory garden, more real than the first, with its trees caligraphically represented as if they were in an herbal,

lined up as they are with their extension of greenery on a black background. The detail of the garden room belonging to the Empress Livia, conserved in its complete original form in the Museo delle Terme in Rome, also offers information about the layout of Roman gardens. People in the room feel as if they are in a garden pavilion. The area dedicated to the garden is reverently limited by a small fence made of woven canes. There is a second decorative stone wall parallel to the first, which is sometimes extended to enclose a tall tree. A lawn with small flowers and herbs lies between the two. Beyond the second fence is the big garden with fruit trees, flowers, and tall trees inhabited by birds.

*Pliny the Elder, *Naturalis historia*; Lucius Iunius Columella, *De re rustica*.

PLATE 7

Hero of Alexandria was the very famous Hellenistic author of the works on pneumatics and automata. As a designer building extraordinary machines and scientist anticipating the steam engine, Hero invented amusing devices in gardens for the leisure time of Alexandrians. Elegant gardens in the cultural capital of the Mediterranean were enlivened by the cries of mechanical birds and the rustle of artificial leaves, almost as if nature itself was not enough to create wonder.

One of Hero's theorems is called "How to create the various songs of various birds"; another, "In places where a channel provides running water, how to build an animal, made of copper or any other material you desire, that roars continually: but when it is given a bowl full of water, it drinks it all in silence, and once finished, starts roaring again." The illustration comes from the first edition of the Italian translation of Hero's works, published in Ferrara in 1589. It describes the hydraulic mechanisms for moving automata (here, the scene of the dragon guarding the golden apples that hisses at Hercules, who is armed with a club). Hero was the disciple of Ctesibius, the Alexandrian founder of these studies (which are believed to have distant roots in Egyptian culture), and a contemporary of Philo, another inventor of mechanical devices. The enchantment of these inventions last-

ed for centuries; it conquered medieval Europe and the Renaissance, and the Arab world as well– so much so that automata, mechanical plants, and animals became the indispensable wonders of Islamic gardens, an implicit demonstration of the elegance of the gardens at that time and in those places. When Rome met with Greek culture, the latter had already elaborated a *classical* conception of its artistic history and its golden age at the time of Pericles. The Romans assimilated this conception but merged it with Hellenistic culture, which, on the other hand, in founding classic philology, had in fact promoted the *classic* conception. The history of the Roman idea of the garden followed a course laid down by these frames of reference.

Gli artifitiosi et curiosi moti spiritali di Herrone, tradotti da M. Gio Battista Aleotti, Ferrara 1589; Albert de Rochas, *La science des philosophes et l'art des thaumaturges dans l'antiquité,* Paris 1977; Paolo Portoghesi, *Infanzia delle macchine,* Bari 1981.

PLATE 8

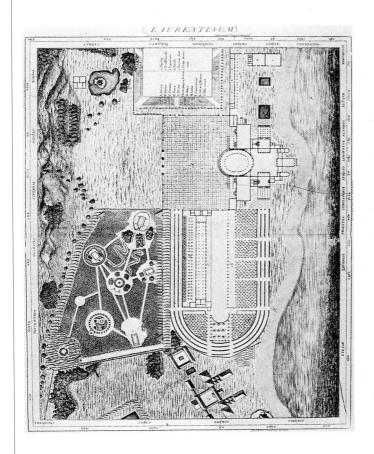

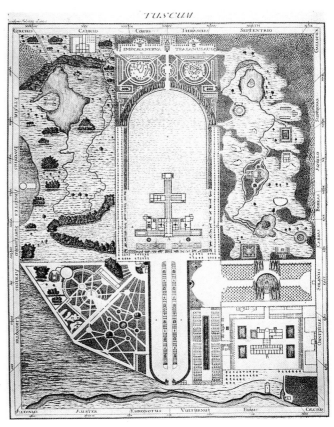

In the age of eighteenth-century revivals, history was always a question of accommodation. For Robert Castell, the English architect and archeologist who published *The Villas of the Ancients Illustrated* in London in 1728, reconstruction was not just a philological operation but the time for spreading the idea of a new eighteenth-century English garden with the instrumental backing of a filtered version of history.

Pliny the Younger's detailed description, in a letter to his friend Apollinaris, of the gardens of his two villas, at Tuscum in the Apennine foothills and at Laurentum by the sea near Ostia, gives us a fascinating literary account of the great Roman garden. It has also made an infinite series of essays possible on the *graphical reconstruction* of their layout. There are a total of twenty reconstructions of the villa at Laurentum, ranging from that by Vincenzo Scamozzi in 1615 to the most recent in the nineteenth century. Castell was the friend and associate of Richard Boyle, the third Earl of Burlington, the leading spirit behind English Neoclassicism in the first few decades of the century (the so-called Palladianism). Burlington's circle included the poet Alexander Pope, who renewed the idea of the garden, infec-ting the canons of the French formal garden with the new principles of asymmetry and the aesthetic reappraisal of natural plant scenery. These two engravings illustrate excellently the historical and cultural setting. The Roman garden is organized geometrically according to visual axes linked to the villas' architectural constructions, as Pliny's description of the villas prescribed. However, at the sides of these general layouts, in areas where the description could lead to diverse interpretations, the result is not a philological reconstruction but rather an example of the latest fashion in English gardens. Unknown and complex geometrical patterns weave poetic shapes, while the fundamental goal of all this confusion seems to be *natural design*.

*La Laurentine et l'invention de la ville romaine, Paris 1982.

PLATE 9

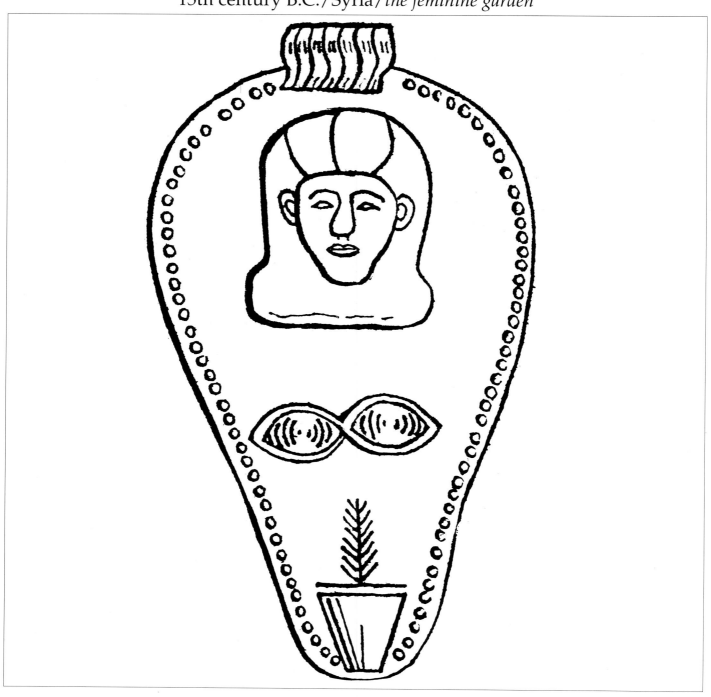

Right from the very first pictures, the plant world seems to be taken as a metaphor of life, and is very often expressed in terms of opposition between male and female. This is a drawing reconstructing an antique pear-shaped gold pendant (1 1/2" x 2 3/4") with a woman's head, stylized breasts and an urn containing a tree, the allegory of the female *pubes*, the womb of life, which symbolizes the relationship between fecundity and fertility.
Aphrodite, the goddess of love, had a garden at Lesbos.

The femininity, fecundity, fertility chain is to be found in all anthropological and cultural projects and is a part of the idea of the garden. The very sense of a biological product which takes root, grows, lives, and dies is strictly tied to the need of being carefully and lovingly cared for, a specifically feminine characteristic. In the garden, femininity is not just a question of fertilization and planting: care as growth occurs, cultivation, continual feeding, love, and tenderness are fundamental. This dimension is not always prevalent, or at least explicit, in the history of European gardens. Yet it is essential in the English figure of the gardener and his history, and it is also essential every time the idea of the garden encompasses the observation and respect of nature rather than the possession or domination of it. Therefore, the garden can never be a static or stable composition, because time is a fundamental component of its very essence. A garden of this kind could never be observed aesthetically as if it was a picture. In this garden man lives together with his plants, quite aware that it changes and is transformed over time, and that the possible aesthetics are of a biological nature, to be appreciated only by those who observe life with fond affection.

Da Ebla a Damasco, 10.000 anni di archeologia in Siria, catalog, Milan 1985; Massimo Venturi Ferriolo, *Eros e Afrodite. Alle origini dell'idea di giardino*, in AAVV, *Il giardino, idea natura realtà*, Milan 1987; Massimo Venturi Ferriolo, *Nel grembo della vita. Le origini dell'idea del giardino*, Milan 1989.

PLATE 10

In the masculine archetype, the concept of fertility is reduced to the instrument and moment of penetration. In this drawing from an alchemic source, which shows how death can give birth to new life (do not seek to extract the secret of philosophy from mercury because mercury draws the soul and the spirit from the flesh), the tree is phallic. The allegory announces that the relationship between man and nature has a generalized anthropological and cultural origin.

In the Middle Eastern and European tradition the relationship between man and nature is one of total domination. Man sows his grain in parallel furrows which will grow in straight lines like soldiers obeying their general. The benevolent relationship between man and plants, a reciprocally respectful friendship, is a specific characteristic of Asian farmers who work with the cuttings of individual plants, as ethnobotany teaches us. This relationship is alien to the history of European gardens at least up until the revolution of the eighteenth-century English landscape garden. In the Italian gardens of the past, the epistemological innovation of the idea of the garden—the orderly sequentiality of repeated trees, hedges clipped into geometrical shapes, orchards with regular plantings—was a continuation of the agricultural practice of dominating nature. And a masculine concept of the idea of fertilization can be inferred here: predictable and unchanging growth is planned so as not to leave any margin of independent variableness to nature. In general terms the planting of a tree has the meaning of a finished task: the tidy arrangement of that planting is man's putting the world in order, a world whose natural state he refuses to tolerate. We can infer from this that every symbolic and ritual, religious, or secular planting commemorating a fact or an event, right up to the widespread eighteenth-century custom of holidays for planting revolutionary liberty trees, contains this marked significance of the masculine will to govern, dominate, and transform nature.

*André Georges Haudricourt and Louis Hédin, L'Homme et les plantes cultivées, Paris 1943; Roger Cook, The Tree of Life, London 1974; Jacques Barrau and Ugo Fabietti, headword plant, in Enciclopedia, volume XIV, Turin 1981.

PLATE 11

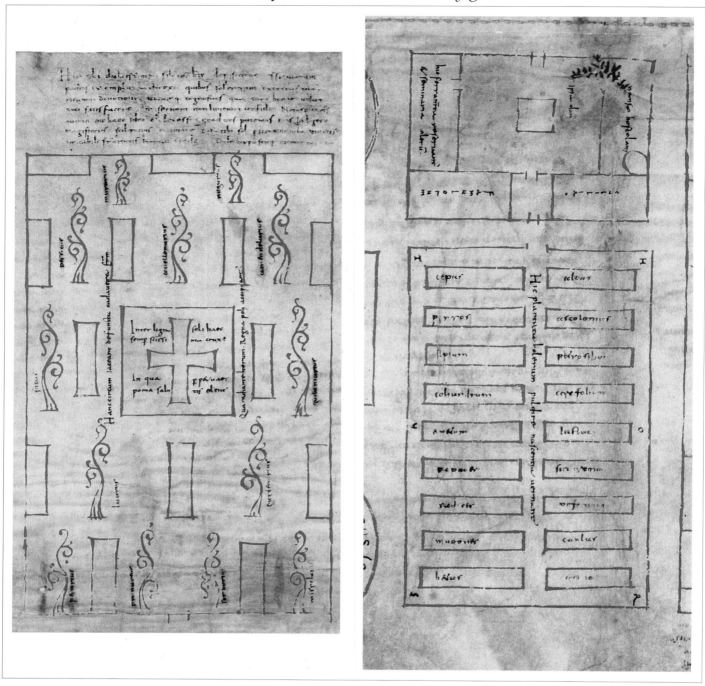

These extraordinary details of the plan of St. Gall's Abbey date back to the first few decades of the ninth century, but the picture is a copy of an even earlier document. It illustrates in minute detail the tiny medieval town that was the monastic order. With its exceptionally complex character due to the interdependence of all the parts, the monastery included three gardens: the kitchen garden, the orchard in the cemetry, shown here, and the physick garden for the cultivation of medicinal herbs.

From late antiquity to the time of this picture, there are only fleeting traces of the destiny of the European garden. Byzantium was the link between the ancient knowledge and refinement of Alexandrian culture, and Greek and Roman customs. This empire established different relations with the old and new East capable also of stimulating the formation of the new Europe. The classical works of Theophrastus, Pliny the Elder, Dioscorides, and Columella were treasured and copied in monastery libraries, thus carrying on a tradition of distant historical and cultural origins which was soon to be integrated both with Hebraic tradition and the new culture from the Islamic world. Kidney beans, garden cress, fenugreek, rosemary, mint, spearmint, sage, rue, water cress, cumin, and fennel, as well as roses and other

flowers were cultivated in the physick garden. The orchard, shown here on the left, was divided into thirteen arable plots, while another fourteen were left as the burial ground for the monks. Two rows of small beds in the kitchen garden contain, from the top left downwards, onions, leeks, celery, coriander, dill, opium poppies, radishes, poppies, beets, garlic, shallots, parsley, chervil, lettuces, cress, parsnips, cabbages, and fennel. The two illustrations also help to understand the arrangement of a medieval monastery garden and the concept of the landscape so eloquently expressed by the orchard that includes the cemetery as well.

*Margaret H. Thomson, *Textes grecs inédits relatifs aux plantes*, Paris 1955; Margaret H. Thomson, *Le jardin symbolique, texte grec tiré du Clarkianus XI*, Paris 1960; Lorna Price, *The Plan of St. Gall*, Berkeley, Los Angeles, London 1979.

PLATE 12

This is a diagram showing the complex layout of a typical medieval garden according to the analytical reconstruction made by Francesco Fariello. The flower beds (2) are inside the entrance; behind them there is a lawn with a fountain and pavilions (3). Other beds with herbs (6) are grouped with the ancient figure of the labyrinth (4) and with the bathing pavilion (5). The other areas comprise the orchard (Pr), the kitchen garden (V), the viridarium (Vr), and the fish pond (Ps).

The significance of water in medieval European gardens is one of exotic refinement, which was its semantic attribution at this time in Islamic gardens. The diagram illustrates this with the sequence formed by the central fountain covered by an architectural construction, the bathing pavilion, and the fish pond. According to the literature of that period, which had strong ties with the Roman classics, the *pomarium* was the orchard where trees were planted in a quincuncial pattern and divided up according to their species. The *viridarium* was the place where evergreens grew (pine trees, cypresses, firs, laurels, and olive trees). It was the best place for protection from the heat of summer and the birds. The kitchen garden or herb meadow was the space dedicated to the cultivation and production of medicinal, culinary,

and essential herbs: mint, sage, rosemary, thyme, basil, and rue. Roses, violets, lilies, jasmine, hyacinths, and lilac were grown in the flower beds. Medieval gardens were enclosed by fences because the area detracted from the wider agrarian context with its requirements of contemplation and special production. It was an area set apart for privileged uses. This circumscription, which is also symbolic and reverent, is multiplied inside the garden in the subdivision into sectors and beds. The garden was an infinite chessboard of various preciosities classified in an easily understandable and culturally acceptable way.

*Frank Crisp, *Medioeval Gardens*, London 1924; Francesco Fariello, *Architettura dei giardini*, Rome 1967; John Harvey, *Mediaeval Gardens*, London 1981; Teresa McLean, *Medieval English Gardens*, London 1981; Marilyn Stokstad and Jerry Stannard, *Gardens of the Middle Ages*, Lawrence 1983; Dieter Hennebo, *Gärten des Mittelalters*, München, Zürich 1987.

PLATE 13

With the birth of printing in Europe in the fifteen century, the idea of the garden met with new instruments of dissemination. Incunabula improved the spreading of information both quantitatively and qualitatively compared to the age of copying manuscripts. Wood engraving, which was used to complete these editions, was moreover a form of communication using figures that was concise and effective from the point of view of technique (the detailed character of a miniature was not possible with engraving) and for the new significance it attached to the image.

The woodcuts in the first printed books were never a form of decoration, as the miniature had sometimes been in manuscripts. They were an irreplaceable and fundamental part of the communication of the text, its emblematic summary. In this case, the very communication is complex. *De Ruralium Commodorum*, which was printed in Florence in 1495, had been written and distributed as a manuscript in about 1305 by Pietro de Crescenzi from Bologna. Of the twelve volumes on the management of a model farm, the eighth dealt with "how to contrive gardens and pleasant things, trees, herbs, and their fruits." From the theoretical point of view, it was based on the ancient Roman classical tradition and on medieval experience. *Contrive* meant that the garden had to be designed with wisdom so as to become the expression of the

modern view of nature being dominated by man for his own benefit and pleasure. This is what makes the illustration so important. It can communicate immediately the sense of the modern garden, as if it was the putting together of its indispensable ingredients. The garden is partly enclosed by a trellis fence, while pots for flowers decorate the wall. The herbs are also on show for a little rabbit, the symbol of fertility. The humanist design is expressed in the architectural system of treillages, here covered with a grape vine. There is a basin fountain in the center of the construction. The picture also teaches how one should live in the garden: the woman (in the presence of the rabbit) must listen to songs and music with tender emotion. If this was a message intended for everyone, it means that this was how a garden was used in that period.

PLATE 14

Giovanni Boccaccio gave a detailed description of a private Italian garden halfway through the fourteenth century in his book *Decameron*. This illustration from a fifteenth-century edition shows a vine-clad pergola ("paths of unusual width, all straight as arrows and overhung by pergolas of vines") in an extraordinary flowery lawn ("there was a lawn of exceeding fine grass, of so deep a green as to seem almost black, dotted all over with possibly a thousand different kinds of gaily-coloured flowers").

The proem of the Third Day of the *Decameron* brings us into a fourteenth-century garden and defines it with a description of its various parts: "The whole place was decked with seasonable flowers and cuttings, and by way of repose they seated themselves on a loggia overlooking the central court....The vines were all in flower, drenching the garden with their aroma, which, mingled with that of many other fragrant plants and herbs, gave them the feeling that they were in the midst of all the spices ever grown in the East. The paths along the edges of the garden were almost entirely hemmed in by white and red roses and jasmine... and surrounded by a line of flourishing, bright green orange and lemon trees, which, with their mature and unripe fruit and lingering shreds of blossom, offered agreeable shade to the eyes and a delightful aroma to the nostrils.... In the middle of this lawn there stood a fountain of pure white marble, covered with marvellous bas-reliefs....The sight of this garden, and the perfection of its arrangement, with its shrubs, its streamlets, and the fountain from which they originated, gave so much pleasure to each of the ladies and the three young men that they all began to maintain that if Paradise were constructed on earth, it was inconceivable that it could take any other form, nor could they imagine any way in which the garden's beauty could possibly be enhanced. And as they wandered contentedly through it, making magnificent garlands for themselves from the leaves of the various trees, their ears constantly filled with the sound of some twenty different kinds of birds, all singing as though they were vying with one another." This description is also an anthropological and cultural declaration of the significance that the governing class of the time attached to the garden, making it, moreover, an irreplaceable element of the scenery of everyday life.

PLATE 15

A new kind of botanical book, the *Tacuinum sanitatis*, was popular in Europe between the fourth and fifth centuries. Unlike the old *herbal* , which was a classification of plant life for medical purposes as well, the *tacuinum* was a serious treatise on medicine which became well-known because of the interdependence of diverse schools of medicine (the *Scuola Salernitana* was to have a similar experience in its relations with the Greek, Hebrew, and Islamic cultures).

The object of that complex and psychosomatic medicine was man, with his humors and his way of life. The scenes in the *tacuinum* are realistic and sometimes show life in the garden. The *tacuinum* was descended from the wisdom of Arabian medicine, and its name derives, in fact, from the Arabic *taqîwm* (but *tables* would have been a better translation). The two tables here show the garden of the time while illustrating a medicinal plant. The center of this garden adorned with precious herbs (from the probably late fifteenth-century *Codex Casanatense*) is the great rosary. One girl is picking roses; the other is crowned with a garland of roses and is making another garland. While giving a detailed description of the scene and of the plant life in it, the picture does not have the same frames of reference as the *herbal*, which just gives a closeup view of the botanical subject for the necessary comparisons with real plants. The scene represents a likely way of living in the garden, the medical aims of the publication being complementary and independent. The attitude and manner of the two girls, and their clothing, testify to the semantic value. The text, however, explains the medical importance of the rose without reciting its botanical description (which is to be found in the herbals): "Nature: cold in second degree and dry in third. Best: those of Suri and from Persia. Relief: to a hot brain. Harm: brings on a headache in some cases. Removal of the harm: with camphor."

*Luisa Cogliati Arano, *Tacuinum sanitatis*, Milan 1979.

PLATE 16

The fourteenth-century garden was a place where the cultivation of plants was attended to with technical skill and loving care. It was the same in physick gardens, where medicinal plant life was cultivated and reproduced. This garden scene is characterized by the vase which contains life-giving food. The vase, like an urn, communicates a sense of treasure, while a vase for cultivation proves the existence of the preservation of life inside it.

The container is a man-made product linked to the future of man's material culture and possible only in a civilization capable of producing it. In a garden, a vase facilitates the mobility of plants and soil, and aids the cultivation (with changes according to the seasons) of plants in hothouses. The subject of this illustration from the Vienna Code, which probably dates back to the end of the fifteenth century, is sweet marjoram. The text reads. "Nature: hot and dry in third degree. Preference: the tiny and aromatic one chopped. Relief: it is good for a cold and damp stomach. Harm: none. What it produces: purified blood. It is good for cold and damp temperaments, for old people, in winter, in autumn, and in cold regions." The gar-

den in this scene is briefly and symbolically denoted by two tall trees and the mass of herbs on the ground. The table also shows that this site is a place of botanical work. The couple are dressed with an elegance that testifies to their lineage and, perhaps, to their specific botanical and medical professionalism. The woman is using a precious vessel to water the sweet marjoram. The vase is also a precious commodity, with many patterns painted on it. It is fashionable, like the clothes of the two figures. The impression given is one of a secular and mundane utilization of the garden, even of the physick garden. The garden of the time is characterized by both permanence and the biological mutation necessary to human existence.

PLATE 17

In thirteenth-century France, the didactic heroic poem *Le roman de la rose,* whose first part was written by Guillame de Lorris, described the relationship between the hero and an extraordinary, beautiful, and highly symbolic rose he immediately fell in love with. The rose is surrounded by other symbolic figures: Beauty, Riches, Kindness, and Youth. The hero will succeed in kissing the rose with the aid of Venus. The garden as a metaphor of the goal of the rite of passage was a widespread literary theme.

This picture is a wood engraving, from an edition printed in 1481, it illustrates the lines describing the entrance into the garden. Apart from the metaphor, it is interesting to observe the representation of the immediately recognizable and well-known figure of a garden, and that without this particular, the metaphor would not be possible. The few, essential symbols clearly form the scene common to every garden: an enclosed place to make the area sacred and to protect it from animals. Its entrance absorbs allegorically all the symbolic values of the gateway to happiness, wisdom, and love. The espaliers are the botanical wings of the image of the rose garden. Traces of precious herbs on the lawn are suggested by a few strokes. The well-dressed young man, with his elegant hairstyle and a precious feathered cap has the rare privilege of being in that garden. He seems to express the knowledge of the importance of being able to use that privilege. He is holding a rose, the flower of the poetic romance, which is a real flower at the moment. The relationship between man and flower in this picture is eternal. It expresses the feelings of every gardener in every past and every future as he enjoys the sight and the scent of the product he has lovingly labored to cultivate. The aesthetic pleasure of a relationship with a flower is tied to the sentiments of man in all ages, without any reference to different societies or different cultures, and it is based on the beauty of natural life inherent in the blossoming of the plant world.

PLATE 18

The effort needed to take care of a garden has been the subject of many pictures in all civilizations. This is one of those scenes, taken from a Parisian edition of Pietro de Crescenzi's *De Ruralium Commodorum*, published in 1486. Here, too, the symbolic representation of those efforts is expressed through the grouping of various tasks that are well-known to everyone.
In the garden it is time to take care of the plants.

The garden is enclosed by a trellis fence that isolates it from the surrounding environment, which is presumably given over to agriculture. The predominance of the figure of the enclosure in every representation of a garden is of great significance in that it accentuates the exceptional character of the use of an area. It has a sacred significance that refers to a form of production not necessarily tied to the needs of survival. Its role is to defend an artifact, conceptually rather than materially, from the more general context. Plants climb up the trellis fence. Herbs and flowers in the lawn reveal a special form of cultivation. Three men are working around three trees, symbols of the orchard and the viridarium.

Pruning and planting are the necessary tasks for making and maintaining a garden. They must be carried out regularly, according to the garden's seasonal needs. The woodcut implies that these efforts must be eternal; the very existence of a garden and its significance require it. A lack of management will lead to the decay of this precious microcosm of *artificial nature* created by man for his pleasure, and maintainable therefore, only thanks to his efforts and to his love. The rest is wilderness. And that will never be a garden; not even when some naturalistic-style projects, in an attempt to demonstrate the possible aesthetic understanding of the whole of nature in all its manifestations, come to propose this in the future.

PLATE 19

This miniature from a codex drawn up for François I is open to infinite symbolic and iconological interpretations. It also informs us about the character of late medieval gardens before the anthropological and cultural innovations of the humanistic and Renaissance period. On the borderland between two worlds, the garden at the end of the Middle Ages expressed all the semantic values it had accumulated in the one thousand years of its European history.

The first interpretation concerns the relationship between the little city, the castle, and its territory. The landscape that embraces the large construction includes another castle in the background. The two castles indicate that the network behind this presence is the political, economic, and also cultural power structure. A large wood on the other side of the river and cultivated fields are signs of the presence of the agricultural world which sustains that economy. Wild flowers and insects can be seen outside the walls, in the foreground. The big wall marks the separation of the garden from that territory. It is a boundary that makes it sacred and private, reserved for the elite who may enjoy it. The allegory places Nature at the entrance. She has the keys to the door. Venus, the goddess of love, is inside, naked beneath a tree. Juno, the Queen of the gods, proposes virtue as a model for life. And lastly, there is Pallas Athena, the goddess of wisdom. This garden, a medieval *hortus conclusus*, is arranged in regular cultivated beds with precious herbs and flowers and tall trees at intervals. A long bed runs along the wall: it defines the area for a special form of cultivation. Roses and other espaliers are grown here to cover all the wall. Therefore the illusion, inside the garden, of being in a complete and precise microcosm—such as the *hortus conclusus* tends to be by definition—is a feasible project. The courts used for feasts in other castles and urban residences were soon to be temporarily decorated by trellises woven with flowers, with the intention of recreating the plant scenery of a *hortus conclusus*.

PLATE 20

The garden was also the place for cultivating sentiments. Madrigals and heroic poems were composed and enjoyed in late medieval gardens. This miniature, painted by Missel de Renaud de Montauban midway through the fifteenth century, portrays a typical scene in a garden used with the aim of sharpening sentiments. It establishes the irreplaceable role of the garden as the context for demonstrating the capacity for refined feelings.

The highly elegant clothing of the two figures illustrates in particular the type of social intercourse to be experienced in a courtly garden of the time. The large brick seat in the heart of the garden forms a raised bed and is designed for relaxation and conversation. Although the garden is sited in a courtyard, it is still surrounded by a trellis fence to show that it has a different significance from its neighboring buildings. Herbs and flowers are grown in the garden, but the presence of material and artistic culture is predominant. In particular the fountain, the source of the sap of life in its symbolic structure of a basin placed on a column, is the kind most commonly seen in the late Middle Ages. The two shapely and decorative pots show the refinement of taste, and, apart from their utility, they serve to indicate the state of progress of the fine arts and the application of all their qualities to an article of everyday use. The territories of the two pots, which are different from that of the garden, exhibit two special and refined examples of cultivation. The first is a small cylindrical wicker frame that supports the stems of flowers, implying a friendly and aesthetic relationship with those flowers that is different from the attitude toward the other plants. The second is a little tree that has been clipped geometrically according to the style and techniques of *ars topiaria* into umbrella-shaped tiers to demonstrate the wonders of artificial nature.

PLATE 21

A scene of life in the garden is to be found in a mid-fifteenth-century
manuscript of a treatise on astronomy and geography called *De Sphaera*
attributed to Gregorio and Lorenzo Dati of Florence. This reproduction of
the miniature reveals the whole composition and its interdependencies in
an urban context, illustrating how a secular and private *hortus conclusus* in
the heart of the city provided a moment of *dolce*
distraction from the exertions of everyday life.

Many similar pictures of life in the garden show
that this kind of evasion was also, apart from its
practical side, a sort of experiment with a life in
contrast to the usual bothers, a life that was not
just temporary but stable, that was perhaps
pursuable even though it was limited to the
privileged. *Eros* was the center of this urban
garden. The rediscovery of the relationship
between the body and water, rooted in the
recollection of the Roman classical world, was
expressed here in the large basin symbolizing the
Fountain of Everlasting Youth. The pleasure of
bathing is realized here, demonstrating the
predominant presence of *eros*. The feeling of the
couple in the foreground announce that the
garden is the place designated for the cultivation

of sentiments. Music is a special aspect of that life:
songs, wind instruments, drums, and lutes are a
necessary source. Tall trees, including one clipped
into umbrella-shaped tiers, encircle the herb and
flower garden. Flowers are also growing in the
pot on the table laid for a meal which will include
the fruit in the basket on the ground. Two people
are busy supplying the company with wine.
Several flasks and two little casks are already
lying on the ground. One woman in the water is
about to drink from her glass; another glass has
been left on the edge of the fountain. Literature
and the fine arts confirm this model of behaviour
in late medieval gardens, almost as if, more than a
description, it was a declaration of ambition
regarding a precise style of life.

PLATE 22

Special research on the history of the illustrations of the various manuscript or printed editions of *Le roman de la rose* could yield interesting evidence about the consolidation of the late medieval idea of the garden. This miniature comes from a fifteenth-century manuscript, a century during which many printed editions were spreading woodcut pictures that were concise and limited with respect to the analytic precision of these precious tiny paintings.

The picture shows the *hortus conclusus* circumscribed by the high walls in the foreground and background, which seem to enclose the vast garden as if it was a small city. Passing the threshold is always an initiatory task, as the woman who leads the young man toward the door demonstrates. Along the inside of the crenellated high wall there is a continual rose garden growing on latticework structures. The great architectural fountain in the shape of a covered chalice, with its ground level pool, is the central feature and documents the adoption of complex hydraulic mechanisms. The water is channeled through a stone gully for the needs of the walled garden and it then comes out through an opening at the base of the wall. A flowery mead surrounds the fountain: it is the seat of life in the garden. There is song and music; the young people with their elegant attire, to illustrate the close relationship between culture and domesticated nature, are exchanging languorous glances. In this *garden of sentiments* a wooden balustrade separates one part of the garden from the other, whose entrance is through the archway. There the garden is arranged in regular square beds for cultivating herbs and flowers. That the garden was an excellent habitat for birds is shown by the large number of them swooping down on it. But decorative birds are also necessary, as the presence of the peacock on the balustrade informs us.

PLATE 23

The unicorn was the medieval symbol of purity, which only a virgin could approach. First linked to the cult of the goddess-mother, this allegory was later adopted with reference to the Virgin Mary and assumed a Christian significance. The *hortus conclusus*, whose walls and fence surround the Virgin and the unicorn, is a common figure in this symbolism which often utilized realistic parks and gardens.

Hunting the Unicorn, a late fifteenth-century French tapestry preserved in New York, portrays the struggle between *homo selvaticus* with his fierce dogs and the legendary animal. The myth about the unicorn's magic horn was alimented by the ingenious medieval trade in the teeth of the sea-unicorn undertaken by northern European fishermen. In order to appear more credible, the allegorical composition had to be supported by a realistic scene that was familiar to all. The scene here is a thick forest, the hunting ground of the lords or their vassals, a sort of living dispensary or biological container for the life of any kind of wild animal, from which the common people were excluded. The ancient glade in the forest, the sacred site of pagan rites, has been substituted by the garden, a *hortus conclusus* circumscribed by a fence designed as an espalier for roses. Rose bushes grown on espaliers are the most usual form seen in the iconographic material of the age, defining the sacred space of the garden. In ancient times the rose was dedicated to Venus. But it also entered into the categories of Christian symbolism: the Virgin Mary was called a *rose without thorns* evoking the legend that roses had no thorns before the Fall. This garden in the forest, the unicorn's garden, is therefore highly symbolic, but at the same time, the setting is of a realistic nature and its components, with their various allegorical aspects, are the real components of every garden.

*Odell Shepard, The Lore of the Unicorn, London 1930.

PLATE 24

Sometime during the first few decades of the seventeenth century, at the start of the laborious construction of the front of the duomo in Milan, an unknown artist sculpted some bas-reliefs illustrating verses from the Bible. "Israel, the vineyard of the Lord" is shown here. Cultural records of the age of the Counter-Reformation are also documents for the history of sculpture serving as original Neo-Renaissance links between Manneristic practices and future Baroque inventions. At the same time, they register the idea of the Renaissance garden with its beds, balustrades, and these architectural pergolas.

The other panels that utilize the iconography of the Renaissance garden to illustrate verses from the Bible are the large garden with a well and balustrade in the foreground and fence in the background (*The well / The source of everlasting water*); the tree near a stump (*The fig tree that produces fruit and the sterile one, cut down*); and the great tree in front of a walled garden (*The solidly planted tree*). These bas-reliefs show unusual garden scenes compared to the image derived from social heritage, laden as they are with the special architectonic values of Renaissance culture applied to gardens. They seem to be a *form of communication and propaganda* in service of the new taste for the elegant Renaissance garden, spread by means of sculpture by the city's most important building. The iconography of the garden, in contrast to the natural landscape, has always been used as an instrument of communication of both religious and secular myths and metaphors, symbolizing the profound significance that cultivation, which transforms nature, has in the history of human society. This example is accompanied by an infinite number of others to be found in painting through the ages, from miniatures to early prints, from tapestries to goldwork. Sometimes decorative, other times documentary or deliberately propositional, these images can always be interpreted as a re-proposal of the Latin *topia* (from the Greek *topos*), the model of the idea of the garden which the Greeks and Romans in the Hellenistic age placed in the peristyle as an example to be adhered to by the owner and the gardener (*toparius*) in their work.

PLATE 25

The iconography of alchemy also offers various different scenes of gardens in its complex symbology. Alchemic metaphors actually use figures from real life, and, among these, the garden enjoys a privileged position. Being the place for taking skillful and loving care of nature so as to transform it into a project of continual improvement on the road to the utopia of perfection, the garden is a good symbol for representing the approach of *alchemic science* to man.

All the myths of the Greek and Roman classical world are open to alchemic interpretations. This scene shows the passage in Book VI of Virgil's epic poem, *The Aeneid*, when Aeneas breaks off the Golden Branch that will let him cross the infernal regions unscathed. The drawing comes from *Splendor Solis*, a sixteenth-century manuscript by Salomon Trismosin. The tree is the tree of life planted in the garden inside a golden crown. The three figures are the main characters of the epic: Aeneas, Silvius, and Anchises, who are dressed in red, white and black alchemic costumes. The birds flying over the treetop represent alchemic sublimation. The black crow with a white head means that black produces white. The symbolic scene is enclosed in the proscenium of a possible theater. It is a picture of a landscape with a garden full of flowers in the foreground and an enclosed area near a distant house in the background. In front of this there is the representation of another traditional scene of garden life: people bathing in a large marble pool whose water gushes from a precious sculptured fountain (on top of a column a putto is riding an animal and blowing his horn). Two women are bringing perfumes to the elegant bathers who have carefully braided hair and wear precious necklaces. The spectators at the sides and in the boxes seem to be hidden and to be outsiders. They observe the two pictures: the first definitely alchemic one on the stage; and the second, more three-dimensional and realistic one of the bathers in the garden on the proscenium.

*Edgar Wind, *Pagan Mysteries in the Renaissance*, 1958; J. Van Lennep, *Art & Alchemie*, Bruxelles 1966.

PLATE 26

Voghamo ancor de suoi libretti ornate
Chesono de eloquentia larghi fiumi
Riceue adunqp sue sublime carte
Et fa che anostri studij sia benigna
Cum opra & cum ingegni in omni parte
Accio che di maior ti facci degna

MONS · ELICON ·

GRAMATICHA EST SCIENTIA ·

· RETTORICA ·

ASTRONOMIA · GRAMATICA ·

The nine Muses lived in the woods covering Mount Helicon, as is announced by this second alchemic illustration. At first the Muses were the nymphs of the mountain's sacred springs. The old crowned man is surrounded by the Muses, who are Apollo's assistants and personify purity and harmony. Astronomia and Gramatica are helping Rettorica hold up Mount Helicon. The wise old man playing his instrument and the other Muses stand at the foot of the mountain.

The nine Muses were Clio (the Muse of history), Euterpe (music and lyric poetry), Thalia (comedy and pastoral poetry), Melpomene (tragedy), Terpsichore (dance and singing), Erato (lyric and love poetry), Urania (astronomy), Calliope (epic poetry), and Polyhymia (religious music). The mountain begins to rise from the flowery meadow where the old man and the Muses are standing. The mountain of the Muses is shown, in this miniature by Nicola d'Antonio degli Agli dated 1480, as a geometrical hemisphere that is cared for as if it was a *delightful mount*, part of a real garden. The symbolic tree is clipped according to the techniques of *ars topiaria*. It, too, is a hemisphere, showing that the place is not abandoned to *savage nature* but is destined for the cultivation of nature by man, a parallel with the myth that tells of the transformation of the nymphs into Muses and the natural source into sacred and magic water, capable of inspiring the Muses. This was, in fact, Hippocrene, the spring that Pegasus brought to life with a kick of his hoof on the rock, which was channeled into a precious fountain. Here the spring is in a red stone pool with a polygonal base. Twin jets of water flow out of the large sphere on top of the column, another figure of alchemic symbology, and fill the pool. The *delightful mount*, the clipped tree and the architectural fountain represent the constituent parts of the Italian humanist and Renaissance garden.

PLATE 27

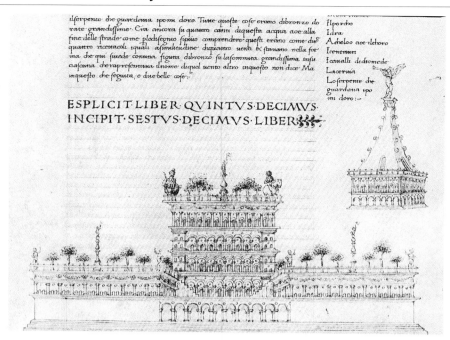

Toward the end of the fifteenth century, Antonio Averlino, known as *il Filarete*, designed a special building, a *palace-garden*, where the humanist age relived the myth of hanging gardens. It was one of the first attempts to integrate the new style of architecture with the garden instead of placing it, as was the custom, to the sides of the building. At the end of the century, Leonardo da Vinci designed pavilions for the layout of the large park belonging to the Sforza family in Milan.

Il Filarete presumably wrote his treatise on architecture, which was dedicated to Francesco Sforza whose *signoria* governed Milan, between 1461 and 1464. It was the first theoretical work to be written in the vernacular, and described the project for the construction of an ideal city, Sforzinda, which was considered indispensable for that dominion. The *Ca' Granda*, the ancient hospital in Milan, testifies to the greatness and significance of those proposals and that dream. This drawing, which comes from *Il Filarete*'s book, proposes a *palace-garden*, an unusual project in which a complex system of hanging gardens transforms the rooftop into one long garden. Leonardo da Vinci worked at the court of the Sforza family in Milan during the last few decades of the century. His studies and projects, as well as his achievements, involve town planning, navigation, architecture and hydraulics, sculpture and painting, nature, and science. His contribution to the design of the huge garden-park behind the castle in Milan, which was the ducal residence, was not sufficiently documented. This drawing is a preparatory sketch for the construction of an architectural pavilion in the park, nothing of which remains. But the sense of that park, of the life within it and its architectural wonders as well, can be found in literary evidence, which shows that hunting and feasting took place there continually. A great fresco preserved (with rather questionable restoration) on the vault of the so-called *Sala delle Asse* in the castle forms an elegant trompe l'oeil with a pattern of plants, a kind of extension of the park inside the building.

PLATE 28

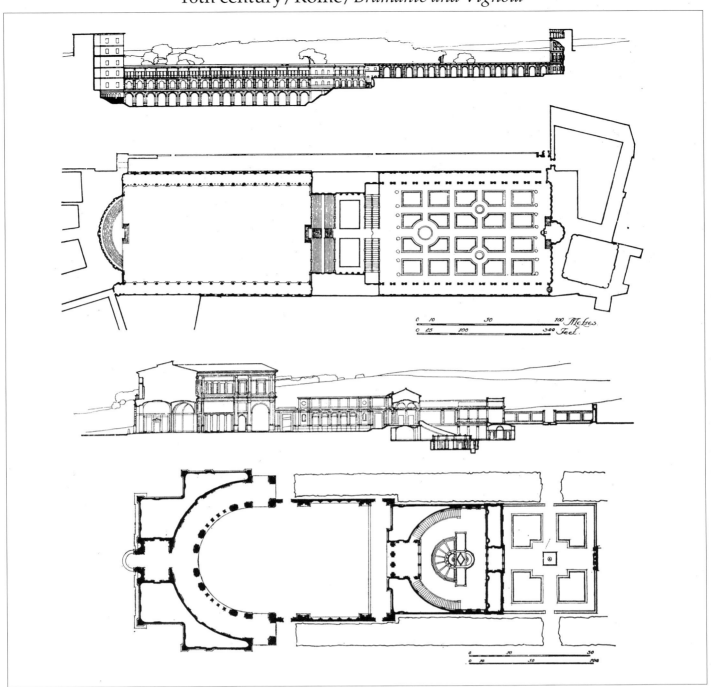

Architecture and the garden were melded together in the early Italian Renaissance, creating a new kind of palazzo that included an area for the cultivation and contemplation of the plant world. It was an original interpretation of the medieval *hortus conclusus*, which was pragmatically sited within the walls of a castle or monastery. Here the garden, with the magnitude of its axes and perspectives, becomes the central part of the whole structure.

In *De re aedificatoria* by Leon Battista Alberti, a treatise on architecture crucial to Renaissance culture (in circulation in 1452 and printed after 1485), the garden was considered an essential component of a home, with specific characteristics and prescriptions. Its layout was to be symmetrical and coordinated, or rather integrated with the building. There were to be waterworks corresponding to the renewed interest in hydraulics. Steps should connect changes in levels. There should be grottoes and nymphaea, and evergreen plants were to keep the garden in a kind of unchangeable state. One of the first fully preserved gardens that put these proposals into practice was the Belvedere in the Vatican, built by Donato Bramante between 1503 and 1504. At the top of this page are drawings of the plan and a section. The traditional court of a large palace became an entire garden whose symmetrical layout was no longer enhanced by plant sequentiality, but was furthered by the orderly collection of the various *botanical wonders* offered to the eye within the entirely architectonic scene that limits it, and distributed along the complex changes in level from which the channeled waters fell. This was to be the model of the garden in an urban palazzo and the cultural reference for every *Italian garden* during the period dominated by Renaissance philosophy. The continuity of the model is demonstrated, below, by the plan and section of Villa Giulia built in Rome between 1551 and 1553 by Jacopo Barozzi (known as *il Vignola*), the architect who personified the period of transition between Mannerism and the Baroque style.

PLATE 29

In 1499, Aldo Manuzio, the publisher and humanist, printed *Hypnerotomachia Poliphili*, a monument of fifteenth-century book illustration, written by Francesco Colonna. The tale of Polia's lover's dream about a love contest has an ancient structure which goes back to medieval narrative styles and, though written in Italian, is incomprehensible to anyone who does not know Latin. A large number of the system of 196 illustrations are dedicated to modern gardens.

The wood engraving shown here illustrates the part of the tale during which Polia meets Polyphilo in front of a small grove where a group of people are sitting. The meeting takes place in a garden with flowers and bushes in the foreground, and under a pergola whose walls and barrel-shaped roof are covered with climbing plants. The *virtual* building, a pavilion that forms a transparent space, is composed of precious marble columns that support the semicircular framework of the roof. There are two benches for resting and conversing inside the pavilion. These are the pictures that propagandize the Renaissance idea of the garden, or rather, considering the modest distribution of the first edition, that register the predisposition toward a wide antiquarian culture that was in fashion in the later half of the century in Venice and its vicinity, in Pa-

dua and Mantua. The Renaissance garden is nothing less than the revival, in hypothetical terms, of the garden in the *Golden Age* of classical Greek and Roman culture. Architects, painters, sculptors, and epigraphists searched for traces and documents in the Venetian area to utilize as historical and scientific backing for the new taste. The design of these exceptional woodcuts, whose author is unknown, communicates primarily the sense of the new garden and how to live in it. The alternation of printed and illustrated pages seems to be the realistic and anticipative documentation of a near and possible future.

*Maria Teresa Casella and Giovanni Pozzi, *Francesco Colonna, biografia e opere*, Padova 1959; Francesco Colonna, *Hypnerotomachia Poliphili*, critical edition and comment by Giovanni Pozzi and Lucia A. Ciapponi, Padova 1964; Emanuela Kretzulesco-Quaranta, *Les jardins du songe, "Poliphile" et la Mystique de la Renaissance*, Paris-Rome 1976; Maurizio Calvesi, *Il sogno di Polifilo prenestina*, Rome 1980 and 1983.

PLATE 30

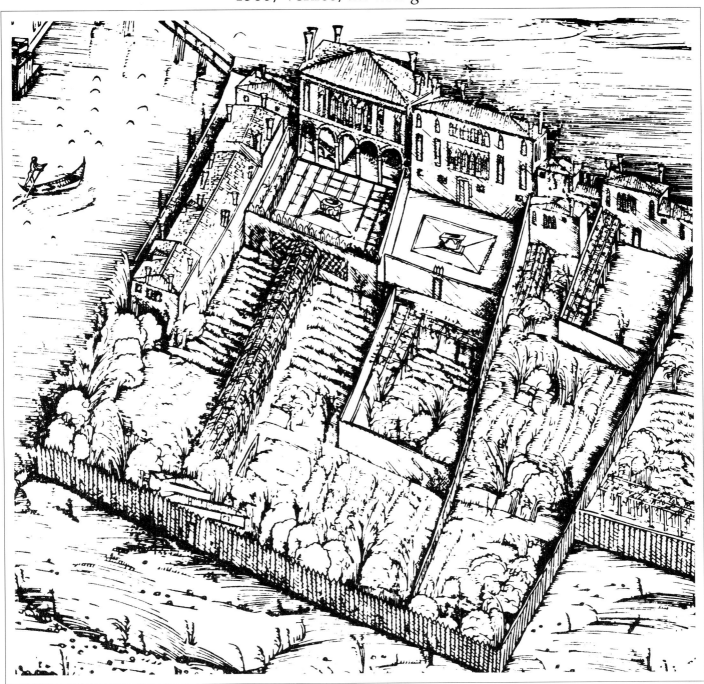

A year after *Hypnerotomachia Poliphili* was published, Jacopo De' Barbari's extraordinary bird's-eye view of Venice was printed at the conclusion of more than three years of detailed surveys of every corner of the city. The island of Giudecca and its wonderful gardens are shown in the foreground of this big print. They are the same as those shown in the woodcuts in Francesco Colonna's incunabolum, to confirm that reality actually coincided with the project.

This detail of the bird's-eye view of Venice shows a part of the island of Giudecca with its buildings to the north on the canal of the same name looking towards Venice, and the gardens to the south on the lagoon side. Until the end of the thirteenth century the island was made up of a narrow strip of land emerging from the water and inhabited by fishermen and craftsmen. When it was decided to enlarge the island on the lagoon side, the land recovered was assigned to some noble families to carry out the necessary drainage. The island of Giudecca never became an organic part of the city of Venice, which could be crossed on foot thanks to a complete system of bridges connecting all its islets. Instead it became the place of feasts, delights, and holidays after the nobles turned the reclaimed land into the very

famous Venetian gardens, which were relatively large compared to the ones in the city. Famous artists such as Pietro Aretino and Michelangelo, princes and noblemen, guests of the Republic of Venice and ambassadors visited them. These gardens were arranged according to the principle of the interrelation of the elements constituting the pattern of the *hortus conclusus*. The garden was on the other side of the villa's architectural courtyard. It was also a place for botanical experiments and for cultivating exotic plants. The main feature of these gardens was the pergola used as a support for climbing plants and for grapevines in particular. The literary descriptions of the life in those gardens confirm the cultural and architectonic analogy with the woodcut pictures in *Hypnerotomachia Poliphili*.

PLATE 31

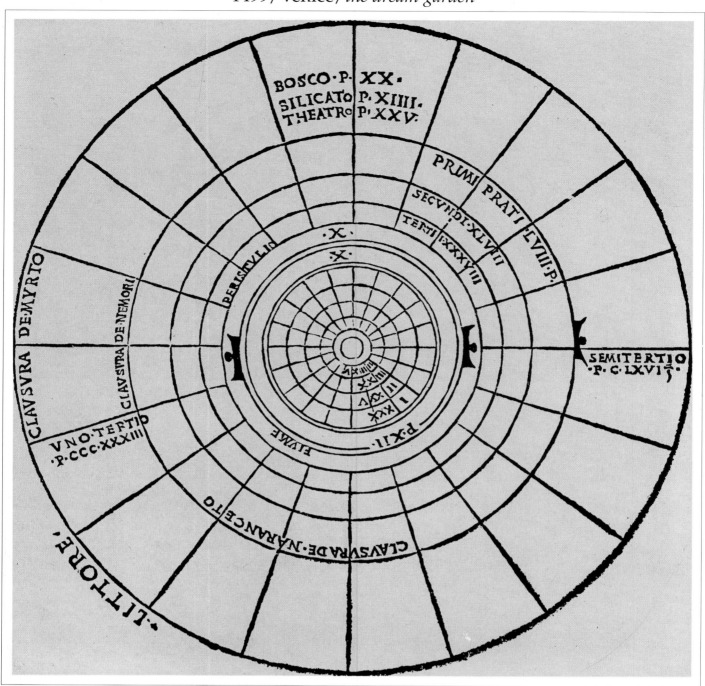

The island of Cythera presented in *Hypnerotomachia Poliphili* can be considered as one of the ideal Renaissance cities, and also as the first proposal of a *garden city* rather than a vast and geometrical park. In Francesco Colonna's extraordinary book, the island of Cythera is shown as being circular, with a diameter of about one mile, and surrounded by transparent salty water. Metal trophies, corroded by the water, lie submerged: they are memories of an ancient civilization that once lived there.

The perimeter of the island, along the coast, is covered with a grassy lawn and a row of perfect cypresses, all exactly alike, planted three paces apart. Their trunks are covered with an espalier of myrtle one and half paces high. The leaves of the plant spread two feet above the support. Twenty radii part from this crown of myrtle and converge at the center of the island. This is on a higher level than the shore thanks to the system of architectural and scenic terraces formed by tiers of short cylinders which, from the lowest one with a diameter of one mile, are continually reduced until the last one forms the large circular amphitheater at the top. The theme of the terraces stepping down to the sea constitutes a never-ending sequence of continuity in formal gardens. Each of the twenty sectors, marked by balustrades of sculptured marble, contains a grove full of herbs and various kinds of trees planted in the most propitious position. In the middle, there is a marble door crowned with an arch. The climbing plants are honeysuckle, jasmine, convolvulus, and campanula. The groves are formed of laurels, oaks, wild cypresses, pines, elms, limes, ashes, firs, larches, chestnuts, olive trees, and topiary boxwood. Animals live in harmony in these groves. Orange and lemon trees surrounded by circular marble flooring make up the next level. Then there is a kitchen garden, divided into separate lawns and likewise with architectural and sculptured decorations. Its main feature is the system of rosaries climbing up columns. The pergolas that shade the longitudinal alleys are covered with white roses. Lastly, aromatic herb gardens alternate with lawns.

PLATE 32

Francesco Colonna made the first definite proposal in Venice in 1499 of the *aesthetics of ruins*, as this wood engraving from his book *Hypnerotomachia Poliphili* shows. This theory successfully combined archeological passion (which here implied a precise relationship with the plant world) with the romantic fascination of an image that brought about, by an act of the imagination, a return from the past of the idea of the golden age of culture.

From the time the humanists started searching for ancient ruins, every discovery produced immense joy, as well as literary documents and pictorial reconstructions, to a point that the very image of the ruin, presented as it appeared to the discoverer, was capable by itself of provoking feelings and emotions. In this way, the viewer experienced through his imagination and specific culture all the potentialities of an extraordinary, but solely *virtual*, past. The ruin as a source of a sentimental and romantic as well as archeological and scientific method of reasoning was then to become such an irreplaceable feature of human culture that a new phrase was coined, the *aesthetics of ruins*. The impressive up-to-date character of the picture is to be found in the way this complex semantic value is communicated, together with its relations with the plant world expressed by the presence of a symbolic nature which tends to submerge a distant culture that might have been lost forever. The kinds of plants that were to become the standard were mentioned explicitly: herbs, weeds, and exotic species. From that time on, every image of a ruin was systematically enriched with the botanical ingredient, its counterpart in the overall scene and an indispensable component. Taken together with the necessarily casual heap of ruined artefacts, the romantic characterization was achieved. It was almost as if the cult of classical antiquity would not have developed as it did, if the ruins had been found largely intact, or experienced only through the copies of the treatise by Vitruvius.

*Jeannot Simmen, *Ruinen-Faszination*, Dortmund 1980; Günter Hartmann, *Die Ruine im Landschaftsgarten*, Stuttgart 1981.

PLATE 33

This woodcut from *Hypnerotomachia Poliphili* illustrates the significance of European gardens at the end of the Middle Ages through the symbolic representation of all the fundamental components necessary for creating the humanistic Renaissance garden. It is characterized by the predominance of human intervention, a consequence of the cultural influence of the new architecture that aimed at the revival of the classical past.

On the plant side, the protagonists are those of the garden in all times: precious herbs and flowers in the lawn, flowery climbing plants on the pergola, groves of tall trees. The limit to the garden is a cane fence intertwined in various patterns that were to become the subject of specific research in decorative motifs two centuries later. The great pergola with its barrel-shaped roof, a simulation of everlasting heaven and symbol of a precious microcosm on the earth, is also built with latticed canes. The great tank is made of marble. Water flows out of a decorative spout into the hexagonal marble pool. Water in a garden is always the source of life, while the tank is the reserve of life. However, in a Renais-sance garden the fountain is also the metaphor and symbol of the *fons sapientiae* as well as being an ingenious contrivance from the hydraulics point of view. This was the reason for the emblematic importance of an artifact that had to be architectural and sculptural, made of precious materials such as marble and metals, and sited in a central position of the garden, almost as if it was the material representation of its axial center. It was the heart of the perspective, but served also as a frame of reference for the structural organization of the garden which depended on that centrality.

*Elisabeth B. Macdougall, *Fons Sapientiae Renaissance Garden Fountains*, Dumbarton Oaks Colloquium on the History of Landscape Architecture, Washington 1978.

PLATE 34

Topiary was a highly developed and widely utilized art form during the Renaissance in Italy, and became known abroad as the essential and characteristic element of the Italian garden. But its historical roots go back to classical Greek and Roman times. The interpretation of antique texts that described the artifice of clipping plants into figures, a bizarre dimension of the dominion of man over nature, contributed in no mean way to the rebirth of those cultures.

Hypnerotomachia Poliphili is an illustrated romance that can also be read as a treatise on the humanistic and Renaissance garden as is shown by these four wood engravings. The reader can study these models for clipping trees into geometrical volumes and put them into practice in his own garden. In ancient Greece, in the Hellenistic age, a *topia*, the painting of a model of the ideal garden which was to be of practical reference for both the owner and his gardener, was placed in the gallery surrounding the garden. This desire for perfection was assimilated in Rome in the first century B.C. with such semantic emphasis that Cicero was forced to define his refined gardener *toparius*, on the basis of a metonymical revival of the Greek term indicating those elegant practices which tended to *transform a garden into a work of art*. Humanistic culture revived this word, giving it a special meaning (which was also relevant to the Greek and Roman past). It re-ferred to the transformation of plant forms into elementary geometrical forms or even complex groups of figures, and proposed the mathematical cultivation of the botanical world. Francesco Colonna used the adjective *topiary* to define the plants that were *artfully clipped*. Shaping natural volumes into artificial forms was certainly not a mere question of decoration in the period in which it became popular. Topiary required patience and skill, which lay outside the confines of a definition of triviality. That these figures were symbolic devices representing the government of man over nature was clear to everyone. To those who practiced topiary and to those who looked at it with curiosity and amazement, it gave a sense of satisfaction concerning man's capacities and the new taste it symbolized.

*Miles Hadfield, *Topiary and Ornamental Hedges*, London 1971; Geraldine Lacey, *Creating Topiary*, Northiam 1987; Ethne Clarke, George Wright, *English Topiary Gardens*, London 1988.

PLATE 35

From the age of rock carvings to the present day, man's figurations have always represented the plant world either concisely or analytically, realistically or symbolically. Part of the knowledge of our botanical past comes from the documents of the whole of the European visual arts. The system of these figurations, like a vast archeological survey, explains the rational and emotional significance of the garden of a period, but it also gives us a description of the species that were in it.

Very little research has been done in this field, and it only started to be truly scientific in the last ten years. The first results, however, are extremely interesting. Mirella Levi D'Ancona has analysed *La Primavera*, which was painted by Sandro Filipepi, known as Botticelli, in 1478. The great tempera on wood, measuring about 79 x 118 inches by three, represents the time of flowering that is connected to various complex symbolic meanings. The goddess Flora is shown on the left. She is walking among flowers, has flowers on her dress and in her dress, a garland round her neck, and a wreath in her hair. The detailed examination of the painting introduces us, among other things, to the botanical preferences of the time. The author of the study identified forty floral species in the large painting, which was analysed minutely. The work was also confirmed philologically by ancient and modern herbals. The flowers are spread over the landscape and on the various figures in the scene. There are three species on Flora's dress that can be seen in this illustration: 5, carnation, 10, corn-flower, 36, rose. She then gave a vast and complex explanation of the symbolism of each flower which was unique to the humanist Florence of the Medici family. This is emphasized in the book's subtitle: "A Botanical Interpretation Including Astrology, Alchemy and the Medici."

*Mirella Levi D'Ancona, Botticelli's Primavera, Florence 1983.

PLATE 36

Every society in every epoch has given symbolic meanings to plants. Apart from their corporeal entity, plants, flowers, herbs, and shrubs tended to denote sentiments, moral or religious convictions, declarations of love or appraisals of specific acts, and complex allegorical figures. Mirella Levi D'Ancona has researched this aspect of Italian painting during the Renaissance, to reconstruct the symbolic system of the time.

One hundred and seventy-one plants have been amply analysed by Mirella Levi D'Ancona in her book, which covers the world of figuration and literature as well as painting. Each of the plants is presented with the different symbolisms that Renaissance culture assigned it semantically and the relative documentation from the visual arts, with an index of the works confirming each symbol. The pomegranate has been chosen to give an example of the results of this research. Here it is shown in an illustration from a Renaissance edition of the work by Pietro Andrea Mattioli, a contemporary of the artistic, historical, and literary period studied by Levi D'Ancona. The book supplies thirteen symbolic meanings for the pomegranate that are to be found in Italian paintings of the time. 1. The pomegranate is a symbol of fertility, sensuality, and marriage (it was the only tree planted by Aphrodite in Cyprus; the *golden apples* of the Hesperides were pomegranates). 2. In Christian symbolism, it is the Church that sows its seeds everywhere in unity. 3. It symbolizes the chastity of the Virgin Mary. 4. For pagan mythological symbology, it is rejuvenation (Proserpina's periodical return to earth in spring). 5. In Christian symbolism, the juice of the pomegranate represents the blood of Christ during the Passion. 6. It is also attributed to Mary Magdalene, as her apple. 7. It also means virtue, good works, election for eternal life. 8. It represents the apostles, united for the salvation of the world. 9. The pomegranate is also man in a state of perfection (humble, charitable, prudent, and pious). 10. When the pomegranate is open it symbolizes Christian charity towards humanity. 11. It is also strength against fatigue. 12. It is the flower of Paradise and the tree of Paradise. 13. Lastly, more generally, the pomegranate is the tree of knowledge (its fruit is full of seeds).

*Mirella Levi D'Ancona, *The Garden of the Renaissance, Botanical Symbolism in Italian Painting*, Florence 1977.

PLATE 37

In 1537 Sebastiano Serlio, the architect and late Renaissance architectural theoretician, published the fourth volume of his *Treatise on Architecture* in Venice. The work totalled seven volumes, published separately over a period of forty years. The first editions of the seven volumes were published alternately in Paris and Venice. An eighth volume remained unpublished until this century. A part of the fourth volume discusses gardens, but in a purely formal way concerning the beds.

In contrast to the significance of the humanist garden as laid down by Leon Battista Alberti in his treatise, which was full of indications stimulating new developments, Serlio's work tends to give credit to the hypothesis that the garden, as a whole, was already codified in the Manneristic period, and therefore, in a certain sense, not open to debate. Following the list of rules he set down for the ornamentation of the composite order, inside and outside the buildings, the author wrote: "The gardens are still part of the ornaments of the fabric, for which these four different figures below (the first two are shown here) are compartments of the same gardens even though they could be used for other things, apart from the two labyrinths, to the side (here shown next to the first two drawings) which in fact have this purpose." Manneristic and formal cynicism merged one of the oldest and most complex figures in the history of mankind, the maze, with the banality of Manneristic decorative patterns, useful for decorating walls and ceilings and also for forming beds in gardens. This gratuitous decorativeness not only implied disinterest in the plant life that was to be inserted inside the diverse partitions of these beds, but also a more general indifference toward the garden where the complex beds were to be placed. This was soon to be codified in treatises on French baroque gardens ("Traité du jardinage" by Jacques Boyceau de la Borderie, published in Paris in 1638, and "Le jardin de plaisir" by André Mollet, also published in Paris in 1651). The *compartment de broderie*, the bed designed in an elaborate embroidery pattern, had to form a kind of vast carpet, with little plant life, in front of the main façade of the building. The repetition of a Manneristic design, considered as the indispensable form of decoration, was to be elaborated throughout.

*Eugenio Battisti, *Rinascimento e barocco*, Turin 1960; Paolo Santarcangeli, *Il libro dei labirinti*, Florence 1967.

PLATE 38

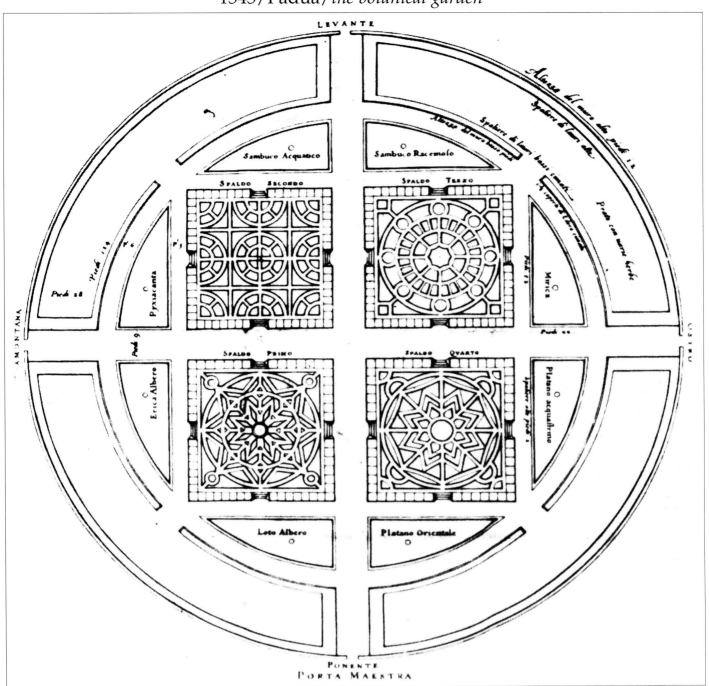

On June 29th 1545 the Senate of the *Serenissima Repubblica di San Marco* decreed the establishment of a physick garden, the first botanical garden in Europe, to be set up in Padua on the Venetian mainland. For centuries Padua had been the seat of a famous university whose studies and botanical experiments were grounded on ancient learning. The plan shown comes from the first book on the botanical garden printed in Venice in 1591. The botanical garden is the expression of an epistemological revolution.

The practical terms of the document founding the botanical garden stated that it was "to plant fruit-bearing and suffruticose herbs and those things which the experts want, resulting in our having some things, as if they were from foreign parts, and from our islands of Candia and Cyprus where there are the most praised herbs and minerals, and from any other places they want." Candia and Cyprus were the meeting grounds of the Islamic world and Europe on a botanical level. In 1591 the Paduan botanical garden accounted for 1,168 species arranged in a classificatory complex of beds. During the European Renaissance, man's interest in the plant world brought to the physick garden the ancient wisdom of the monasteries and the medical practices of the recent past. What history had handed down, that is to say, what was considered useful and suitable for every future, was preserved there for its cultivation and reproduction. The year before the foundation of the botanical garden in Padua, the famous and successful book by Mattioli, presented as a comment on Dioscorides' classical work, was published in Venice. It represented the now more solidly scientific continuity between contemporary botany and that of the past. The character of new herbals, however, was modified more and more by the presence of exotic plants, especially those coming from the Americas, which were soon to preside in the botanical gardens. Unlike the ancient physick garden with its medieval heritage, the Renaissance botanical garden became the place for observation and experimentation, the laboratory for studying the old and the new plant world, and an arena for new productive possibilities as well.

*Margherita Azzi Visentini, *L'orto botanico di Padova*, Milan 1984.

PLATE 39

Eros and garden are two words that were merged into a single semantic meaning in all European culture during the secular Renaissance. This picture of a German garden overlooking a wood shows a scene of aristocratic life in these *pleasant places*. After the late medieval and humanistic feasts involving large numbers, garden life, in the high Renaissance period, was, perhaps, limited to more intimate groups.

The picture shows three couples. Apparently mature but certainly not impotent bearded gentlemen are flirting with young women on the borderland between the cultivated garden and the savage wood. The clothes they are wearing are not just elegant, as the fashion of the time dictated, but are quite luxurious, as can be seen in the elaboration and richness of the drapes and fabrics. They serve to classify the figures from a sociological point of view and also testify to a certain habit of expressing sentiments in the garden environment. This corner of the garden is circumscribed by latticed fences serving as a back to the grassy raised bed used as a seat. Flowers can be seen on the espalier, on the ground and in the large vase to the left of the scene. The cultivation of sentiments, with the inevitable satisfaction of

desires of the senses, does not ignore the needs of the stomach. The scene describes an extraordinary banquet. There is a large flask of some excellent wine in the foreground. The stone table is covered with a table cloth and laid with precious accessories and utensils (a goblet, a cup, plates, and cutlery). The leftovers seem to be traditional food, but there are also cakes in the large central plate. The garden, therefore, is not an end in itself, an autonomous area with its own special character, good only for a moment of rest inside a property designed for the contemplation of the domination of nature. It is the necessary, useful, and pleasant backdrop for a certain kind of life, a necessary ornament of the house, its extension out-of-doors. The original, ritual significance, characteristic of every garden, has quite disappeared.

PLATE 40

In this mid-seventeenth-century anonymous French engraving, an allegory of the month of May, the scene is familiar, while adding something new. The erotic garden is no longer for private consumption as in the case of its contemporary from Germany. Here there is a sense of a return, after a few centuries, of that *joi de vivre* to be seen in the prints illustrating the late medieval and humanistic crowded feasts.

Eroticism does not seem to be the only feature in this picture. Courting, friendly conversation, cultural or sentimental declarations, and musical appreciation clearly share the stage. Moreover, the scene takes place in a real garden. To the right there is the house with the beds of a *parterre* in front of it. To the side there is a flowery lawn where a group of people are sitting, some playing musical instruments, others singing, and others just listening. Next to them some little girls and young women are wreathing garlands and crowns with the flowers they have picked. Here, too, elegance and finery are an obligation for the garden's guests. The garden extends from the end of the beds in front of the house through the long alley with its barrel-shaped roof completely covered with climbing plants. From the terrace, emphasized by the balustrade, the garden goes down towards the river where some of the guests are boating. The river widens to the right and reveals an island, that, like all gardens of the past and of the future, has a tiny temple in the middle. This building, the latticework pergola, the stone balustrade, and the stone moulding of the eaves of the house announce the complete adherence to the whole of Renaissance culture of Italian origin. People wander through the park as far as the island. Villages can be seen in the distance at the foot of the mountains. There is a wood to the left of the island, the finishing touch to what appears to be a list of the characteristics of a model garden.

PLATE 41

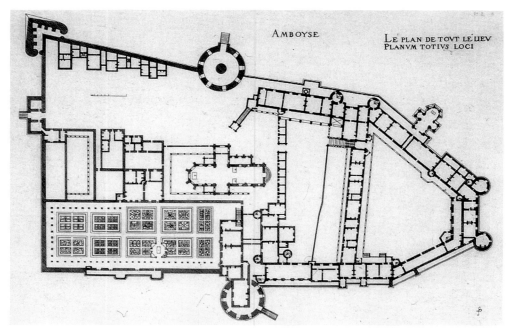

Jacques Androuet du Cerceau, the draughtsman, engraver, and publisher, brought out two volumes between 1576 and 1579 with the title, *Les plus excellents bastiments de France* (a novel idea for that period which was to become very popular in the future). The book presented the residences of the great, often in flattering tones, to the benefit above all of their own vainglory. The author, however, was one of the leaders of the French Renaissance and a highly cultivated intellectual. His books are a mirror of the time.

The author's detailed drawings, mostly based on surveys, look true to life. They were supposed to form a kind of scientific documentation, not to gloss over reality as very often was the case with certain perspectives taken from convenient view points. His elegant engravings serve to analyse the monuments illustrated in minute detail, and offer both contemporaries and posterity a faithful portrait of the palaces and gardens in France in the second half of the seventeenth century. This picture shows a castle of medieval origin with various wings added according to necessity at later dates. There is a *hortus conclusus* inside the castle walls. Not long after the castle was built, its garden was modified according to Renaissance culture and taste, which was then widely appreciated in France as well. There is a large architectural and symbolically important fountain in the center of the garden that can be seen clearly in the plan and partially in the perspective. The garden design of ten large squares is woven into forty beds bordered by hedging that forms asymmetrical compositions. This typical system of organizing regular beds containing various different patterns and species is typical of Renaissance culture, which did not aim merely at decoration. The latter was to become a must in the near future, when symmetry became an obsession. Here we have the clear and immediately comprehensible arrangement all of the plant world that is possible and worthwhile, brought together not just for its botanical interest but also for aesthetic reasons. The garden was a metaphor of the whole world and the world of knowledge.

*Alfred Marie, *Jardins français créés à la Renaissance*, Paris 1955.

PLATE 42

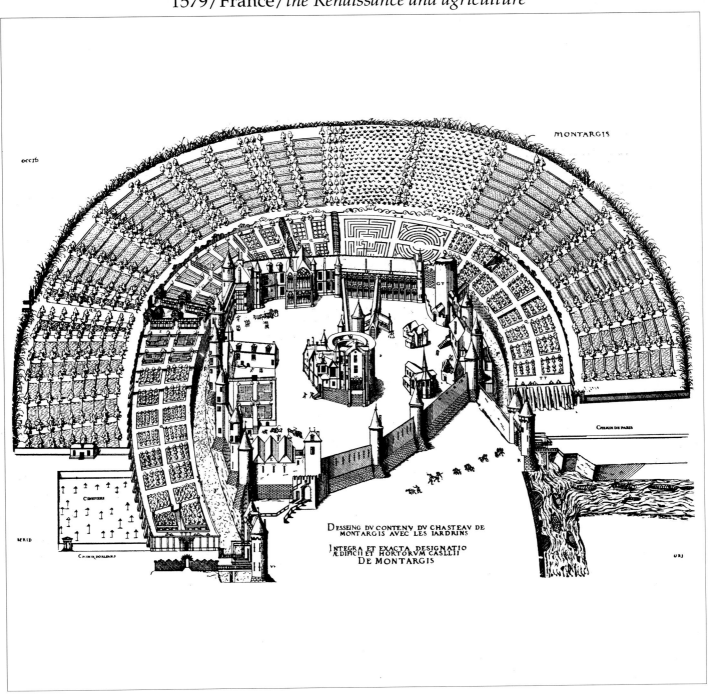

This second type of castle and garden to be found in Jacques Androuet de Cerceau's book is an alternative to the one on the previous page. It does not illustrate the will to modify the taste and culture of a *hortus conclusus* inside its unchanged physical environment. Instead it constitutes a frame of reference for a new, extroverted garden. Here the garden spreads in a circular fashion beyond the walls of the *little city* with the ancient manner house in the center, potentially towards the geographical infinite of a territory to be dominated by botanical domestication as well.

The extraordinary picture shows what this complex structure was like in the second half of the seventeenth century. It was completely destroyed in the early years of the nineteenth century. The tiny walled city formed by the castle is seen here from its center. Beyond the garden, the author writes, there was a huge oak forest. A garden was formed of two concentric circular rings. The first, which was directly linked to the castle moat, was surrounded by a continuous wall with remarkable Manneristic twirly decorations on top of it—a curious and enormous artifact, the complete opposite of the ancient, functional walls of the fortifications. A system of architectural treillages lead into the curvilinear garden, which is formed of a continuity of twin beds used for cultivating flowers and herbs, decorative tall trees, and fruit trees. Latticed fences and barrel-roofed pergolas separating the more important beds can be seen in the central part of the picture. There are two big mazes to the right; one is circular and one square. They represent the recollection of an ancient symbol. The external ring of the garden is divided into sectors for special types of cultivation, separated by tidy rows of tall trees. There is only one gate, to the left, going out of the vegetable garden toward the great oak forest. The last ring is closed in by an impenetrably thick hedge. Beyond it lies the geographical infinite.

*Andrée Corvol, L'homme aux bois, Paris 1987.

PLATE 43

Exceptional evidence of what Tuscan Renaissance gardens were like is provided by the fourteen still-existing lunettes commissioned by the Grand Duke Francesco I at the end of the seventeenth century from Giusto Utens, a mysterious Flemish artist who lived at Carrara, to decorate the Villa of Artiminio in the center of the Grand Duke's hunting ground in the Montalbano hills. The realistic illustrations make the lunettes an irreplaceable documentation of the gardens of the cinquecento.

With the help of maps and architectural drawings, Giusto Utens carried out surveys of the fourteen sites. The subjects were all Medicean villas and their gardens, which became the main features of the paintings. The scenes show the villas built by different members of the Medici family from 1451 to 1599, when the last lunette was finished. This is the villa and park called Pratolino, built for the Grand Duke Francesco I over a period of fifteen years starting in 1569, by the architect Bernardo Buontalenti. It was a monument to the complex Manneristic culture and anticipated the richness of the Baroque style. The park was considered a wonder from the start. It had labyrinthine walks which could only be appreciated by following them. There was no way of getting a general view. It was a garden of sights and sounds, because the various areas were first presented to wonder-struck visitors by the splash of running waters and cascades. The garden was crisscrossed by channels with a masterly succession of pools and cascades forming a double frame around it. The thickly wooded park inside was also intersected by a geometrical network of straight, multidirectional walks which led to various architectural and sculptural spaces. Buontalenti's project did not let visitors ever get a glimpse of the garden as a whole from any point either in the villa or the park. Utens' bird's-eye view is therefore fundamental for fully understanding every scene. It reveals and desecrates the mystery imposed on visitors.

*Luigi Zangheri, *Pratolino, il giardino delle meraviglie*, Florence 1979 and 1989; Daniela Mignani, *Le Ville Medicee di Giusto Utens*, Florence 1980.

PLATE 44

LA PRETAIA

This lunette painted by Giusto Utens shows the Villa della Petraia, a farmhouse turned into a villa by Bernardo Buontalenti for Ferdinando Medici probably between 1575 and 1590. Here, too, the artist's attention is centered on the garden, giving both a complete and analytical view of the whole, while the villa, pictured in precise detail, has become a focal point, fundamental for the perspective view, but not the subject of the primary communication.

Here the Manneristic architect did not propose a continuity of breathtaking curiosities as at Pratolino. Instead he re-proposed, in a more modern version, the fascination of the rationality of early Renaissance Italian gardens. At La Petraia, he applied all his knowledge of and research into hydraulic machinery, automata, scenographic and pyrotechnic happenings. The permanent theater for combining botany and hydraulics to animate the life and feasting of the Medici family and their guests was the garden, here *photographed* at the time of its completion. The villa lies against a backdrop of hills and cypresses. In front of it there is a lawn which looks on to the large fountain and its many waterworks. The villa is flanked by two columns of trees that continue with potted trees as far as the terrace. Under this, to the side of the pool, there is a pattern of symmetrical beds for herbs and flowers, with more potted trees in their centers. Another terrace leads down to the lowest level, where the most conceptual and symbolic part of the garden is situated. Two more spectacular spaces are laid out with twin concentric rings formed of barrel-roofed pergolas completely covered with climbing plants, as if they were labyrinths. Thick groves separate the two pergolas and fill the space outside the largest circle. The two round spaces in the center of the rings are the meeting points at the end of the walks, used for feasting, masques, and music. The park is closed in by a long perimetric wall interrupted by one triumphal entrance in the middle. Its simple layout was essentially a permanent homage to reason, but it was also designed to host the most extraordinary man-made events.

PLATE 45

Martius, Aprilis, Maius, sunt tempora veris · VER Pueriṭẹ compar Vere Venus gaudet florentibus aurea sertis ·

This engraving, made in 1570, is a reproduction of a drawing and painting by Pieter Brueghel the Elder, the great Flemish artist, who also succeeded in expressing moments of material culture in his extraordinary scenes. The picture is a metaphorical representation of spring, shown in the realistic portrayal of the work to be done in a Dutch garden during this season. The print is therefore an exceptional document. It is difficult to find the likes of it in other societies and in other historical epochs.

All the components of a northern garden in the sixteenth century as well as how to look after it are depicted here in this partly anthropological, partly didactic picture. In the foreground a group of men are preparing the beds after the winter, while some women are adding dung to the earth and planting bulbs that will soon transform these geometrically shaped plots into flower beds. Behind them, potted trees, flowers, and shrubs are ready to be transplanted to the centers of the beds or along the pathways so as to complete the scene. There is also a topiary tree clipped like a cakestand. The garden is surrounded by an architectural balustrade and regular clipped hedges. To one side, it leads into a barrel-roofed pergola whose entrance supports are formed of a sculptured carytid and telamon. The sheep pen is behind this, with a small pasture and the sheepcote where some men are shearing. Beyond the pen there is a river where a boat can be seen transporting trees, perhaps for this garden, proof of how much care was taken in looking after gardens at this time. There is an open-air tavern in the background with people drinking, pouring out wine, and making music. An arbor implies the presence of another garden under the castle walls. The whole scene expresses the labor necessary for setting up and preserving a garden. It documents the complex *continual maintenance* necessary to its very existence.

PLATE 46

Hans Vredeman de Vries (1527-1606) was the Dutch theoretician who introduced the idea of the Italian Renaissance garden to northern Europe as the final expression of a new, increasingly popular culture. He was an expert in draughtsmanship and perspective drawing and spread his Flemish and Dutch interpretation of the Manneristic architectural and decorative school through a series of books and tables that had an enormous influence in the whole of northern Europe, including England.

In 1583 he published in Antwerp the first edition of *Hortorum Viridariorumque Elegantes & Multiplicis formae...* which proposed an improbable application of Vitruvian orders to gardens. The author actually presented twenty prints (which became twenty-eight in the second edition published in 1587) showing the *Doric* garden, the *Ionic* garden and the *Corinthian* garden. Although they were intellectual and pre-academic exercises, Vrendeman de Vries' pictures provide documentary evidence, thanks to their detail and realism, of the reconstruction of Dutch gardens during the second half of the sixteenth century. This engraving shows a fairly large garden, by Dutch town standards, contained within a sequence of parallel buildings and probably limited at the far end by a canal. The garden is completely architectural, with a succession of fences, entrances, pergolas, walks, little temples, and geometric beds. The relationship between the architecture and the plant world is shown, for example, in the various kinds of pavilions, from the stone one in the foreground covered with a leafy roof with a statue on top, to one similar to it in the heart of the concentric arrangement of the pergolas, to the twin arbors at the end of the garden where the plants prevail over the treillages. The scene is a slice of life. The elegance of the guests, their behaviour, and the large banquet show that in the sixteenth century, one single cultural model was established for gardens in every European nation.

*C.H.C.A. Van Sypesteyn, *Oud-Nederlandsche Tuinkunst*, 'S-Gravenhage 1910.

PLATE 47

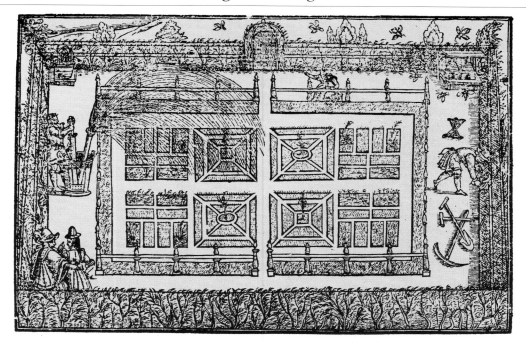

The relationship between man and the garden from the point of view of material culture shows a variety of characteristics, both in the geographical spaces of different societies and in time. In England the term *gardener* means not just an enthusiast but also the person who takes care of the garden, culturally and materially. In the second half of the eighteenth century, Horace Walpole coined a new word for this figure: *gardenist*. This late sixteenth-century English woodcut shows the gentleman gardener and his servants.

The illustration is taken from the 1594 edition of the book by Dydymous Mountaine (a pseudonym for Thomas Hill) titled *The Gardeners Labyrinth*, an enlarged version of the earlier "A most briefe and pleasaunte treatyse, teachyng how to dresse, sowe, and set a garden," published in London in 1563, which was the first book in Europe wholly on gardening. Elizabethan England saw the birth of a new figure, the amateur gardener or dilettante. If the success of the book was something to go by, this figure became very common. Renaissance culture and the Dutch upper classes' passion for flowers and gardens contributed to the establishment of this phenomenon. From its original behaviouristic dimension and symbolic quality, gardening became a passion in the whole of England and a necessary characteristic of the new gentleman's style of life. In the last

ten years of the sixteenth century, the time when this passion was in full swing, 288 exotic species were imported to the British Isles (compared to 127 in Italy over the whole century, which had five botanical gardens, while the first of its kind in Britain was founded at Oxford in 1621). Ever since then, botanical interest (scientific and agricultural, experimental and medical) in England was never separated from the question of the practical management of the garden and its successive contemplation. The book promised to reveal the "new and rare inventions and secrets of gardening not heretofore known," adding that nothing of the like had ever been published before for embellishing every garden of pleasure.

*Roy Strong, *The Renaissance Garden in England*, London 1979; Richard Mabey, ed., *The Gardener's Labyrinth*, Oxford New York 1987.

PLATE 48

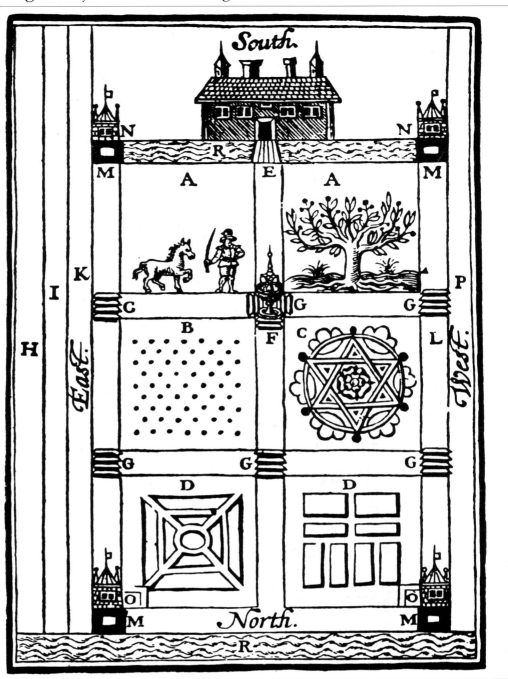

A. Al these squares must be set with Trees, the Garden and other Ornaments must stand in spaces betwixt the Trees, and in the borders and fences.
B. Trees twenty yards asunder.
C. Garden Knots.

D. Kitching Garden.
E. Bridge.
F. Conduit.
G. Stairs.

H. Walkes set with great wood thicke.
I. Walks set with great wood round about your Orchard.
K. The Out fence.
L. The Out fence set with stone-fruit.

M. Mount. To force Earth for a Mount or such like, set it round with quicke, and lay boughes of Trees strangely intermingled, the tops inward, with the Earth in the middle.
N. Still-house.
O. Good standing for Bees, if you have an house.

P. If the River run by your door, and under your Mount, it will be pleasant.

The extraordinary eloquence of a diagram in the history of the ideas of the garden is illustrated by this woodcut, which fully demonstrates the idea of the garden in England at the beginning of the seventeenth century. The print comes from William Lawson's book, *A New Orchard and Garden*, published in London in 1618 and sold together with another of his books, *The Countrie Housewife's Garden*, printed in 1617, which was the first European book for women amateur gardeners.

The woodcut shows a kind of existential microcosm, an obvious reference to medieval monastic models. The house and its enclosed territory contain, virtually, all man's requirements, in total independence from the surrounding environment. The Renaissance idea of the garden and the figure of the amateur gardener were grafted onto this old concept of the garden which was first and foremost a productive unit. The elegantly dressed gardener is to be seen training his horse, not far from the fountain of considerable architectural and aesthetic importance, which is also the heart of the garden's irrigation system. The property is confined within two waterways. A bridge links the house to the garden, which is laid out in six large squares. Lawson wrote that these squares could be surrounded by trees and contain gardens and other ornaments inside them. He proposed the arrangement in an order that follows a classification of practical and mundane uses: the formal flower garden with beds laid out in decorative patterns; the garden for the palate, for the requirements of the kitchen; the orchard (with trees planted twenty yards apart) and side walk; another walk paved with wood; pavilions; beeboles; artificial mounts forming belvederes. The orchard and kitchen garden are the puritanical self-justification for the other garden, the leisure garden for elegant idleness and contemplation, which was, in turn, justified by the practical labor of the owner.

*Reginald Blomfield, Inigo Thomas, *The Formal Garden in England*, London 1892; H. Inigo Triggs, *Formal Gardens in England and Scotland*, London 1902.

PLATE 49

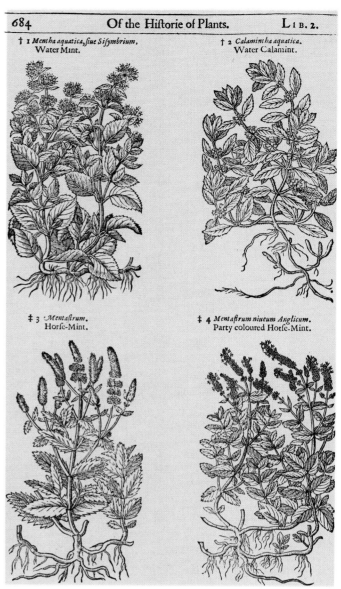

John Gerard's book, *The Herball or Generall Historie of Plantes* whose definitive edition was printed in London in 1633, was a milestone in the history of European gardens. It had its origins in the complex character of sixteenth-century botanical culture (in the typographical transcription of hand written herbals, in the age of the cultivation of new American plants, and of the epistemological leap from the physick to botanical gardens). In England the book was the cultural means for transforming medical and botanical curiosity into interest in the garden.

The first edition of this book was published in London in 1597, fifty-three years after *I Commentari al Dioscoride* by Pietro Andrea Mattioli. The latter book, published in Venice, was the most famous herbal in print and was to achieve an unrivaled success over the following centuries. Mattioli republished the work by Dioscorides, the famous military physician of the first century A.D., for its botanical and medical interest, since it was considered from late antiquity right through to the Renaissance the undisputed authority on classical botany, as numerous handwritten herbals before the age of printing were to document. Gerard drew heavily on Mattioli (whose woodcuts followed the model of medieval and humanistic botanical drawing) for both the description of the plants and for their illustration. In the history of

English culture, where the scientific and medical interest in botany developed several decades after the first editions of the herbal, Gerard's work has a more complex significance. First and foremost it was an instrument supplying knowledge suited to the requirements of every gardener. The aesthetic utilization of botany took the place of scientific use. It also helped settle the profit and pleasure relationship, which many English texts were proposing, by including some micro-productive areas, especially orchards, into the modern garden. Gerard can be seen at the bottom of the frontispiece holding a shoot of the potato plant, illustrated here for the first time in Europe.

*Pietro Andrea Mattioli, I discorsi di M. Pietro Andrea Mattioli Medico Senese, ne i sei libri della materia medicinale di Pedacio Dioscoride Anazarbeo, Latin edition, Venice, Italian edition, Brescia 1544.

PLATE 50

In 1629, only thirty years after Gerard's herbal, John Parkinson published *Paradisi in Sole, Paradisus Terrestris*. Its ingenuous programmatic frontispiece is shown here. The main role in this earthly paradise was played by the English modern garden with its arrangement of trees, flowers, and fruit trees, including a significant number of exotic species introduced only a few decades earlier which were already the subject of curiosity and delight for gardeners.

The complex English relationship between botanical science and the garden was clearly formulated here. While the book is planned like contemporary herbals destined for scientific uses, nearly all the text is dedicated to the knowledge and techniques necessary for creating, under English climatic conditions, a garden of all kinds of pleasant flowers. The two shortest supplementary sections are also on gardens: the kitchen garden and the orchard. England was never to experience a dichotomy between botanical science and gardening. The relationship between the two and their interdependency was to become closer and closer, unlike the experience of other European countries. Proof of this is that extraordinary and unique institution, the Royal Botanic Gardens at Kew, housing twenty-five thousand species. Founded in 1754, they remained a part of the royal palace until the last century. There is an ancient physick garden; a botanical garden; a scientific laboratory for continual experimentation, the heart of botanical research undertaken all over the world; a center of scientific and historical documentation – all imbued with the national passion, shared by kings and citizens alike for the plants and flowers needed to make a garden, credit for this must be given to Sir Joseph Banks, who headed the insitution from 1778 to 1820, establishing its permanent characteristics and significance. English gardeners and European scientists set up an active partnership, producing both scientific and aesthetic results. The Royal Horticultural Society, founded in 1846, with its activities and its Journal, formed a perfect complement to the Royal Botanical Gardens. The Society has marked the development of these interests in England and throughout the world.

*W.J. Bean, *The Royal Botanic Gardens, Kew: Historical and Descriptive*, London 1906.

PLATE 51

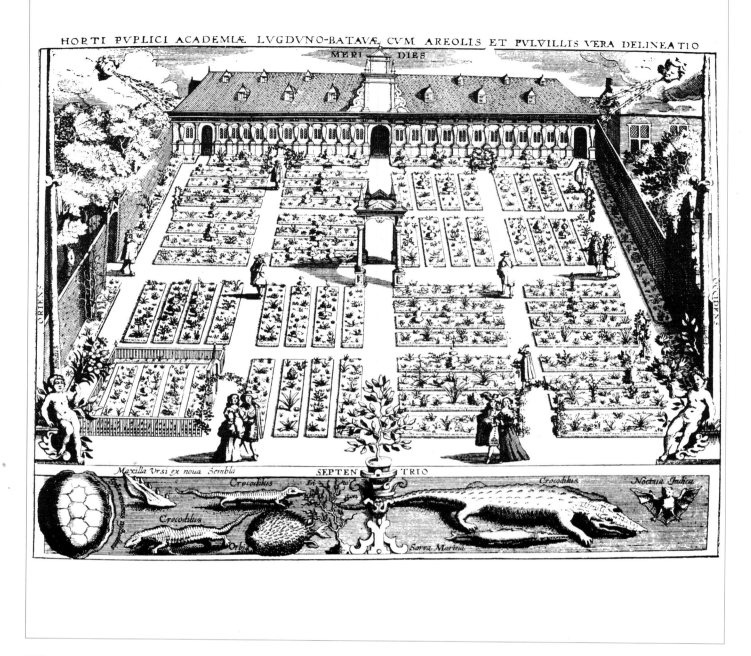

HORTI PVPLICI ACADEMIÆ LVGDVNO-BATAVÆ, CVM AREOLIS ET PVLVILLIS VERA DELINEATIO

This picture, dated 1655, showing the Dutch botanical garden in Leiden, illustrates how, over the years, scientific botanical interest became more and more tied up with exotic curiosities. The animals in the cartouche are evidence of the new geographical discoveries. The botanical garden in Leiden was one of the first in Europe. It was founded in 1577, thirty-two years after the Paduan one. In 1633 its catalogue totaled 1,104 species. One century later there were more than six thousand.

Some of Europe's most important botanists taught at the botanical garden in Leiden, including Charles l'Ecluse or Clusius at the end of the sixteenth century. Pineapples and tuberoses were among various exotic species to be cultivated here for the first time in Europe. Scientific and botanical interest on the one hand and garden enthusiasm on the other came together here, like at Kew, in a system of not easily interpretable interdependency which lacked, perhaps, the continuity of a passion that, in the English case, has been maintained to the present day. The kind of garden suggested by this botanical garden should not lead to a false conclusion. The tidy arrangement of the rectangular beds laid out in squares with one of them protected by fencing, the central pavilion in front of the villa used for studying, the high wall around it, the elegant visitors walking down the paths, are the constituent and descriptive factors of a place giv-

en up to the scientific classification of the botanical world. The orderly division of the plant species is essential for their fostering and to study their life and growth, because it places the whole of nature within reach, simply because it has been rationally organized. It is clear that this kind of structure is derived from a Renaissance idea of order, and it is also evident that the application of such a method of classification to a botanical garden will influence, in the form of a continual bilateral relationship, the development of future Manneristic and Baroque style gardens. Rarities and exotica were then to dominate both in botanical and formal contexts. The idea of the garden invaded the field of botanical science. The first tomato plant that was brought to Europe was considered as a possible decorative element for the garden, in apparent contrast with the culture and practice which made the search for profitable plants their aim.

PLATE 52

In 1614 a twenty-four-year-old Dutch gardener, Crispin Van de Pass the Younger, published a book in Latin called *Hortus Floridus*, which was translated into English the following year. It was an herbal of garden flowers arranged in texts and finely engraved illustrations, and divided into climatic and temporal groups: spring, with 41 species; summer, with 20; autumn, with 25; and winter, with 12.

The immediate publication of an English edition shows how great an interest there was in Dutch floriculture and what an attraction the small flower garden was in England, which was still under the influence of Renaissance culture. This engraving is the frontispiece of the book whose flower illustrations are the best of the time for their realism and detail, as can be seen here in this general view outlining a kind of Dutch model garden at the beginning of the seventeenth century. The beds for cultivating flowers are traced by dividing the area into highly decorative geometric designs. The whole of this symbolic rather than realistic garden is meant for flowers, and the tulip already reigns supreme. The little trees, clipped in topiary shapes, seem to be reference marks rather than main features, unlike the climbing roses in the foreground, winding around the columns of the gallery. The musing owner is leaning on the balustrade while his wife (as her dress reveals her to be) is looking after some tulips. The garden is enclosed by an architectural structure made famous by Hans Vredeman de Vries a hundred years earlier. This is one long barrel-roofed *berceau* supported by caryatids and covered with plants; it forms an old and elegant cultural frame for enclosing the new cultivated treasures of a modern garden characterized by exotic marvels and the various fashionable ways of enjoying them.

PLATE 53

The symbol of the glorious revolution and of the golden century (the seventeenth) of the Dutch middle class's power was an exotic flower, the tulip, the overwhelming passion of every owner of a garden. Tulips, in all their various colours, had been imported to Europe at the end of the sixteenth century. The flower won the hearts of the Dutch, who formed commercial companies for speculating in it. The peak of the rise in its price, in 1637, brought about one of the first modern financial crashes and the ruin of immense fortunes.

Looking back, it seems as if the whole social existence of the Dutch revolved around tulips, from the garden, obviously, to the house, to the china factories in Delft, which produced complicated multiple-mouthed vases for exhibiting infinite series of cut flowers. Tulips came from China originally and were brought to Vienna by the Austrian ambassador to Constantinople (the place from which the interest in tulips spread through Turkey). The commercial adventure of the tulip involved to a greater or lesser extent the whole of Europe but it became established as a fashionable plant in Holland, where some special varieties were worth their weight in diamonds and others were considered to have the value of a dowry. (A hundred years later, another plant craze in Holland followed in the footsteps of the tulip: this time it was the hyacinth.) These are some of the illustrations of tulips published at the time. One of the first known European drawings, by Konrad Gesner, is to be seen at the top left. This was used in

De Hortis Germaniae liber, the botanical work by Valerius Cordus published in 1561. To the right there is a Turkish design for printed decorations dating back to the early years of the seventeenth century. The other two illustrations come from the book containing thirty-eight prints of tulips painted by Nicolas Robert (1614-1685). They are part of the immense heritage known as the *Vélins du Roi*, the name by which French botanical portraits were known ever since Louis XIV (for whom Robert worked) acquired the library and collection of botanical drawings from his uncle Gaston, the Duke of Orleans, who had started it in his castle at Blois as a parallel to his loving cultivation of the garden. The *Vélins du Roi* established a new aesthetic and scientific method of illustrating flowers in Europe.

*W.S. Murray, "Tulips and Tulipomania", in *Journal of the Royal Horticultural Society*, March 1909; Arthur Baker, "The cult of the Tulip in Turkey", in *Journal of the Royal Horticultural Society*, September 1931; Wilfrid Blunt, *Tulipomania*, London 1950; Tom Lodewijk, *The Book of Tulips*, New York 1979.

PLATE 54

The *camellia* is a flower with about one hundred and ninety varieties. It originally came from the area between the twentieth and thirtieth parallel N., which includes Japan, a part of Korea, south-east China, and the outskirts of the Indochinese peninsula. Its road to success in Europe was unusual. It was taken into consideration as a possible producer of tea (the Chinese still refused to give Camellia sinensis to Europeans) but the species imported were a clamorous aesthetic and botanical success.

The genus was established by Carolus Linnaeus in his *Species Plantarum*, volume II, 1753, and dedicated to the Moravian Jesuit botanist, G.J. Camellus, who was not an expert on camellias. An English captain introduced the first plants to England in 1739. These were taken to Lord Petre's garden and placed in the greenhouse. They died because their natural conditions of growth were not known. A later introduction involved Italy: Lord Nelson gave Lady Hamilton a plant which still survives in the romantic part of the former royal garden at Caserta. The first, careless introduction of this flower to Europe was followed by a second, and there were others of epic proportions. Taken away from the garden for the few, or isolated from its botanical and aesthetic habitat, the camellia was to become a symbol for all. Alexandre Dumas the Younger wrote a novel, inspired by a dramatic autobiographical experience, which was to make him famous. It was called *La dame aux camélias*. The play,

which was criticized by the censor, was put on, with other great successes, in 1852. Giuseppe Verdi's *La Traviata*, whose libretto was inspired by Dumas' work, was presented for the first time in 1853. Camellias became the rage. Every lady had to wear one or more of them. The flower became the star of popular novels. Nurseries started to speculate with their production. The camellia greenhouses in St. Petersburg were the most famous in all Europe. This watercolor comes from a series of about two hundred (preserved in Milan, in the Natural History Museum) probably painted by an anonymous Flemish artist in the first few decades of the nineteenth century, the time when Luigi Sacco had formed a collection in the museum of about twelve thousand. The various contemporary cultivators of camellias are members of national societies which are brought together in the *International Camellia Society*.

*Tom Durrant, *The Camellia Story*, Kingswood 1982.

PLATE 55

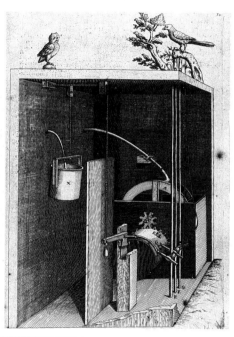

Salomon de Caus, the French architect and engineer of Huguenot origins, sought refuge in protestant England during the reign of James I. When James' daughter, Elizabeth, married Frederick V, the Elector Palatine, de Caus went with her to Heidelberg, where he designed one of the most interesting Renaissance gardens in the whole of Europe. Salomon de Caus was fascinated by the machines invented by Hero of Alexandria for gardens. He did not simply translate the ancient texts describing the great Greek engineer's machines as the Italians had done halfway through the sixteenth century. His creative spirit led him to invent and build new ones.

The stature of this extraordinary intellectual, artist, and ingenious technician in the first half of the seventeenth century can be seen in the European dimensions of his publishing activity. *La perspective, avec la raison des ombres et miroirs* was published in London in 1612; *Les raisons des forces mouvantes*, from which the fourth illustration is taken, was printed in Frankfurt in 1615. The same town and the same year saw the publication of *L'institution harmonique* from whose second volume on the decoration of villas and garden the first three illustrations are taken. *Hortus Palatinus*, the description of the garden at Heidelberg, was published in Frankfurt in 1620. Lastly, *La pratique et demonstration des horloges solaires* was printed in Paris in 1624. All these books reveal a scientific attitude towards the subject of enquiry even if the aims of the study were simply those of making a garden more pleasant. The four drawings are illustrations of projects described in the texts. The first shows Memnon, the mythical statue of ancient Egypt which Hero had taken for a subject. This hollow metal figure apparently spoke by means of solar heating and a hydraulic sonorous machine hidden inside it. The second is a complex fountain for a grotto with waterworks that implied the knowledge and utilization of new techniques of hydraulic engineering. The third is a hydraulic machine for animating some mechanical birds in a natural setting. The last one is a real hydraulic organ. The text describing this included the transcription of modern, mainly Italian, music. By using specially regulated running water, a small, continual concert could be guaranteed in the garden.

PLATE 56

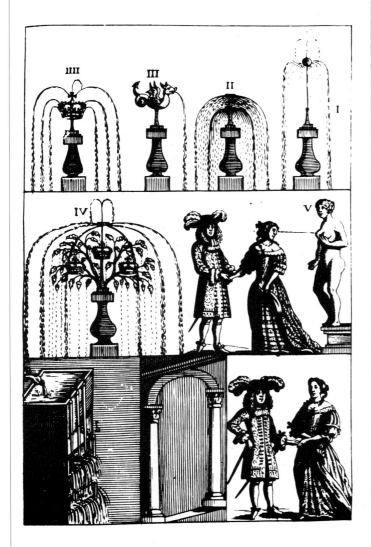

The term *hydraulic game* underwent a semantic change in just a few decades. From the refined intellectual Renaissance meaning based on the complex character of the machine and the fascination of the artifice, which had its roots in Alexandrine classical antiquity and before that in the distant past of Egyptian magic, hydraulics came to be associated with superficial, easily forgotten enjoyment, or with the simple symbolic allusion to the decorative form.

These two illustrations date back to 1677. The one on the left comes from John Woolridge's book, *Systema Horti-Culturae, or the Art of Gardening*, which was printed in London. This is the frontispiece of the chapter on fountains that gives a simple and concise technical grounding on the subject. One of the simplest amusements achieved by the waterworks is a supreme joke: the breast of a female statue that squirts water in the eye of the beholder. Similar devices were distributed round the garden to surprise guests. The picture on the right comes from *Le Labyrinthe de Versailles* by Charles Perrault (the brother of the classicistic architect, Claude Perrault) which was published in Paris. In the *labyrinth*, one of the most bizarre and wonderful terminuses to the intricate course the Roi Soleil obliged visitors to his park to follow, Perrault organized the representation of Aesop's thirty-nine fables in lively three-dimensional scenes. (Jean La Fontaine's rhymed version of the fables was then in fashion.) Plant environments as rigid scenery, ornaments as furnishings, sculptures as actors: these elements transformed thirty-nine areas into thirty-nine theaters or, better, dioramas, where hydraulic machines were a structural component. This scene, based on the movement of jets of water, turns the swan and crane into the actors round the didactic fountain. Here the host could remind his visitors that when the crane asked what was the news, the swan replied that he was about to die.

PLATE 57

The history of *chinoiserie* has nothing to do with the more ancient and complex relationship between Europe and China. For chinoiserie China was an imaginary continent, full of every possible fascination, and imbued with convenient interpretations, especially as far as the European garden was concerned. It was a fashion which built its theoretical and pseudoscientific bases on our continent toward the end of the seventeenth century and became the rage during the early years of the following century.

Seventeenth-century rococo style decorations came in the form of excessive curiosities, but these were also the result of scientific interest in another, asymmetrical, non-Eurocentric branch of aesthetics. William Temple, for example, published *Upon the Gardens of Epicurus* in London in 1692, where he described, in the form of an improbable-sounding aesthetic theory, a kind of asymmetry unknown to Europe and defined by the Chinese as *sharawadgi* (a term of uncertain origin) which at the time was believed to have been invented by Temple. Unusual symmetry was to become the theoretical foundation of the aesthetics of the *curved line*, or *serpentine*, later the subject of a book by William Hogarth. These three illustrations, all on the same subject, artificial rock formations, serve to study the methods used to spread this taste for chinoiserie. The first comes from the book *An Embassy...to the Gran Tartar Cham Emperor of China* by Jan Nieuhof, the Dutch ambassador, printed in Lon-

don in 1669, fifty-nine years after the death of Matteo Ricci, the Italian Jesuit missionary. The picture did not attract any special attention immediately. But when Johann Bernhard Fischer von Erlach, the Austrian architect and theoretician, had his illustrated history of world architecture, *Entwurf einer historischen Architektur*, printed in Vienna in 1721, he inserted this old, perhaps forgotten drawing into the part on bizarre, unusual, and exotic styles, full of examples from the seventeenth century. Lastly, Ercole Silva, the Italian *aesthetic terrorist* and propagandist of the romantic garden, published as an example a perfect copy of the Austrian's picture eighty years later in his book, *Dell'arte dei giardini inglesi*, Milan, *Anno IX* (for the Republic, otherwise 1801).

*William Hogarth, *The Analysis of Beauty*, London 1753; Fiske Kimball, *The Creation of the Rococo Decorative Style*, New York 1943; Arthur O. Lovejoy, "The Chinese Origin of a Romanticism", in *Essays in the History of Ideas*, London 1948; Hugh Honour, *Chinoiserie. The Vision of Cathay*, London 1961.

PLATE 58

The garden is often the scenic backdrop for life. While theatrical scenery can certainly represent a garden, the stage is an unlikely place to try out a new type of garden, although in theatre, experimenting with new types of cities has became feasible. In this sense the theater works as a *diorama* for the garden, reproducing the marvels of imaginary or real normality.

Giacomo Torelli (1608-1678), the architect and mathematician, was also an innovator in Italian theatrical scenery during the second baroque period halfway through the seicento, thanks to his extraordinary perspective effects of a hypernatural, illusory character. The backdrop was all sky in realistic shades of blue which suggested the spatial infinity of the scene. The architectural or naturalistic wings were silhouetted, again realistically, against this enormous sky. A projecting element standing in the center, around which the actors or dancers moved, guaranteed the three-dimensional illusion of spatial depth. In this picture the wings simulate a thick forest. These were painted on transparent cloth, which assured the perfect scenic fusion with the sky. The centerpiece is an apparently artificial grotto. It represents Mount Helicon, the mountain of the Muses, who are, in fact, sitting on the top. Three different vistas, to the center and sides of the grotto, create the illusion of tree-lined avenues disappearing in the distance, painted on the backdrop from where the sky sweeps upward. The intelligent alternation of artificial lighting and deliberate shade makes this scene very real, or, at the least, fascinating as a credible imitation. The audience seems to be inside a huge modern garden, as the relationship between wilderness and order in the plant composition suggests, and as the great architectural and symbolic manufacture in the center confirms.

PLATE 59

The monumental complex at Bomarzo is a mysterious garden full of curiosities and monsters that perhaps lived inside the sacred glade of the wood not far from the home of its inventor, an enigmatic humanist, Vicino Orsini. More than a composition designed to amaze visitors, Bomarzo seems to be the architectonic and sculptural framework for the rite of passage of a select group admitted to a private cenacle. But it could be interpreted, as it was, in another way.

From the puzzle of the monsters and the meanings of this Manneristic invention (Bomarzo was built around the middle of the sixteenth century), the world of the garden took hold of wonders and rarities to transform them into the ingredients of a banal and gaudy form of aesthetics available to all. Separated from its still mysterious context, this leaning pavilion, shown here in a recent drawing, slides down a scale of values to the banality of the unusual. Even though the site and its monuments are in an advanced state of decay, they still comunicate to anyone that their entire being and interdependencies have an undeniably complex and deep significance. A single component, taken in isolation, destroys and desecrates the sense of Bomarzo even though it still conserves its secrets. The aesthetics of *bad taste* feed on exceptionalness,

distorting its significance and worth. The garden was soon to become the popular theater of objects of bad taste, both big and little. As in a catastrophe (according to Ren Thom's theory) an eyesore can slip into a garden almost unnoticed, but its very presence sets off an inexorable repetition that turns the series into triteness. This was the case, for example, with a little statue which Swiss folklore called the *gnome of the forest* whose presence was a good omen. In 1840 an English woman took one home as a memento and put it in her garden. From that time on it multiplied, taking over English gardens, whence it spread, in even worse taste, to gardens all over Europe.

*Eugenio Battisti, *L'antirinascimento*, Milano 1962; Horst Bredekamp, *Vicino Orsini und der Heilige Wald von Bomarzo*, Worms 1985.

PLATE 60

Christian Cay Lorenz Hirschfeld, professor of philosophy and the fine arts at the University of Kiel, was an enthusiastic observer of the artistic aspects of the new English romantic garden between 1779 and 1785. He published in Leipzig a monumental five-volume treatise which codified all the English ideas. The book came out simultaneously in two languages, *Theorie der Gartenkunst* and *Théorie de l'art des jardins*. It aimed at formulating in both theoretical and practical terms the new aesthetics and the techniques regarding plant scenery.

This picture comes from Hirschfeld's treatise. Using the methods and complex structure of a modern encyclopedia, it proposed to found a new subject of study and to define it both holistically and in every specific part. It was arranged in the form of didactic examples, but it was soon used as a sort of paper pattern for do-it-yourself copies in any garden where the owner felt inclined to adopt the now romantic aesthetics of exceptionalness. The frame of reference here is the fully integrated *aesthetics of ruins* that led to the production of projects and buildings of fake ruins capable of embellishing semantically the garden scene. The little Tuscan temple, *partly in ruins*, as the author emphasizes, is enriched by the presence of plants: weeds grow between the stones of the broken roof. There is a square pool in the center of the portico which is now open because of the deliberate ruin of the roof. Once the perimeter of the portico and its top have been closed in with netting, the building becomes a functional aviary, with the little building serving as a cote. Everything has been thought out beforehand, from the romantic image of the building, to the decision that this container is a pretty home causing doubtless delight to its inhabitants. In this perspective, exceptionalness has become the ingredient for creating picturesque environments (like those found in landscape paintings) which satisfy the now widespread taste for a form of *Romanticism* that has been codified in its most elementary dimensions.

PLATE 61

In 1620 the French architect Salomon de Caus, an exiled Huguenot, wrote a book in Heidelberg in the tolerant Palatinate describing the garden he had designed for Frederick V, the Elector Palatine. The book, *Hortus Palatinus a Friderigo Rege Boemiae Electore Palatino Heidelbergae extructu,* was published in two editions, both with a Latin frontispiece but with texts in German and French. Rosicrucian manifestoes aiming at the transformation of the Palatinate into a place of tolerance and peace had been printed or hand copied just a few years earlier.

Frederick V's social and political project to create an area in central Europe of greater tolerance between Catholics and Protestants failed. The terrible Thirty Years War broke out two years before the publication of the book on his gardens. The war caused the death of more than half the Palatinate's inhabitants. Salomon de Caus' book describing the garden built for the Elector is a document of profound significance for that Utopia. All the technical and artistic details of gardens of the period deriving from innovations or Alexandrian historical roots were rearranged according to the author's Renaissance culture. Salomon de Caus reintroduced, for example, the machines created by Hero of Alexandria in this huge formal garden grounded in reason and sensibility. His interest in hydraulic and musical machines is documented in his other books. The garden in Heidelberg was formed of a series of regular terraces set between the hilly woods and the river to the side of the Prince's castle. It was designed with beds and square plots for botanical and especially for floral cultivation, with pergolas and wonderful waterworks and musical inventions. It was an exhaustive model of the most refined Renaissance garden and was more complex than its classical and glorious Italian counterpart because it was imbued with the new political and moral values of the Palatinate.

*Frances A. Yates, The Rosicrucian Enlightenment, London 1972.

PLATE 62

The project of the orangery, as presented by Salomon de Caus in his book, is an eloquent document of the scientific and aesthetic significance of the *Hortus Palatinus*. *L'Orangerie d'un fabrique de pierre de taille*, as the author called it in 1620, was an elegant late-Renaissance building, designed symbolically and functionally to hold sixty-year-old orange-trees transported to central Germany from far-off lands to the south, "chose que la plupart jugeont impossible."

The large hothouse with a stone structure was to replace a wooden one, and to store the collection of four hundred large orange trees and thirty medium and small ones, which were kept outside in the garden in the warmer season. The project illustrated the interdependency of the botanical interest in and the aesthetic fascination for exotic plants, and the practical nature of the new Renaissance garden that was highly characteristic on the cultural level. The design of the orangery is simple and intelligent: it is a long rectangle with a row of large windows placed close together (a demonstration of the semantic depth of this sophisticated architecture). The roof is partially hidden from sight by a balustrade with urns containing little trees. With its essential rationality, the orangery can be considered as a perfect example of an independent pavilion in a vast open space. Details of drawings were not considered necessary in similar contemporary projects. Here it seems to prove the sensibility of the architect and his elegant style of design. The large windows are divided up by both the built-in vertical columns and by the molding that runs around the orangery. In the detail of the window, one side is closed with a latticework pane and the other is open, showing the trees inside as evidence that the building was designed for the trees and not as an indifferent container. The coupled columns are didactic and symbolic: they petrify the illusion of a Manneristic trunk decorated with climbing flowering plants.

*Salomon de Caus, *Le Jardin Palatin, Hortus Palatinus*, Paris 1981; Richard Patterson, "The Hortus Palatinus at Heidelberg and the Reformation of the World", in *Journal of Garden History*, 1/1981 and 2/1981.

PLATE 63

Gervase Markham published his book *Country Farme* in London in 1616. It was the second revised version for English readers of Charles Estienne's famous treatise, *L'Agriculture et maison rustique*, dated 1564. This illustration proposes examples of fencing for the garden which are products of the European Manneristic concept of complex decoration. Fences were a practical, symbolic, and graphic necessity for enclosing a sacred place.

Every pattern for a garden fence is partly expression of the culture of its place and time. The very concept of an enclosure is deeply rooted in the idea and lexicon of the garden, ever since the medieval term *hortus conclusus* began to identify its special character. To enclose an area with a fence, even a small bed with a tiny border, means making it sacred, its symbolic value having priority over any other practical purpose. Sometimes even a wall required a supporting structure or treillage on the inside to be able to hold up the wandering shoots of the climbing flowering plants, as if it was a second, sacred, and botanical enclosure. An espalier of roses is therefore a regular feature in every garden in all times. But even a simple fence could become so too, as these two drawings show. The pattern of tied rods is quite straightforward in the lower part, while it develops into various decorative shapes at the top with the aim of creating an intricate overall design. The merlons give a sense of the conclusion or end of the surface defining an area, space, or building in the same way as architectural crenelation. The birds and boats seem like trophies. The author also indicates how to use the lower fence as a treillage for growing climbing plants, turning it into a support that shapes a hedge without having to resort to the laborious task of topiary.

PLATE 64

This anonymous engraving dating back to the end of the seventeenth century shows a German garden laid out according to the old dictates of the Italian style. It is characterized by a central fountain, balustrades, clipped box hedges, and a tulip in the center of a circular bed. *Virtual constructions* of pavilions shaped by a transparent framework have been built into the high surrounding wall.

The cultivation of plants for creating spaces to be used by man in the same way as houses built with traditional building materials presupposes not only very great technical ability but also a long period of time. The system of treillages was considered the most suitable method for creating architectural arbors fairly quickly, even by those who could allow themselves projects for an important part of the garden that would develop over tens of years or even several generations. Pavilions and barrel-roofed arbors made of wooden or marble trelliswork, which the climbing plants were supposed to turn into botanical buildings, had already been proposed in the humanistic period. Later on, fashionable taste made it necessary to revive the method of creating botanical constructions without using supporting structures. But the time needed to do this was so great that a compromise between the two methods was usually found in real gardens. At the beginning of the eighteenth century, the fashion for plant walls forming huge constructive elements was satisifed temporarily by setting up painted wooden walls and tying flowers and leaves on to them for social events, almost as if there was not even the time for creating a wall of climbing plants supported by an espalier. The architectural structures shown here would have been able to turn quite quickly into botanical buildings, modifying and adding to the scenic quality of the garden as well as emphasizing its perimeter, a feature which places a small garden in the category of *hortus conclusus*.

PLATE 65

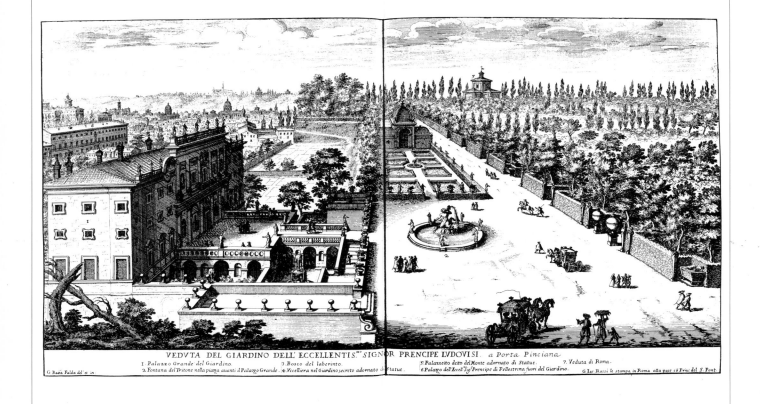

VEDVTA DEL GIARDINO DELL' ECCELLENTIS.^{MO} SIGNOR PRENCIPE LVDOVISI. *a Porta Pinciana*

1. *Palazzo Grande del Giardino.*   3. *Bosco del laberinto.*   5. *Palazzetto detto del Monte adornato di Statue.*   7. *Veduta di Roma.*

2. *Fontana del Tritone nella piazza auanti il Palazzo Grande.* 4. *Vccelliera nel Giardino secreto adornato di Statue.* 6. *Palazzo dell'Eccell.^{mo} Sig.^r Prencipe di Pellestrina fuori del Giardino.*

G. Bara Falda del' tt in.   G. Iac. Rossi le stampa in Roma alla pace c6 Priu: del S. Pont.

The publication, beginning in 1670, of a succession of engravings by Giovanni Battista Falda was very important for the study of Roman gardens at the end of the seventeenth century. These large *garden portraits* were so successful that the author brought them together in a book entitled *Li giardini di Roma, con le loro piante, alzate e vedute in prospettiva* (1683). The technique of a close-up bird's-eye view allowed readers to feel they were inside the garden and could visit all its most secret parts.

The overall composition of Prince Ludovisi's garden (on the area that was once the *Horti Sallustiani*) is easily observable in this drawing. There is a distinct relationship with the architecture of the palazzo through the system of terraces and steps, a repetition of ornamental plants in urns, a large central fountain, a secret garden decorated with statues and an aviary (which was to become an orangery in the next century), and a great walk including a maze, framed by the palace and the green walls which enclose a large wood. It is interesting to observe here a design form which derives from a new relationship between antiquarian culture and the garden. The Ludivisi family collected antiquities and the garden was also considered a gallery for their finds. These were transformed into sculptures and were used as an architectural limit to the wood. They also defined the great walk, the borderline between history and culture on the one hand and nature on the other. The squares formed by carefully clipped plant walls led into the wood. A series of hermae, probably the results of careful archaeological excavations, can be seen in these entrances, almost as if they were intended to revive a form of decoration from the distant past. Two huge antique marble urns placed on an axis with the fountain and the palazzo have the effectiveness and eloquence of those celebrated by Piranesi in the following century. Some ancient marble tombs complete the antiquarian scenery woven into the green walls. Behind them, the wild wood raises its head as if it was a different but not distant territory.

PLATE 66

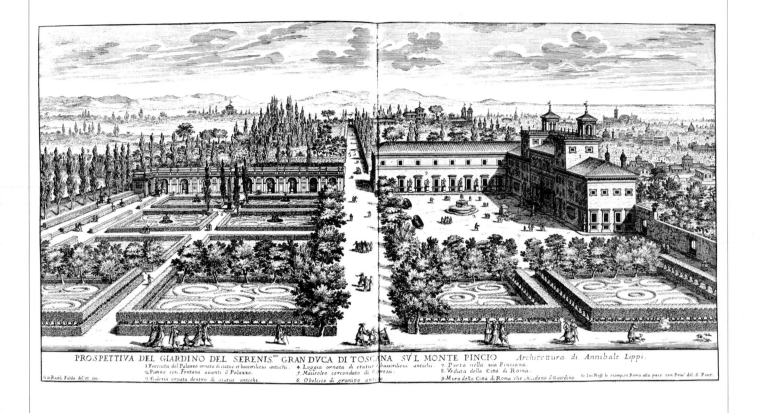

PROSPETTIVA DEL GIARDINO DEL SERENIS.^{MO} GRAN DVCA DI TOSCANA SVL MONTE PINCIO   *Architettura di Annibale Lippi.*

This scene of another sixteenth-century Roman garden was also drawn by Giovanni Battista Falda. This is the garden of the Grand Duke of Tuscany on the Pincian hill, known as *Collis Hortulorum* for the numerous gardens there at the time of republican Rome, including that of Lucullus. It is laid out like a large chessboard of cultivated and enclosed areas in front of the villa. Beyond this closed court is the second part of the garden with the big mount (mausoleum) planted with cypresses.

The architectonic space of this *little city* is defined by the villa and by its extension, a loggia with a series of niches containing sculptures that is linked to the terracing with its clipped hedges and tall trees. The great architectural and sculptural dignity, with its antiquarian connotations (the façade of the palazzo is decorated with antique statues and bas-reliefs, the gallery contains ancient statues, the loggia is embellished with similar statues and bas-reliefs), together with the signs of the Italian layout (the great walk, the fountains, the obelisk, the beds decorated à la française with sixteenth-century *broderie* designs and bordered by low box hedges creating the impression of a little green wall) were the expression of a new creativeness. In fact it was the first step toward the landscape dimension in the organization of the garden at that time. The triteness of symmetry which had spread everywhere and was used for the incessant and obsessive repetition of hackneyed botanical squares was consciously avoided here in a way that actually raised the whole question of their significance as the elementary basis of a potentially infinite multiplication. The large beds in the foreground are limited on the sides that are visible by hedges clipped to form balustrades. The transparent horizontal strip created at eye level by the naked trunks gives a view of the inside of the space with its *broderie*. The bed is bordered on the other two sides by tall trees whose natural growth gives the illusion of a grove. This serves as a backdrop to the series of the three plant communications that complete each other in their juxtaposition.

Paolo Gozza, La musica nella rivoluzione scientifica del seicento, Bologna 1989.

PLATE 67

HORTVS A MAGNIFICO ET NOBIL. VIRO DÑO IOHANNE SWINDIO CONSVLE et Senatore Moeno-Francofortano, conciñatus extruc. tus, ædifica- tur Francofortū ad Mœnū videndus.

M. Merian, ad viu) delin et sculpsit 1641

This perspective shows the garden belonging to Johannes Schwindt, the burgomaster of Frankfurt in 1641. German gardens in the Baroque period re-proposed the elements of Italian classical gardens and the great Renaissance tradition in a Manneristic version. The symmetrical layout, the merger of architecture and garden, the large architectural and sculptural decoration are the basic features of a specific Italianess chosen in that period by the ruling classes in central Europe as a style of life.

This kind of military occupation by Italian taste is clearly discernible in the print. Here the desire to be in fashion prevails over that of relating man and nature in a modern and elegant way in order to enjoy a garden designed on the basis of that union. The grouping together of these features, ornaments, and symbols appears to be quantitatively acceptable, but it is substantially mechanical, full of commonplace semantic significance, resulting in an aggregate that has lost the special harmony of the original Italian models. The great portal is part of an enclosure broken up at intervals by huge windows with urns containing little trees inside them. Between the windows there are columns supporting busts of a vaguely antique origin. The architectural design of this entrance is neither sober nor elegant nor triumphal. It is a haughty Manneristic exercise lacking the fascination of Baroque-style transgression. The internal arrangement also respects these formal criteria. The two large beds containing herbs and flowers, surrounded by potted plants, which are kept in the hothouse in winter, are the fruit of a traditional concept of collection that is certainly not especially botanical in content. The large tree-lined space that connects the two areas of symmetrical beds is characterized by two large human statues, matched at the other end by two obelisks. The barrel-roofed gallery walk covered with greenery that enlarges and emphasizes a large part of the garden wall is more a set quotation of Italian style gardens than a special solution to a landscape problem. The same can be said of the rose espaliers, softening the walls in front of the green porticoes. In the middle of the espaliers, there is a fountain for drawing water, but it is not the Italian fountain, the allegory of the *fons sapientiae*.

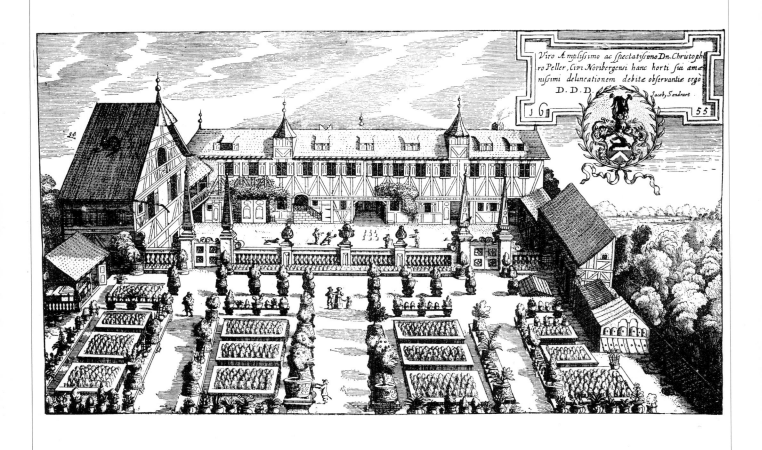

This perspective record dated 1655 shows Christoph Peller's garden, a contemporary of the previous one, in Nuremberg. While still having an Italian framework, this garden differs from the other in its rejection of figurative and symbolic emphasis. It succeeds, in fact, in achieving a creative union between the old timbered and plastered building and the new garden that is as yet free from deference to the Italian style. There is a greater love of flowers here, and pleasure in contemplating them.

The medieval court surrounded on three sides by buildings has not been changed either in its architectural composition or its functions. Here it serves as the setting for a game of skittles. The old court is enclosed by a precious Renaissance balustrade, a metaphor of the dichotomy between old and new, between house and garden. It has two gates flanked by large twin obelisks that seem to represent a passage from the past to a present full of promise. These gates lead into the new garden, which is quite alien from the ideas and culture that produced the buildings. Everything is organized mathematically, suggesting the reasoned arrangement of the Renaissance, not symmetry reduced to decorative triteness. The beds are filled with herbs and flowers. The pattern formed by the plants is such as to stimulate a closer look with the hope of establishing a link with each single flower, not just a rapid glance to get an overall impression. Large pots of orange trees and other plants lie along the paths next to the beds. They are brought out of the glasshouses during the warm season and displayed for continual observation of their botanical wonders. This typical organization of the Renaissance garden is similar, from a conceptual and sometimes from a formal point of view, to the arrangement of botanical gardens designed for the new scientific study of plants and for the consequent domestication of the plant world. Botany and gardening, science and aesthetics are terms which on many occasions during the Renaissance tended to weave creative interdependencies rather than produce insurmountable sectorial, disciplinary, and specialistic antimonies.

PLATE 69

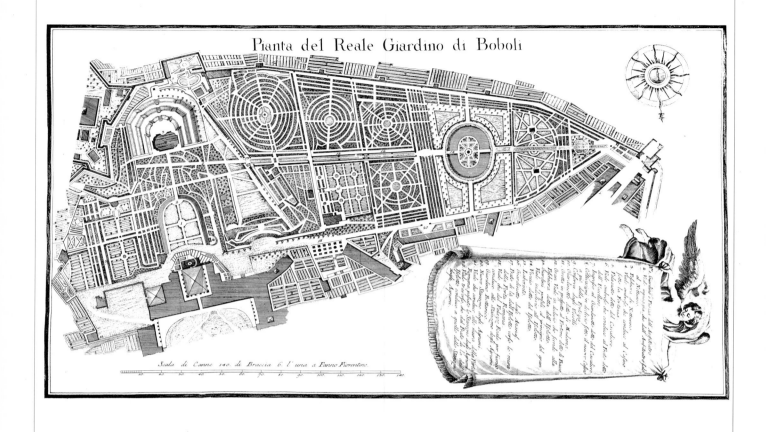

Pianta del Reale Giardino di Boboli

Scala di Canne 140. di Braccia 6. l'una a Panno Fiorentino.

The building of the first garden of Boboli began in 1550. It was designed by Niccol Tribolo, a sculptor, engineer and architect, one of the first architects to dedicate the greater part of his time to creating gardens. The first area of the garden was conceived as a green amphitheater placed in line with the villa. The vast lateral extension designed by Alfonso and Giulio Parigi that forms the extraordinary garden full of concentric geometrical patterns dates back to the beginning of the seventeenth century.

This seventeenth-century engraving giving a more or less faithful picture of the two phases shows the whole of the more modest sixteenth-century garden near the villa (used for theatrical events and naumachiae) and the great seventeenth-century extension. Everything is set up with patient Fland skillful *ars topiaria*, creating regular beds and green walls which host architectural ornaments, sculptures, and fountains. The two general layouts brought together by the sloping avenue which cuts through the first garden and generates the axis of the second, larger one, should be examined first of all. The original garden, whose backdrop is the internal facade of the villa, is a system of amphitheaters placed on various levels. These form an ideal outdoor setting for organizing entertainment thanks to their immediately comprehensible spatial and figurative relationship with the villa, almost as if they were its open-air extension. To the west of the villa there is the complex, more minute structure of the plant composition presented in regular square or rectangular beds. The new garden is grafted onto this existing layout, but it expresses an alternative dimensional rationale. No one can comprehend the design and the precepts for using it without actually walking through it, as is the case with the most perfect Baroque-style architectural spaces. Here, unlike the gentle perspective that revealed everything, real knowledge of these allusions to complex and infinite spaces can only be obtained by actually experiencing them. As if it was as a system of real labyrinths, a common feature of gardens of the time, Boboli has a succession of fake labyrinths (fake because they were concentric parallel walks) lying asymmetrically with respect to the layout. At the end of these there is the large, scenically restful oval fountain with its central island, offering a moment of contemplation at the end of a garden whose framework looks like a little city made up of circular patterns.

PLATE 70

Vuë du jardin et des Batimens, avec d'autres Jardins et Maisons voisines, de Son A. S^me Monseigneur Le Prince Eugène de Savoye.

Prospect Sr Hochfürstl Durchl Prinzens Eugeny von Savoÿen, u. s. Garten und darzu gehörigen Gebauden, sambt andern angrünzenden Garten und Haüsser.

Another model of a garden in a grand style is seen here in this bird's-eye view of Prince Eugène of Savoy's summer residence, the Belvedere palace, in Vienna. This print comes from a collection dedicated to him by Salomon Kleiner in 1731. It reveals the relationship between the residence outside the city and its environment and shows the apparently infinite extension of the park. It was considered one continual garden and laid out to classify all the wonders that the taste of the time could imagine.

Between one battle and another, Eugène of Savoy, a valorous soldier and famous condottiere, attended personally to the construction of his Viennese palace and its vast garden, built between 1700 and 1723. The garden was designed by Dominique Girard as a kind of summary of all the fashions of the time as applied to the art of designing gardens. The French formal style cohabits with several features of the Italian garden. The primary communication of the whole does not derive from the general layout, with its elegant relations between the buildings and the gardens, its mélange of forms, and its composite alignments, but from the use of certain gardening techniques to create a new microcosm. The system of regularly clipped green walls, which circumscribe thick groves or mark spaces, is used on an unusual scale. The great straight boundaries become avenues flanked by botanical parallelepipeds imitating buildings so vast as to give the impression of being in a very orderly urban context. The tiny open spaces and the green galleries form a more close-knit network, but still exhibit spatial qualities of a mini-urban nature. To walk through them is to be in a potential city, a laboratory where the plant world is utilized as it might be in a real city. The importance of the decoration of the *parterres à broderie*, essential for satisfying the taste of the time, is secondary compared to the dimensions and complexity of the extensive pattern of the mini-city.

PLATE 71

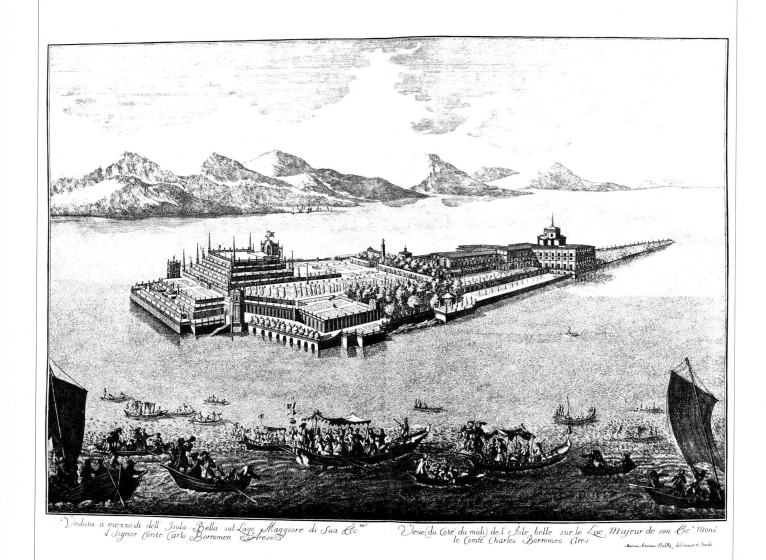

Veduta a mezzo di dell' Isola-Bella sul Lago Maggiore di Sua Ecc.
d'Signor Conte Carlo Borromeo Arese

Veüe (du Coté du midi) de l' Isle belle sur le Lac, Majeur de son Ecc.ᵐᵒⁿˢ
le Comté Charles Borromeo Ares

Marcus Antonius Dal Re, delineavit et fecit

Lake Maggiore, between Piedmont and Lombardy, was once governed feudally by the Borromeo family. The first island to be transformed by the family into a delightful place was Isola Madre, at the beginning of the sixteenth century. It was laid out in terraces descending from the top of the island to the lake and became an elegant Italian garden surrounded by water. Then it was Isola Bella's turn to be converted into a Manneristic curiosity. It took nearly fifty years (from 1620 to 1670) to complete.

The transformation of a natural island into the shape of a great floating ornament was the unusual subject of a project started by Count Giulio Cesare, carried on by his brother Carlo Borromeo III, and completed by his son Vitaliano. While intellectual meetings of poets and musicians took place on Isola Madre in the cinquecento, huge, deliberately stupefying feasts, theatrical masques and naumachiae simulating adventures were organized on Isola Bella one century later (mock naval battles were also enacted around the island). Here Isola Bella is shown in an engraving by Marc'Antonio Dal Re dated 1726. The Borromeos carried out earthworks following the lie of the land and utilized the ancient Renaissance technique of descending terraces in order to build a geometrical macrostructure capable of appearing artifical and therefore more wonderful than and, in this sense, different from Renaissance gardens. Everything is put on show to dazzle those coming to the island. The terracing and the architectural balustrades, the moorage and the pavilions, the permanent scene of the great theater on the top of the high ground, all were designed to form an extraordinary, apparently hanging garden, but which also seemed like a huge barge-garden anchored off the shore. The garden was to be the scenery facing the large palazzo whose lowest floors included vast grottoes with, perhaps, the aim of emphasizing the idea of everthing being pensile and artificial. The Borromeo family wanted to make Isola Bella one of the wonders of the world from the cultural and artistic points of view. The desire to build a prodigy, an extraordinary *Wunderkammer*, a setting for every possible natural or existing curiosity, diverges from the idea of the palace and the garden (and contrasts with the Renaissance taste permeating Isola Madre).

PLATE 72

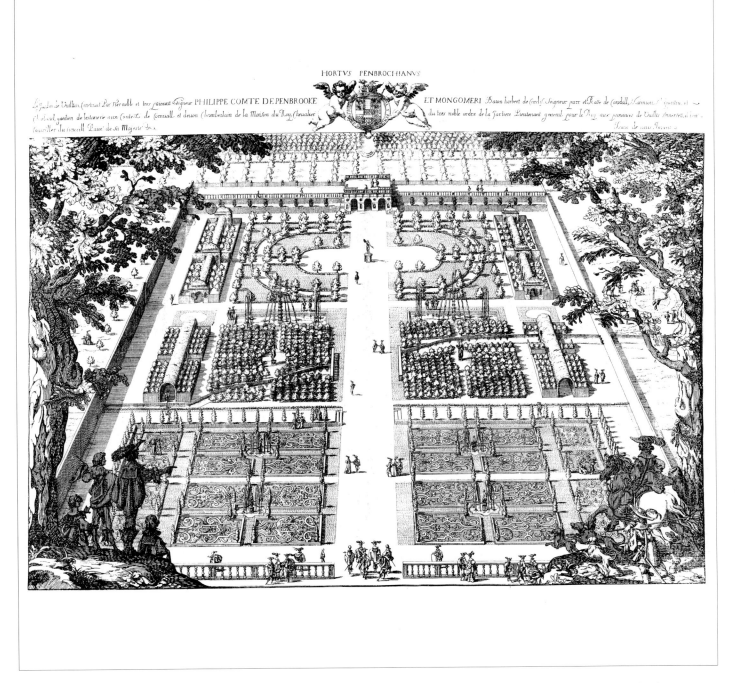

In England, Isaac de Caus followed in the footsteps of his brother Salomon, continuing his studies and methods of design. This bird's-eye perspective gives an overall view of Wilton in Wiltshire, built by Isaac between 1632 and 1635. It can be read as a cultural declaration of the supremacy of the new French formal garden over the tradition of the Italian Renaissance garden, even though there are references to the latter in the layout and in many details.

The definition of space was a novelty in England at that time. Wilton was a scenographic garden designed in the grand manner. A few years earlier Francis Bacon, the outstanding philosopher and forerunner of English empiricism, had expressed his ideas on gardens, establishing what was to become a must, in England in particular but also in other European countries, for every poet in the future. "God Almighty first planted a garden. And indeed it is the purest of human pleasures. It is the greatest refreshment to the spirits of man, without which buildings and palaces are but gross hand-iworks," was Bacon's opinion in 1625, expressed at the beginning of his essay "Of Gardens." Isaac de Caus carried on in England the work and research begun by Salomon. In 1644 "Nouvelles Inventions de lever l'eau plus haute que la source" was published in French in London. It was followed a year later by a book of engravings entitled *Le Jardin de Wilton* (the source of this general view), which aimed at documenting and theoretically justifying the garden he had built. Architectural balustrades and galleries, statues and complicated fountains similar to those made by Salomon, the inevitable, symmetrical *parterres de broderie* as curtain raisers, groves and the great oval circus, treillages forming vaulted *berceaux* and pavilions were all ingredients of this great and new garden where everything was clearly visible and comprehensible. However, wedged between recollections of Italy and French innovations, there is a disquieting sign that was to become a characteristic of all English gardens in the future: the respect for and interest in natural elements. At Wilton, Isaac de Caus did not modify the course of the river that flowed diagonally and in an irregular fashion across the new geometry of the plant composition.

*Roy Strong, The Renaissance Garden in England, London 1979.

PLATE 73

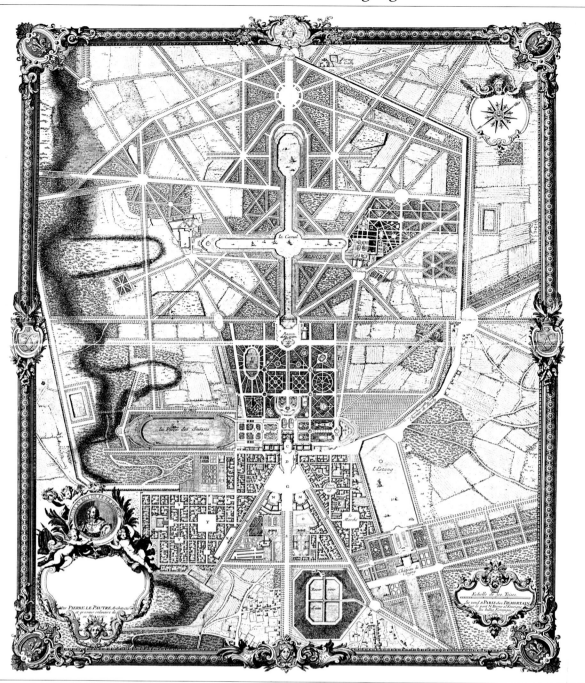

The seventeenth-century garden *par excellence* in Europe was the immense residence of the Roi Soleil and his court at Versailles. Designed as a metaphor of the dominion over nature by one who already dominated a nation and throught he dominated the world, Versailles was the masterpiece, in terms of quality and quantity, of André Le Nôtre (or Lenôtre, Le Nostre, Lenostre, 1613-1700), the landscape gardener.

Le Nôtre came from a family of gardeners and was the first in a line of French landscape gardeners. He worked both for Louis XIII and for Louis XIV. He was the founder of the style and school of French formal gardens, vased on a rigorous *esprit de géometrie* and on gigantesque dimensions. He experimented with his ideas in the park at Vaux-le-Vicomte and brought them to their apotheosis at Versailles where work on the garden started in 1662. The great park, shown here in an engraving by Pierre Le Pautre dated 1710, was designed on an axis starting from the royal palace, the point where all the lines of direction of the urban network converged. The vast scale was evident and an observer also was meant to understand that the government of the territory went way beyond the limits of the consolidated park to include the whole country by means of straight avenues that started at its boundary and disappeared into the distance. Avenues, hunting grounds, woods, gardens, fountains, gigantic stretches of water, and the first modern menagerie for taming, raising and observing animals were the ingredients of the park-city the king wanted for his own and his court's enjoyment. Inside it there was another garden with a residence for getting away from the pompous court etiquette, known as the *Grand Trianon*, to be seen in the engraving to the east of *le Canal*. The practical problems of everyday life in this *virtual city*, but *real capital* of the nation were enormous, involving the satisfaction of the various needs of the multitude of nobles, servants and military living there. But the problems of keeping the immense garden going were even more gigantic.

*Franklin Hamilton Hazlehurst, *Gardens of Illusion (The Genius of Andr Le Nostre)*, Nashville 1980; Kenneth Woodbridge, *Princely Gardens*, London 1986.

PLATE 74

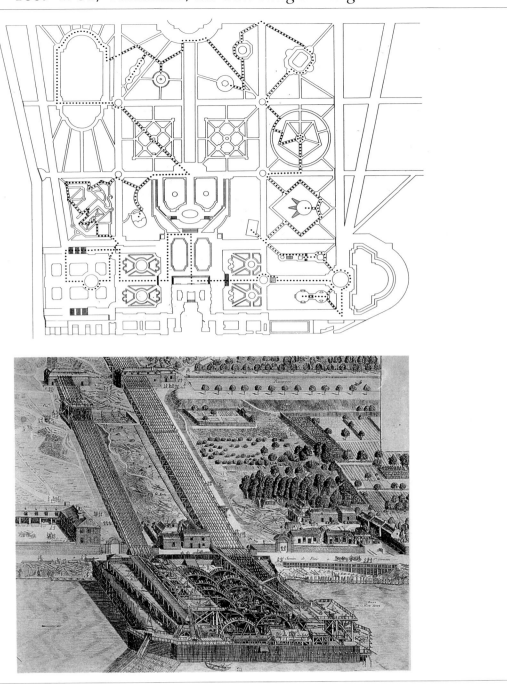

Louis XIV's idea of the garden can be seen in the manuscript he wrote expounding the norms for using the garden at Versailles. The eloquently titled book *Manière de montrer les jardins de Versailles* was published in three versions, the first on July 19, 1689, the second between 1691 and 1695 (which included this diagram), and the last between 1702 and 1704. The Sun King's work reveals all the secrets of the garden of Versailles as if it was the solution to a mystery.

From the course marked out by the king for visiting the garden, it appears that the aim of every walk was to see the terminal features inside the vast and complex beds in the first part of the park. The various wonders to be seen here were the large plant and architectonic settings, the permanent theatrical scenes, the terraces, fountains, statuary, *le Canal*, and the maze. For the king the garden was the opportunity for creating a story for every guest, adapting it to the levels of his interests and his good taste. With respect to this, it is interesting to note that the great straight axes were not destined for fatiguing and boring walks but, as the king showed in his directions, were for the strict comprehension of the enormous dimensions of man's domination over na-

ture offered by the view when crossing them. This explains the real quality of the relationship between the general scenographic significance and the detailed instructions for using every French formal garden. There is a complex dialectic relationship between micro and macro that is not always immediately comprehensible. Examples of the colossal dimensions of Versailles and the obsession for detail are given by the documents illustrating the machinery for supplying water for continual irrigation and for alimenting the system of the geometrical and artifical fountains and lakes. But this gigantic machine built at Marly never actually worked.

*Louis XIV, Manière de montrer les jardins de Versailles, Paris 1982.

PLATE 75

Fontaine de Flore dans les Jardins de Versailles, representant le Printems. Cette Figure, et les Amours qui l'accompagne, sont de B. Tuby, du dessein de M. le Brun.
A. *Allée de l'Etoille.*
B. *Allée de l'Obeliste.*
C. *Allée sablée.*
D. *Autre Allée qui conduit à l'Etoille.*
E. *Allée qui conduit aussi à l'obeliste.*
F. *Allée qui va au bassin de Cerès.*
G. *Allée qui conduit à la grille de Trianon.*
A Paris chez Mortain pont N. Dame.

The central parts of the great plant *compartiments* inside the royal park at Versailles form a system of smaller gardens with an independent existence, almost as if they were a succession of squares in a city. The outdoor life of the court of the Roi Soleil took place here in these various scenes, created with masterly skill and intelligence, in one long protean calendar of entertainments and walks.

This engraving, made in the first few decades of the eighteenth century, shows one part of the park at Versailles. It is one of the innumerable prints that invaded Europe during the seventeenth and the eighteenth centuries (they were sold separately in Paris by *Mortian, pont N. Dame*), spreading the ideology and model of the French formal garden even before the special treatises on the new art of designing gardens had codified the techniques and the taste. This picture shows the *Fountain de Flore*, which is a metaphor of spring. The great green square is the metaphysical translation of an urban scene. Perfectly clipped green walls with natural trees peeping over the tops simulate the scenes and stage of a city. There are many other plant scenes like this in the park—for example, the squares of the fountain of Bacchus, the fountain of Saturn, the *bassin* of Enceladus, the Obelisk, and the square of the Three Fountains. Avenues lead away from the square formed by the complicated system of two-dimensional green walls of precise macro-architectural significance. These, too, have an urban look to them because they define spaces of a size similar to those in an urban complex. They seem to be parts of an abstract and distinct *city of reason*. The center of attraction, the conclusion to one of the possible walks at Versailles, was this waterwork. A powerful jet of water visible from afar rose from the group of sculptures by Jean-Baptiste Tuby in the middle of the fountain. The meeting place could therefore be easily recognized from a distance.

PLATE 76

LE THEÂTRE D'EAU.

Ce Bosquez est de forme circulaire moitié en Amphithéâtre de façon avec des portiques de verdure, sous lesquels sont placés 22. Bassins de rocaille d'ou s'élèvent autant de Jets d'eau. Il y a dans le fond 4 fontaines rustiques avec des groupes d'enfans de metal doré, et trois enfoncements de trois rangs de Jets d'eau au nombre de 75. qui changent de forme ou de décoration 4 fois. Cette variété produit un effet admirable.

Another type of architectonic, scenographic, and social attraction at Versailles is shown in this picture of *Le Theâtre d'Eau*, engraved by J. Rigaud in 1741, part of a remarkable series of similar scenes. Prints were the iconographic material for spreading information about monuments and about the new ideology of the garden. Here the highly domesticated plant component is combined with the wonder of artifically maneuvered waterworks.

The great amphitheater is shaped by the clipped green walls, where deep and narrow niches have been formed at regular architectonic intervals to create a decorative framework around the tall jets of water, the second phase of this repetition. Other vertical fountains fall into chain cascades inside the approaching avenues. All this water architecture presupposes, obviously, an ingenious hydraulic arrangement with complicated conduits capable (thanks to differences in volume and pressure) of creating the mobile liquid geometrics set down in the scenographic and hydraulic project. This was where feasts, theatrical performances, concerts, and elegant ballets took place, but it was also another terminal feature, a necessary meeting place at the end of a walk in the park. The scene illustrates this. Servants are bringing the ladies in curious sedan chairs on wheels to meet their cavaliers for the daily, inevitable round of gossip that was interrupted at intervals by literary and poetic recitals, some reference to the sciences, and by obligations concerning the fatiguing and almost non-stop game of coquetry and seduction. Images of this kind do not just communicate the new forms and the new significance of the garden, but, evidently, also the theory and practice of a new way of life.

PLATE 77

In 1709 Antoine-Joseph Dézallier d'Argenville published in Paris the treatise that codified the French formal garden, whose most famous monument was the park at Versailles designed by André Le Nôtre. It was called *La Théorie et la pratique du jardinage, où l'on traite à fond des beaux jardins appellés communément les jardins de plaisance et de la propreté, avec les pratiques de géometrie nécessaires pour tracer sur le terrain toutes sortes des figures: Et un trait d'hydraulique convenable aux jardins.*

The spatial concept of the seventeenth-century French formal garden, which was to spread all over Europe and right up to the later half of the next century, was strictly linked to the obligation to represent power in its architecture and surroundings. Versailles was the archetype and concrete and matchless example of this. The construction of the residence of the king and his court and its huge garden was initiated by Louis XIV, who followed the progress of the works very carefully. The *parterres de broderie* – the pattern of great beds elegantly laid out with precious designs, clipped hedges as borders, and completed with colored gravel – formed a kind of huge carpet in front of the palace, establishing a model which was to be copied by every one for the next hundred years. This illustration of a parterre and how to lay it out comes from the successful and exhaustive treatise which offered didactically the general diagrams of projects for the great axes and perspectives as well as every possible aesthetic and technical detail. The complicated decorative pattern was composed chiefly of non-botanical material: tiny colored stones, gravel, and ground marble. This scenery on the ground was designed to afford a precise perspective view, and no flowers or herbs could be allowed to impair the rigid perfection of the shapes, color, and general result with their biological life. Plant material was used only for the green frames around the beds and was clipped regularly. It was the artist-gardener's task to reach a maximum of elegance in design.

PLATE 78

VUE DU CHATEAU DE LA MEUTTE ET D'UNE PARTIE DU PARTERRE

This eighteenth-century engraving offers a general view of the Château de la Muette with a part of its parterre in the foreground. It summarizes the passage of a complex aesthetic and structural appraisal of the French formal garden, which, with the logic of the Age of Enlightenment applied to the criticism of past truths, destroys dialectically and polemically its deepest roots.

In late sixteenth-century Mannerism, the presupposition behind the decorative artificialness of every bed was that the laborious graphical plant embroidery served as a dignified framework, linking the palace and its garden. It was a kind of gigantic, sumptuous carpet laid down in front of the entrance of an equally luxurious residence. The fundamental aesthetical and technical principle behind this concept was the rigorous application of the most elementary symmetry, which was capable of repeating its sinuous patterns in a mirror fashion along the main axis of the design. Ground, inert material used to create chromatic variations made the insertion of such unstable elements as flowers quite unnecessary. But a few geometrically and calligraphically clipped evergreens were accepted. The picture challenges the false truths of this aesthetics, showing, with the logic of the king's new clothes, that this symmetry is an illusion because the parterre is perceptible and enjoyable from one standpoint only. A glance at the garden while taking a stroll through it is enough to realize that the obsessive symmetry of the two-dimensional decorative part of the garden is now incomprehensible. It looks instead like a chaotic muddle of signs and colors and the sinuous lines no longer form recognizable figures. The criticism is precise and effective. However, another consideration was to be even more successful in deciding the fate of the French formal garden. This concerned a change in the relationship between man and the plant world which was spreading outside France, in England.

PLATE 79

In the first half of the eighteenth century, the formal garden (this is a German example) was the setting for social events. The garden was organized as if it was a theater by embellishing the fixed scenery with botanical props that the servants here are transferring from the greenhouse to the parterre to be set in a repetitive mathematical arrangement. Unlike his English contemporary, the gentleman owner here is indifferent to the change of scenes. He will come on stage, like the star of the show, when the garden is ready.

The picture is a detail from a print by Salomon Kleiner, the prolific engraver who cataloged the great Austrian and German residences and their gardens in a collection of views. This table comes from *Gartenpalais Liechtenstein in der Rossau. Das Orangen-Boskett* printed in 1738. The scene is interesting from the anthropological and cultural point of view. The garden is a vast theater, subject to continual productions where there is no difference between man-made objects and trees. These are regulated by a concept of design based on serial arrangement and achieved through the repetition of types that have been domesticated geometrically by topiary. They serve to create vistas that must represent the allegory of power. This power is expressed on more than one level,

the most significant of which is not the traditional sociological one of the rich and noble over the less rich and less noble. What is most important (and unconsciously so, for those who practiced the aesthetics of the formal garden) is the power of man over the plants, repetitively prostrate before his whims. The direct interdependence, in England in the seventeenth century, between the owner or dilettante and his garden had estabilished the premises for a new relationship, that between man and a single plant, which was to become the basis of the epistemological revolution implicit in landscape gardening. The naturalistic garden, as opposed to the formal one, which developed in the later half of the eighteenth century, was known as the English landscape garden.

PLATE 80

VUË DU CHÂTEAU DE TRIANON DU COTÉ DU PARTERRE.

Cette vuë est dessinée du haut du Perron au bout de l'aisle qui avance dans le Jardin et d'ou l'on découvre en entier le beau parterre émaillé de toutes sortes de fleurs les plus rares. Ce qui produit un coup d'œil admirable le Canal paroit dans l'Eloignement.

The *Grand Trianon* was the place inside the park at Versailles where the king liked to rest after the exertions of court life. J. Rigaud's engraving, part of a series on the gardens at Versailles dated 1741, shows how the courtiers relaxed. Like a theatrical scene of life, the garden stage has been set, thanks to the work of numerous servants who prepared every detail at dawn.

The conspicuous architecture of the pavilion, the plant walls clipped to form regular surfaces, the *wild* trees to be seen behind them, are the fixed elements of the scenery. The hydraulic system has been set in motion and the jets leap to their planned heights. Even the urns and cubic containers for the little trees have been taken from the hothouses and everything is ready for the scheduled event. The garden at *Le Grand Trianon* is smaller in size, more private and reserved for the smaller number of habitués, compared to the great park near the royal palace. In that area, the smaller gardens were the terminal features of a walk, alternative menus for the court's geographical life. Here, it is the unique scene for the privacy of the king and his most trustworthy intimates. The result is a kind of private garden, where the dimensions are psychological more than physical, to come to every day with a small following to contemplate an unvarying scene with no alternatives. Symbolically, every large park is a land to be discovered continually, presenting all kinds of surprises and stimulating innumerable adventures and sensations. It is the place and metaphor of never-ending knowledge. A smaller garden does not offer the same range of possibilities, not even to occasional visitors. Where dimensions are limited, an overall view is enough for anyone to understand it all, although only from the point of view of the macro-morphological structure. Therefore, like a great hall in a palace which needs only a glance at the architectural space and the system of decoration to make everything clear, this garden becomes the scene, without any simulation, of the *theater of life*.

PLATE 81

Bosquets en quatre.   Prospect eines viereckigten Bosquets

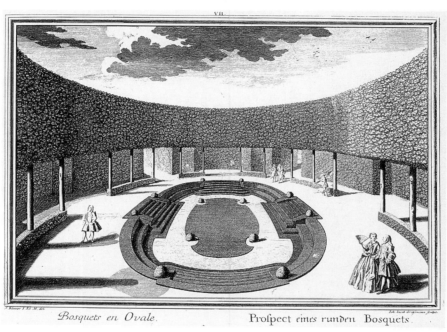

Bosquets en Ovale.   Prospect eines runden Bosquets

Every edition of Antoine-Joseph Dézallier d'Argenville's treatise on the French formal garden following the first one in 1709 was further enriched with pictures serving as models for those who wanted to catch on quickly to the images of this modernism. By using them as scenes to be applied to his own garden, a landowner and his gardener could choose the layout to adopt for various parts of the landscape.

Engravings printed as loose sheets illustrating the most famous parks in the new style and Versailles in particular were one of the most successful means of spreading the aesthetics of the French formal garden. But the technical side to things had to be explained too, and this was the reason for the success of the famous treatise. (It was translated into English in 1712, and saw numerous editions in France during the early part of the century.) Other books using this material, bound in more manageable editions and containing reproductions of the original illustrations, were printed and sent throughout Europe. This German example drawn by Salomon Kleiner in 1737, showing Prince Eugène of Savoy's garden in Vienna, offers readers two different kinds of architectonic and geometrical solutions for groves based on the uniform clipping of the upper part of the plants. The message is clear: a meeting place in the garden, the ancient sacred glade in the wild forest, must be governed by good taste and with forms that demonstrate that this is the Age of Reason, which is also shown in the acceptance of the mathematical ordering of the plants. One continual green wall as the backdrop to the two scenes and the little tree trunks holding up the geometrical foliage form a significant organization of space. There is a complementary *parterre de broderie*. The owner can decide whether the grove should be rectangular or oval. But he should also know that it would be better to have both shapes in his garden.

PLATE 82

TITLE OF BOOK _____

I bought the book at _____

I received the book as a gift _____

MY COMMENTS: _____

_____

_____

My business or profession _____

_____

Please check off subjects of interest below:

1. ☐ Art
2. ☐ Architecture
3. ☐ Photography
4. ☐ Interior Design
5. ☐ Industrial Design
6. ☐ Graphic Arts

7. ☐ Fashion
8. ☐ Jewelry
9. ☐ Gardens
10. ☐ Judaica
11. ☐ Native American Arts
12. ☐ Travel

13. ☐ Cultural History
14. ☐ Music/Performing Arts
15. ☐ Fiction
16. ☐ Illustrated Gift Books
17. ☐ Nature
18. ☐ Social Science

☐ Yes, please send me the Rizzoli catalog

NAME _____

ADDRESS _____

CITY _____ STATE _____ ZIP CODE _____

TELEPHONE NUMBER _____

All Rizzoli titles are available through your local bookseller

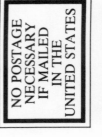

BUSINESS REPLY MAIL
FIRST CLASS PERMIT NO. 1083 NEW YORK, N.Y.

Postage will be paid by

RIZZOLI INTERNATIONAL
PUBLICATIONS, INC.
300 PARK AVENUE SOUTH
NEW YORK, N.Y. 10160–0673

Another two pictures from the series by Salomon Kleiner (1738) which attempted, by means of concise, easily comprehensible engravings, to spread through Germany the syntactic and grammatical principles of the theory of the French formal garden. These prints were documents of the epistemological sense inherent in the idea of the garden during the Age of Enlightenment, before the revolution introduced by the idea of the English landscape garden.

The two scenes here are also complementary, and not alternatives. The philosophy of the time worked, ideologically, like a huge amoeba, with such a level of tolerance as to englobe apparently totally contradictory forms and models. Here the scene of the arrangement of straight walks leading into a large open space reveals how much effort was necessary to maintain perfectly clipped structures. The geometrical formation of the rows of trees- each one like its neighbor, as if it was the result of modern clonating is emphasized by its positioning in front of the smoothly clipped green walls. At this time, it could have seemed like the only configuration for converging avenues in a space. But the second picture, following the first in the original album, shows that diverse solutions were acceptable, deriving from different but not incompatible concepts of nature. Here the trees do not form regular lines based on serial arrangement: they are wild groves. The combination means that during that period, the aesthetics of natural plant life could coexist with the former style, without being an alternative as it was to become not long after in England and then all over the Continent. Not only a pre-eclectic attitude accepting all kinds of styles, this comparison seems an enlightened classification based on scientific curiosity and on the desire to comprehend all the possible aesthetic and operative solutions. Better still if they were all presented in one large omnivorous garden.

PLATE 83

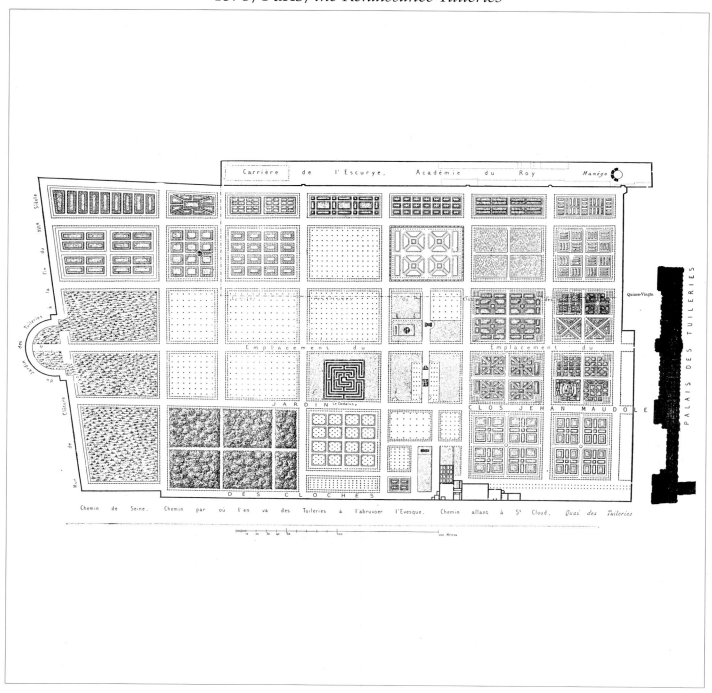

The diagrams on these two pages should be compared. They show the gardens of the Tuileries, the royal palace in Paris, that had the most important and significant system of parterres in the whole of France. The two layouts of the same garden show it half-way through the sixteenth century and half-way through the seventeenth: from the old-fashioned perseverance of the European tradition to the rapid change imposed by the new taste.

This picture comes from a book by Jacques-Androuet du Cerceau, who made an illustrated record of the palaces and gardens of the French nobility half-way through the sixteenth century. The garden layout contains the sense of the *hortus conclusus*, of the physick garden, and of the novel botanical garden: there is knowledge sufficient to master every idea of the garden, even with aesthetic and contemplative goals. The classification that can be derived from this engraving is one of a regulative and cognitive kind. Herbs, flowers, and trees were cultivated in different positions on the chessboard as if they were books on shelves in a library which could be of interest at one time and then be replaced for future consultation later on.

This garden, which included groves and a labyrinth, was to be experienced through the succession of plants laid out in such a way as to offer any visitor the *colony* of a species, or a rich combination of varieties. Each cultivated square was a terminal feature demanding specific attention, never a gratuitous space serving as mere scenography. Symmetry was used as the foundation of a complex structure based not just on formal interdependencies relating to the knowledge of the plant world, but on cultural ones, for the alternation of the species and for their relationships, and on scenic ones too, for the juxtaposition of the planted squares.

*Marcel Poëte, Au jardin des Tuileries, Paris 1924.

PLATE 84

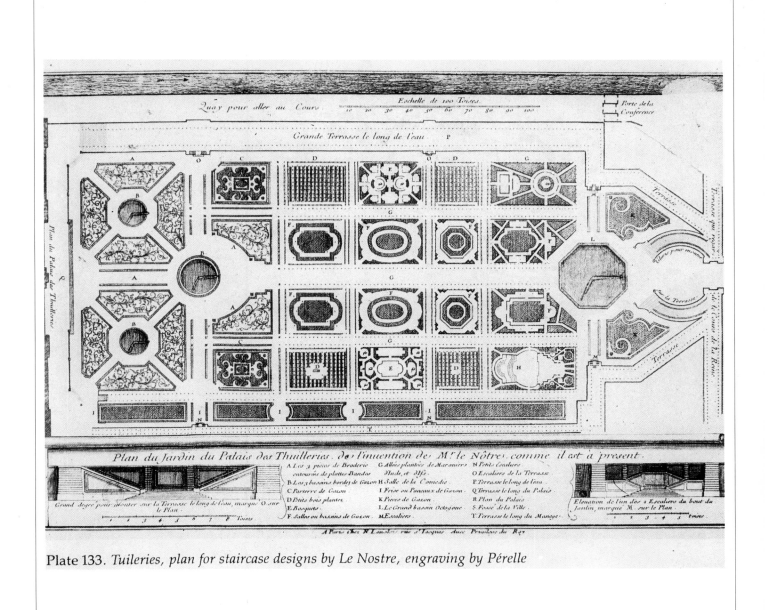

Plate 133. *Tuileries, plan for staircase designs by Le Nostre, engraving by Pérelle*

André Le Nôtre, the great architect of the seventeenth-century French garden and author of the park at Versailles, transformed the gardens of the Tuileries according to the requirements of the new taste. His family history was closely tied up with that of the royal gardens. His grandfather Pierre had looked after them during the second half of the sixteenth century for Catherine de Médicis; his father Jean was superintendent at the time of Louis XIII.

This task, for Le Nôtre, meant confronting what is now seen as the Freudian myth of the destruction of the image of the father (and also that of the grandfather). The reform of the garden was total and epistemological because it was the new *science* of the garden that had to be communicated. The late Renaissance aesthetic and botanical interest in the plant world was turned upside down. Plants themselves were no longer the subject of study and contemplation. All they had to do was provide a visually pleasant scene for man's elegant and refined presence. Symmetry then was turned to meet the simple requirement of forming a perspective axis generating the mirror-like arrangement of a calligraphic decoration. The design was so perfect that it had to be immobilized permanently and this was impossible if plants alone were used, given problems of growth and seasonal variations. The garden, that huge carpet in front of the palace, was therefore interlaced more and more with colored inorganic materials and less and less with plants. The important thing was that visitors could appreciate the *wonder* of this decorative symmetry and its complex forms. Potentially infinite serial arrangement and botanical repetition were implicitly the visual expressions of the dominion over nature by a real, concrete and ever-present power, a symbol of the riches necessary to build and maintain a garden of this kind.

PLATE 85

During the later part of the eighteenth century, gardens in Europe became the indispensable setting for social behaviour based on extensive private entertainment. This garden, the largest in Lombardy at the time, was conceived by Jean Gianda, the French architect, as the decoration necessary to complete the villa owned by a nobleman called Giuseppe Antonio Arconati-Visconti, and designed by Giovanni Ruggeri, the Italian architect. It was a scenographic space shaped by natural and artificial walls which formed a refined and metaphysical microcosm for an elegant style of life.

While the landscape garden was gaining ground in England in the first half of the eighteenth century, a highly creative period was fermenting garden design on the continent and unsettling the static character of the French formal style. Cabinets (arbors whose space was defined by closely planted and pleached trees, successfully experimented with on a large scale at Versailles) were replaced by real plant architecture which created a kind of micro-urban complex. The garden became a network of walks and spaces according to the geometry of rococo culture, reserving continual surprises for its visitors. The material protagonists were the regularly and periodically clipped huge green walls, capable of demarcating both linear and winding pathways and the spaces these led to. It required a few dozen years to shape these walls by patient cultivation. Many of these illustrations exaggerate the real size of the walls through carefully angled perspectives. They were often formed of two-dimensional trellises that acted as supports for climbing plants; on other occasions they were painted wooden walls designed for the ephemeral and temporary application of flowers and leaves. But they always created a new and original configurative and spatial system whose specific character and autonomy still has to be fully researched. This engraving by Marc'Antonio dal Re in 1743 shows the garden as a kind of laboratory for experimenting with a possible, fantastic city of the future built around metaphysical spaces, absent from cities as we know them.

PLATE 86

In the Age of Enlightenment a nobleman's private garden was no longer sufficient to cope with the complex behavioral patterns of the ruling classes. Public gardens came into being as the meeting place of aristocrats, intellectuals, and the rich bourgeoisie in response to the interdependent requirements of taste, fashion, eroticism, culture, and cosmopolitanism. This was Milan's first public garden, and one of the first in Europe, laid out in 1787. The print shows the garden at the time of its revolutionary and Jacobin period (1803).

The first public gardens were created during the second half of the eighteenth century in the Europe of the Age of Enlightenment. The French and German theoreticians of the new landscape garden defined its social connotations. One of the models was the Ausgarten in Vienna whose entrance bore the inscription "Place of pleasure, dedicated to all men by their friend (Joseph II)." The construction of a public garden in Milan, the capital of Austrian Lombardy-Veneto, was decided upon in 1777 and took place between 1782 and 1788. It was designed by Giuseppe Piermarini, the architect and champion of the new architectural classicism in the city. The public garden became the place for expressing new collective behavioural patterns: right from the start, horses and carriages were excluded. Pedestrianism was not just a rule, it was a psychological dimension. During the period of the revolution, the public garden became the scene of complex political and ideological propaganda, promoted by the new ruling class. The print shows a temporary arrangement, in republican times, of the final part of the *Giardini Pubblici*, the part which links it to the center of the city. It is a geometrical system of limes, elms and rhododendrons (immediately called the *Boschetti*). This picture was sent to Paris to document the political demonstrations in Milan in the second year of the Republic (1803), but the date was changed and it was used to describe the holiday the following year. It was an extraordinary invention of green architecture. Thanks to the volume of the foliage high up (creating a sheltered walk), the straight tree trunks seemed like a close-knit architectural colonnade covered by a mass of leaves.

PLATE 87

Still-life paintings had introduced didactic multicolor scenes for the contemplation of flowers into private homes. Toward the end of the seventeenth century, pictures of another kind began to propose a new method of enjoying the plant world. Apart from Flemish landscapes showing real and universal scenes, attention was paid to the details of the Italian landscape, pregnant with new semantic qualities that were indispensable for the renewal of aesthetic sensibility.

The fundamental sources were Claude Lorrain (1600-1682, whose *Pastoral Landscape* dated 1638 is shown here), Salvator Rosa (1615-1673), Gaspard Dughet (1615-1675), and his maestro and brother-in-law, Nicolas Poussin (1594-1655). When Joseph Warton, the English poet, wrote a poem in praise of *Capability* Brown, the father of the English landscape garden, he invoked Lorrain, Rosa, and Poussin: "What e'er Lorrain light-touched with softening hue, Or savage Rosa dash'd, or learned Poussin drew." Architectural ruins set in a Roman countryside, suitable only for raising sheep, were the visual evidence of what the English critics were to call the sublime and the beautiful in landscape painting. Here the plant world chosen in preference to the infinite possibilities of agricultural landscapes was the natural, savage, and incidentally autonomous one. It was a completely new way of contemplating nature for European culture and for all its genetical projects. Similar trees and similar scenes were nowhere to be found in existing gardens. When William Kent, the English painter, architect, poet, and landscape gardener, went to Rome in 1710 with the Earl of Burlington, the advocate of English Neoclassicism, he found these paintings an aesthetic revelation. Soon it would be possible to understand the the meaning of the words of the poet, Alexander Pope, in relation to European gardens: "All gardening is landscape painting."

*Helen Langdon, *Claude Lorrain*, Oxford 1989.

PLATE 88

The epistemological revolution in the relationship between man and nature consisted in hypothesizing, for the first time in Europe, the balanced interdependence between man and a single plant, which is similar to the south-east Asian tradition where farmers maintained a friendly relationship with the plant, which was world based on reciprocal respect.

Another painting by Claude Lorrain, *Oak Tree in the Countryside*, probably dated 1638, demonstrated the thesis of the new aesthetic concept by filling the scene with a tree as the only aesthetically, and not just technically, self-sufficient actor. William Kent proposed that the innovation should become the method for creating a new naturalistic garden where nature (or, better, the idea of nature that was being developed) prevailed over artificialness. In this way a landscape could be considered, conceptually, an infinite garden. This was why Horace Walpole, at the end of the eighteenth century, called William Kent the father of modern gardening, of landscape gardening. If William Kent had leaped the concep-tual fence of the historical limits of the European garden, it was Capability Brown who was to leap the physical limits, the boundary walls of every garden no matter what the size. The destruction of enclosures through the invention of ha-has (a wall set in a ditch to keep animals out of the garden while permitting an unlimited view far into the distance) created new dimensions and with them, new ideas about nature and complex aesthetic standards. The *hortus conclusus* gave way to the whole wide world. Imitation inherent in the fashion for *chinoiserie* and the discovery of a new aesthetics based on asymmetry were included in this process as well as a new sensibility that soft-ened the rigidity of the Neoclassic style.

PLATE 89

A single-room pavilion in a garden represents the central, vertical axis of a sacred space. It has no front, no back, and can be seen through. Only the dome-shaped roof, a metaphor of the firmament, protects with cosmic effectiveness the axis of sacredness that sinks into the ground. Unlike the fountain, the *fons sapientiae* in the heart of a garden, the pavilion can be used to create various centers of geographical sacredness in a park.

The meaning of the *genius loci* of the garden is clear in this English painting of about 1745, attributed to Joseph Higmore, which shows the Drake-Brockman family inside their *rotunda* at Beachborough in Kent. The little circular temple-like pavilion with a lead roof supporting a statue of Mercury and six Ionic columns without a balustrade, placed on a slight rise (the Renaissance *belvedere*), reveals the very nature of the family of the time. Two women are lingering inside the temple, which is furnished with some chairs. The owner is sitting on one of these and adjusting a spyglass, probably to explore the landscape, while his young son is crossing the scene in front of the building. A village near a hill-side can be seen far away, beyond the wooden fence. Unlike other ornaments in the garden designed to complete a picturesque scene to be seen from afar, the small pavilion is a place to stay in, chosen before the others, and has become a symbol of the spirit of the garden exactly because of its multidirectional character. It was the terminus of every walk, a chance goal for visitors, but a must for the owner. The Neoclassic pavilion seems like an outgrowth of reason, fitting harmoniously and coherently into the plant world that surrounds and accepts it. Its precise aesthetic purpose was comprehensible and natural for anyone in that period.

PLATE 90

Between the end of the eighteenth century and the beginning of the nineteenth there were people who believed that inert building materials used in a garden could make the site chosen for a little temple less sacred. In adopting the eighteenth-century hypothesis that all classical Greek and Roman architecture was nothing but the ritual and declamatory *petrification* of the primitive wooden hut, it was suggested that plants should be used as a new type of building material.

The *green pavilion* was partly a continuance of the art of topiary which succeeded, by means of treillages supporting climbing plants or independently by the geometrical clipping of shrubs and trees, in creating spaces and volumes similar to those formed by man-made constructions. But the semantic values attached to it were far greater. This *Temple de Verdure* dedicated to Ceres was a project designed by Jean-Jacques Lequeu (1757-ca. 1825), the creator of fantastic architectural drawings at the time of the revolution. It was one of the numerous proposals for an autonomous plant architecture that was not just a repetition of the anthropocentric qualities of many barrel-vaulted galleries covered with plants or even shaped by the vegetation alone with considerable analogy to architecture. Its meaning is plain. Nature becomes culture by means of plants alone. This indicates a possible course for man to govern it better and to live with it, evidently in the complex context of all things curious that this eighteenth-century culture was offering for even greater and more widespread consumption. The difference with respect to the complicated figurations of the early eighteenth century, like those proposed by Antoine-Joseph Dézallier d'Argenville, which every one could copy in his own garden, is exactly this: the new relationship between man and the plant world is no longer merely scenographic, it is of a symbolically vitalist nature.

*Philippe Duboy, Jean Jacques Lequeu, une enigme, Paris 1987.

PLATE 91

This engraving from William Chamber's eighteenth-century project for a small trelliswork gazebo and seat for Kew Gardens expresses the refined, not merely Neoclassic elegance required for the construction of garden furnishings. It is a modest wooden pavilion to be placed as a resting place along a garden walk. But it is full of architectural and environmental significance.

The pavilion frames a scene destined for a tête-à-tête, for day-dreaming, for a nature lover's contemplation of the garden, as if it was the proscenium of a theater. The classical architectural dignity of this square shape with a gable is delicately upset by the concavo-convex curves, that converge decoratively on the illusionistic keystone. Trelliswork, the virtual walls of a deliberately transparent construction, fills the space inside the triangle of the gable and the curves forming a protection between the pavilion and the environment. This product of the mid-eighteenth century is refined and unobtrusive, and so light as to seem ephemeral. It fits into the plant environment with unfanciful elegance and with suitable reserve. It contrasts with the visual exaggeration and configurative aggressiveness of many Neoclassic products, which were soon to become Neo-gothic and more generally eclectic, designed more to testify to the magnificence of a garden than to offer comfort. This seating arrangement was part of a more general culture that tended to insert particularly discreet features into the garden and spread them out according to practical needs. Only a few constructions were assigned the task of being architectonic attractions, with the aim of affirming the primary communication of the plant scene (the natural elegance of artificial organization).

PLATE 92

This little architectural garden pavilion is the work of Quinlan
Terry, the English architect (born 1937) and controversial restorer
of the classical forms of eighteenth-century architecture, using the
techniques and materials of that period. It
had royal approval from Prince Charles.

The material composition of this magical site is a
modest pavilion, closed by brickwork on the two
sides that back the two long benches, with an
essential and purist gable roof covered with
wooden shingles and supported by seven
columns of the *rustic order* (which Sebastiano
Serlio, the sixteenth-century architect, wanted)
made of natural tree trunks showing the knobs of
former branches. Quinlan Terry's scrupulous
research into philological and material problems
has served on other occasions for other buildings
to recreate the fascination of antiquity (leaving
aside any contemporary criticism of the
modernism of the International style) as if it was
an ahistoric quality which man must always refer
to for improving his cities, his environments, and

his gardens as well. This is a synchronic category
in contrast to the diachronic future of the
enormous quantity of ornaments made of
abominable materials whose consumption is
inevitable in modern gardens. It has, first and
foremost, an ethical and moral significance, which
has thus become a precise aesthetic frame of
reference. As far as the use of materials is
concerned, like *art pauvre*, this construction offers,
didactically and maieutically, the profound
meanings of old and natural materials. Where
there is a desire today to preserve the deepest
sense of the garden in particular, they appear to
be irreplaceable.

*Clive Aslet, *Quinlan Terry. The Revival of Architecture*, Harmondsworth 1986.

PLATE 93

Vue Perspective de la Colonne.

In 1774 M. de Monville bought an estate in the village of Retz, near Marly. It took him ten years to transform it into an Anglo-Chinese model garden, with his own house forming a symbolic and integral part. His *maison chinoise* in front of a pond was perhaps the only example of a middle class home of its kind in Europe. But at the beginning of the eighties de Monville was dissatisfied and knocked down the eighteenth-century folly to replace it with a broken column.

The fifteen meter diameter of the base of the presumably Doric or Tuscan column suggested an overall height of about one hundred and twenty meters. In 1785 there were about twenty architectural follies throughout the park and they formed its main source of attraction, like Bomarzo in the sixteenth century. The bizarre nature of the broken column implied specific symbolic values, but most of all it served as an extraordinary, gigantic scenographic machine, its purpose to stupify like every playful exaggeration. The residence inside the remains of the great column was designed in a calligraphically baroque style without any deviation or transgression. It was formed of four floors and two basements. The rooms, eight on each floor, were arranged around the great central circular staircase. The picture shown here, from Georges Louis Le Rouge's collections of prints, illustrates the significance of the follies inside the park in terms of landscaping. Its emphatic quality and its giantism correspond perfectly with the fundamentals of the *aesthetics of ruins*. The details, too, are in line with this theory, with a variety of hanging plants that descend from the roof of the attic hidden behind the crown of the broken walls along the fluted face of the column-building. The owner derived his pleasure not from using the folly but from seeing the amazement it provoked on the faces of his guests.

*Véronique Willemin and Gilles-Antoine Langlois, *Les 7 folies capitales*, Paris 1986; Sylvia Soudan-Skira, *De folie en folie, la decouverte du monde des jardins*, Genève 1987.

PLATE 94

A system of fake ruins, based on a few real memories, was part of the layout of the Princess of Monaco's garden at Betz built between 1780 and 1784. The princess wanted to create a model for the garden of *sentiments*. Even the plants were to be melancholic: Italian poplars, sycamores, cypresses, plane trees, and Chinese thuyas. This picture can be taken as a symbol of the theory and practice of the *aesthetics of ruins*.

This view, drawn by Constant Bourgeois, is taken from Alexandre De Laborde's book *Description des nouveaux jardins de la France et de ses anciens chateaux*. It was printed in Paris in 1808 in three languages, French, English, and German, which gives an idea of the success of these kinds of publications. The picture is overflowing with semantic messages, which rooted themselves in the fertile ground of both the figurational and sentimental social heritage. Who could deny the emotion felt when seeing the architectural remains of an ancient civilization, especially the medieval one, handed down from the past in the shape of ruins? The remains in this scene are also potentially perfect. The very tower is menaced by a *catastrophic* crevice, a premonition of future,

irreparable disasters. A similar fate has been prepared for the squat support of the rotting bridge and for the great archway framing the scene. Not surprisingly, this picture was reproduced in many forms and became one of the most eloquent symbols of the *aesthetics of ruins*. An appraisal of the scene eliminates any conjectures about its possible restoration. The message lay in the romantic interpretation of decadence, in its irreversible and infinite nature. The semantic interpenetration of ruin and vegetation is also complete. Weeds grow like parasites in the cracks of the buildings. The unchecked advance of wilderness announces that man no longer belongs here. The place has been given back to nature.

PLATE 95

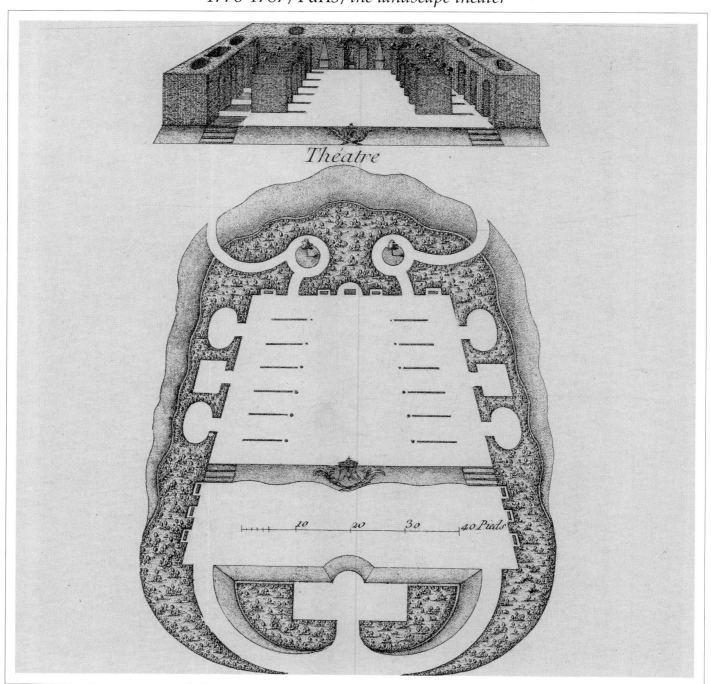

Nature can be a building material for creating useful architectonic environments. This was the sense of Georges Louis Le Rouge's popular engravings. From the high Renaissance onwards, green theaters were an indispensable part of European gardens. This table showed eighteenth-century readers a typical example that could be copied anywhere.

The plant mass has been molded into an elementary stereometry. On the inside it has been hollowed out to obtain various elliptical or rectangular rooms of theatrical utility leading on to the stage, as well as the amphitheater itself. The stage, which is slightly higher than the natural pit, comprises a symmetrical series of six wings, also formed by green walls, to be used in all the various events. At the back, beyond the two topiary pyramids and the statue preserved in a plant niche, there are two secret cylindrical rooms with a bed and tree in the center, which connect the stage to the garden behind it. They can be used for private theatrical games. This little theater testifies to the refined and rational organization of the permanent theatrical space. It was used for plays and for musical and literary events, which were considered functional and organic components of the idea of the garden. The garden itself was taken as a cultural container in the wider sense of a setting for the performance of the theater of life. In eighteenth-century gardens, curiosities were combined with the commonplace in these theaters, and in the behavior and the imagination of their audience. The time and effort needed to create such a plant construction were so great as to make it a marvelous and precious object in itself.

PLATE 96

Between 1776 and 1778, Georges Louis Le Rouge, the engraver and publisher, ran an original publishing project in Paris linked to the growth of interest in the new garden. The periodical sale of a series of 493 plates collected in 21 notebook offered readers a real encyclopedia of modern gardens. Its title was significant: *Détails des nouveaux jardins la mode. Jardins anglo-chinois.* This print shows a naturalistic grotto with a *jardin d'hiver* and banqueting hall inside the rocky structure.

This project (from the tenth notebook, dated 1782) documents the plan to build an artificial, naturalistic grotto in the Parc de Monceau. It was not an environment with a permanent scene that could be taken in at a glance. The grotto had to be walked through if one was to enjoy the various side-scenes and special areas such as the *jardin d'hiver* (for pineapples and exotic flowers), the diningroom in the rocks, and the architectural *cabinet*. It was a microcosm with a configuration and functions that were typical of eighteenth-century interest in unusual and bizarre composition. Le Rouge proposed this *jardin d'hiver* to the readers of his periodical plates in order to document the existence of its singular character, and also to suggest to architects and owners models of reference for other constructions. The other examples were all drawn using the same methods, with the aim of forming a collection. This classificatory information was planned, first of all, to illustrate the taste of the time, and this is why it is useful. But its practical purpose was that of following what had become the dominant and consolidated fashion of suggesting models (suitable for typological repetition at least), and the publishing project confirms that many were interested in that taste. At the same time, the structure and method of distribution of the periodical contributed to spreading that taste in a completely new way, quantitatively and qualitatively, differing from other methods of communication (treatises on gardens, architecture, and botanical science). After all, real models of existing gardens could not be visited by everyone. The images in similar publications transmitted all the eighteenth-century curiosities in the idea of the garden before the actual event.

PLATE 97

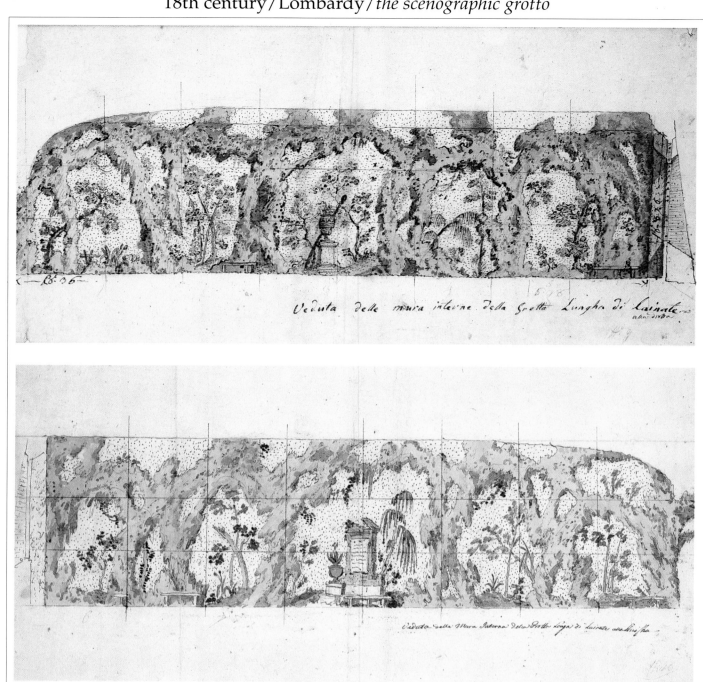

Veduta delle mura interne della Grotta Lungha di Lainate

Veduta delle Mura Interne della Grotta Longa di Lainate

This project, probably the work of Sandroni, the Italian architect, in the last decades of the eighteenth century, was the blueprint for a grotto completed in the garden of the villa belonging to Antonio Visconti Arese Litta and described by Stendhal as a "jardin rempli d'architecture." The natural cave and the artificial one formed by *rocailles* are the main features of the idea of the garden. They were the containers of sacred spaces, within the wider sacred territory (separated by practical uses) of the garden. With picture-writing, man created his own anthropological and spiritual monuments in caves. From classical times to the present day, the artificial grotto proposed to revive the primitive states of mind that had generated those paintings.

The landscape garden was conceived as a succession of permanent natural scenes similar to the model of landscape paintings. These were to be masterfully designed as perspective vistas to be seen by those walking along its pathways. The garden as a whole was therefore an artificial assembly of a series of scenes created three-dimensionally with plants, some constructions, and a few ornaments. The aim of this scenographic and pictorial concept of the garden was not just of an aesthetic and romantic nature, but involved morals as well. In fact, people soon started writing about the moral effect of the garden. The English architectural style used for the buildings overlooking these gardens was also based on principles that might be termed scenographic. The architectonic culture, in reality, did not follow any one style but embraced a wide variety of them. Unlike the experience of many European cultures, such as the Neoclassic eighteenth-century one, in England architecture was not considered a religion, but rather an instrument serving mankind. An architect designed in a Neoclassic, Neo-gothic, Neo-Indian, or Neo-Chinese style according to the cultural or sentimental necessities of his client (John Nash was an example). A garden, in particular, which was the setting for certain kinds of behaviour, could require a romantically Gothic or romantically Classic fixed scene with suitable and complementary plant species. It could provide the setting for lovemaking or for intellectual debate. Even the ornamental elements reflected these requirements, as the project for this scenographic grotto demonstrates.

PLATE 98

This photograph shows a detail of the grotto as it is today. The project can be seen on the opposite page with its clear intentions of achieving scenographic results. Simple materials, such as stucco and a mosaic of pebbles, are the technical means for reproducing the design in the sketch and preserving the original eighteenth-century sense of this *rocaille*. This is a fake grotto, but it is able to suggest a natural image.

In former times, aesthetic taste and Renaissance skill led to the reconstruction of nature in the artificial grottoes by using extraordinary illusory effects. But in the romantic age this was no longer necessary and the scenographic dimensions satisfied the need for an overall image. In formal seventeenth-century and early eighteenth-century gardens, materials were mostly used for similar ends. The patterned and multicolor order of the *parterres de broderie* was guaranteed more by the use of gravel and ground stones than by botanical material. Often, while waiting for real hornbeam hedges to grow, plant material was attached temporarily to painted trelliswork to give the illusion of clipped green walls. It was a quick way of solving the problems of scenery for a reception or feast. This photographic detail emphasizes the multitude of tiny parts used to create the scenic whole. The grotto was slightly illuminated by daylight thanks to a carefully limited opening, but at night the artificial lighting was at its feeblest. What counted was that the overall design gave the impression of being inside a grotto, or better still, inside the *idea of a grotto* in a fashionable garden. Multicolor pebbles and stucco and pieces of brick instead of precious stones were enough to create that specific sensation. But the illusion planned was a double one, because the illusory grotto was built with huge lateral openings from which the *idea of the garden* of the time could be seen. And this garden was illustrated with trees, dead trees, shrubs, urns, inscribed pillars, and even a classical ruin.

PLATE 99

Belvedere is an Italian word coming from the Renaissance. It denotes a place, usually on high ground and sometimes characterized by a small, transparent, and multidirectional one-room pavilion, from which a *lovely view* could be observed. Like the Italian musical terms of the time, this word spread over Europe together with the culture that gave birth to it.

An elemental and elegant little *belvedere*, a detail of a print from Georges Louis Le Rouge's collection, can be seen at the top of this page. It shows that the relationship between the site containing this construction and the landscape to contemplate, the subject of the very sense of *belvedere*, was not tied to exceptional altitudes. The height of a man, as in the case of this little cylinder with its internal staircase, was enough to bring the eyes to an unusual and satisfactory level in order to enjoy a lovely view. Another term was coined in the eighteenth century in England, the home of the new garden. This was *gazebo*, a word to define a construction like the one built on belvederes. The word *gazebo* comes from the verb *to gaze*, that is to

look with curiosity or wonder. The term was soon used all over Europe and then throughout the world, as a result of the spreading of the new English landscape idea of the garden. Therefore an area of the garden formerly designated for contemplation was now destined for observation, a form of behaviour that required and privileged curiosity more than aesthetic pleasure. The gazebo in public gardens in the nineteenth century (this is a stereotyped picture from that period) took on the significance of the *sacred place*, the primary connotation of the Renaissance original, and added a few innovatory semantic overtones. It was to embrace, for example, the new ambiance of promenade orchestras.

PLATE 100

Vue du BELVÉDÈRE de S.^T LEU.

A View of the BELVEDERE at S.^T LEU.   Ansicht des BELVEDER'S von S.^T LEU

This scene with a *belvedere-gazebo*, presented by Alexandre De Laborde, is typical of the new European landscape garden. The eloquence of the illustrations in this book has made it a sort of codification and rather late ratification of what was by then the generally accepted taste for landscape gardening all over Europe.

In the large plates in De Laborde's book, engraved by masters in the art of portrayal, there are gardens which have been immortalized in their most exquisite forms as landscapes. In this view, for example, everything is landscape, including the artificially designed lie of the land, the winding of the waterways, and the alternation of grass and trees, arranged to seem like a natural scene. The very *belvedere* has become an integral part and positive feature in the landscape. The picture is offered as the image of a specific *idea of the garden* before being considered as an actual site. The little temple is unidirectional because it is located on a rise that displays only one view. It has an elegant structure with slim columns, a conical roof made of sheeting decorated with triglyphs. It is an example of how a discreet building, if it is placed in a suitable place in a suitable garden, can meld with the plant matter without altering the specific qualities of the natural-artificial landscape whose every detail has been constructed according to a precise aesthetic formula. The presentation of this panorama is in itself a communication and a form of didactic advice: this is how a romantic garden should be contemplated correctly. The wings should be in the foreground, and here they are composed of the *belvedere* and a great tree which frame the deep and plastic stage reaching into the far distance toward the real garden. Teaching how to contemplate a garden also means teaching how to build one, because, as this print shows, it makes both the morphological composition and the significant details clear and comprehensible.

PLATE 101

Giuseppe Castiglioni, a Milanese Jesuit, went to China in 1715. He was an advocate of exceptional cultural tolerance and respect. He did not melt into the ranks of local intellectuals, nor impose his knowledge as a precious treasure to bargain over. He entered the cultural world of the time, establishing a bilateral relationship with it, and became one of its main exponents.

Castiglioni became famous as a painter in China with the name Lang Shih-Ning. He was the founder of a new school of painting that combined oriental axonometric drawing with European perspective in a really unique form of extraordinary creativeness. Between 1737 and 1766, the year he died, Castiglioni built, on behalf of the religious order and with the help of seven brother Jesuits experts in engineering and hydraulics, a palace and a garden on the outskirts of Peking which were both examples of the European style. The whole operation could be considered, on the one hand, as an experiment in consuming European exotica in China, or, on the other, as the Chinese form of observing European models based on scientific curiosity. Between 1783 and 1786, about twenty years after his death, a few copies were made of twenty engravings, illustrating the palace and its garden. One of them showing the garden is reproduced here. Leaving aside preconceived styles, the building and garden were attemps to help the Chinese grasp the *sense* of Europe (which was responsible, thanks to the Anglo-French armies in 1869, for destroying the whole complex). The engravings were made by Chinese artists personally supervised by the Emperor, who wanted to conserve a record of this work. The print was made using the Chinese pictorial style of engraving filtered through the European formula of the bird's-eye view. It shows the labyrinth with a central pavilion inside it in a large garden whose high walls were lapped by streams flowing toward two artificial lakes.

PLATE 102

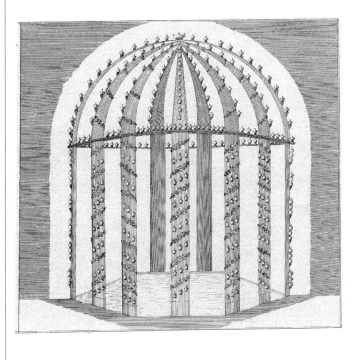 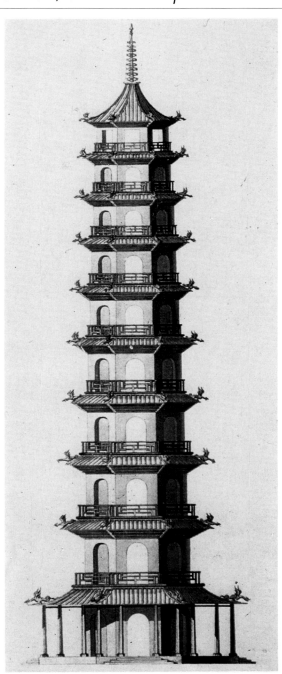

China in Europe. Here are two pictures of a virtual China seen in the calligraphic version of an exotic style designed to characterize the landscape of a garden. When *chinoiserie* was in fashion, daily life was disrupted by scenes and objects that, apart from their specific nature, were supposed first of all to document that exoticism. This was the case with both the pagoda and the complex lighting machine shown here.

Georges Louis Le Rouge published an illustration of this extraordinary pavilion in his collection of prints. It was one of the first European constructions designed, according to the vague indications of an ethnographic literature that always glorified the Far East, for the artificial illumination of a special part of the garden. The reconstruction illustrated here has a European air about it, which is evident, for example, in the fashionable elegace of the oil lamps placed on the outside. But the significance of this practice lay far away to the East. The project of the second picture, the great *pagoda*, as it was immediately called by the English, was drawn up by William Chambers. He used his nine years' experience of the East to construct a 165 foot high building in Kew gardens, the then royal gardens, in 1761. More than a philological and archaeological reconstruction of a Chinese type of architecture in England, the construction of the tower brought into the landscape of European gardens a pictorial demonstration of *chinoiserie* on a colossal scale whose extraordinary style and dimensions were enough to leave anyone thunderstruck. It was, in fact, its size that implied a sense of volume that the little pavilions, the follies that anyone could build, could not achieve. Here the idea and the project have turned into a great work whose motivation could not be assigned to the category of bizarre *capriccio*. The image of the pagoda has become an integral part of the landscape of Kew Gardens, not just due to the establishment of a familiar form in the social heritage, but also because the idea that sparked it off harmonized deeply with the original conception of these gardens.

*Jean Denis Attiret, *A Particular Account of the Emperor of China's Gardens near Pekin*, London 1757; William Chambers, *Designs for Chinese Buildings, Furniture, Dresses, Machines and Utensils*, London 1757; William Chambers, *A Dissertation on Oriental Gardening*, London 1772; John Harris, *Sir William Chambers*, London 1970; Patrick

PLATE 103

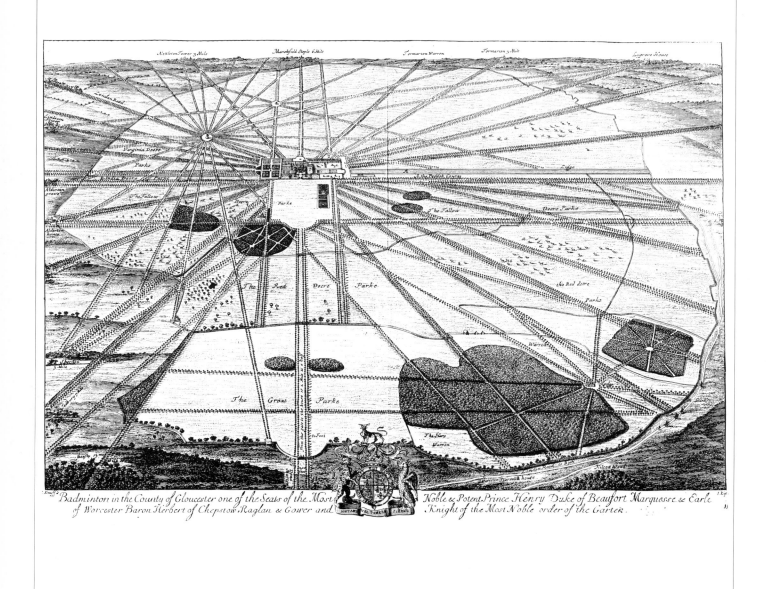

Badminton in the County of Gloucester one of the Seats of the Most Noble & Potent Prince Henry Duke of Beaufort Marquesse & Earle of Worcester Baron Herbert of Chepstow Raglan & Gower and Knight of the Most Noble order of the Garter.

The Badminton House estate in the county of Gloucester was the home of the Duke of Beaufort. It comprised a villa, garden, and vast park, shown here in a sweeping bird's-eye view of the whole territory. The picture comes from a collection of engravings called *Nouveau Théâtre de la Grande Bretagne: ou description exacte des Palais de la Reine, et des Maisons le plus considerable des Seigneurs & des Gentilshommes de la Grande Bretagne*, published in London in 1708.

The book was conceived as a faithful catalog of the residences of the leading class of the time. It was a kind of self-examination of those in power. Not much later on, this printed form of stark documentation was to be used in a captious way by the Earl of Burlington's Palladian circle to spread the new Neoclassic taste. Among the tables illustrating ancient buildings were included others on the new architectural style with all its innovatory semantic stimulus. This divulgatory mission was brought to an end with the publication of *Vitruvius Britannicus, or the British Architect,* written by Colin Campbell, the architect, whose first two volumes were published in London in 1715 and 1717. However the editorial purposes of the book illustrating Badminton did not go beyond the task of mere registration. This layout looks like a mathematical and geometrical demonstration of seventeenth-century science. The garden, in England, in Europe, and in the world, had not yet *leaped the fence* of its traditional enclosures, firmly rooted in the *hortus conclusus* tradition, to decree the concept that *all nature was a garden.* All the same, this picture suggests that even before the revolution there was, perhaps, a wider conception. The garden of the residence is a small formally arranged space. But the territorial composition including woods and fields, designed with avenues, and proposed and imposed on the designer by the landowner, demonstrates that *reason* (expressed by the network of countless directions) is the means for governing the whole wide world, without end.

PLATE 104

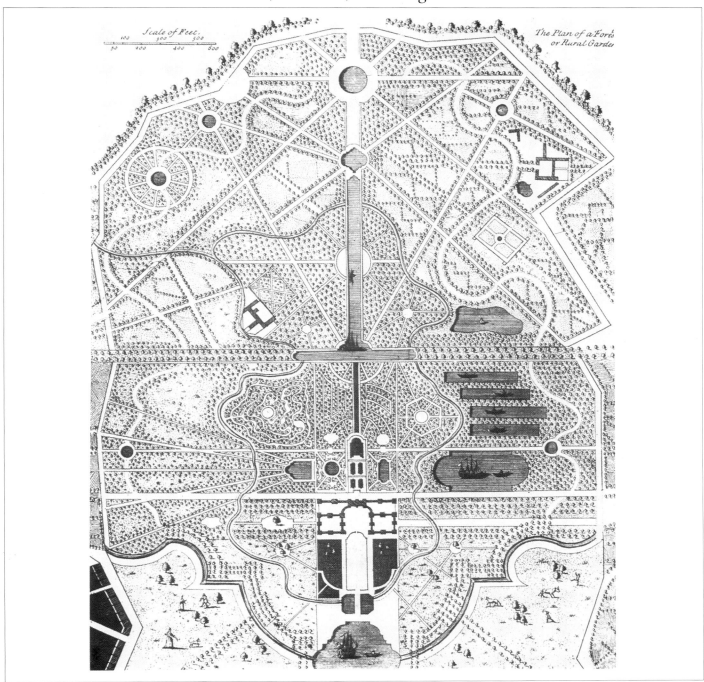

The Plan of a Forêt or Rural Garden

In 1718 Stephen Switzer published in London his three-volume study, *Ichnographia Rustica: or, the Nobleman, Gentleman, and Gardener's Recreation*, an enlargement and revised version of an earlier work dated 1715. Not many years had passed since the publication of d'Argenville's treatise, which had been fundamental for spreading the French formal garden, but Switzer's book was to invalidate those principles. This is the picture of a possible and desirable garden. It unites the Dutch taste for attention to detail and the French *Grand Manier* with *Rural and Extensive Gardening*.

A few years after the publication in France of the architectonic treatise written by Antoine-Joseph Dézallier d'Argenville on the French formal garden based on great symmetry, its teaching was challenged in England. The change was radical and implied a complete modification of aesthetic values. The *parterre de broderie* was already reduced in size and the great cross-shaped canal and transversal walk had apparently assumed the significance of a Cartesian system of reason onto which other geometries, those of experimental complexity, had been grafted. The curved line or *serpentine*, borrowed conceptually from the oriental aesthetics of asymmetry, was to become the main feature of the English landscape garden in its victorious struggle against the French formal garden. Here serpentines (the watercourse and the external avenue) connect varying complex botanical patterns as if this garden had to contain every possible future eighteenth-century European garden by trying out all the new sensibilities with respect to the canons of the formal garden. Another technical manual on the new possible garden, *New Principles of Gardening* by Batty Langley, came out in England in 1728. These were the years when William Kent, the father of the landscape garden, was developing the principles of the new aesthetics of the garden (before these books were published) soon to conquer England and then Europe. At the same time he began his first practical experiments, applying the principles to his own projects.

PLATE 105

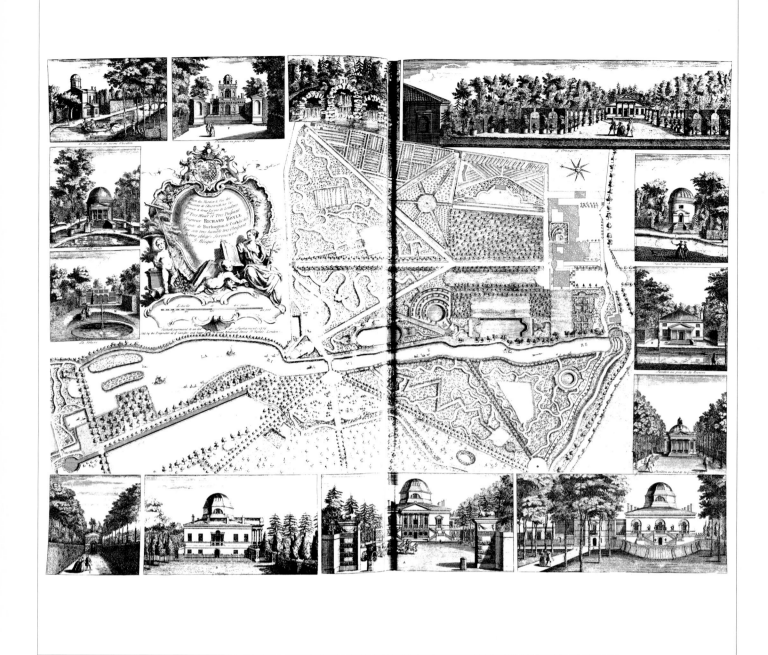

In the fourth volume of *Vitruvius Britannicus* by J. Badeslake and J. Rocque, printed in London in 1739, one engraving by Rocque dated 1736 (they were originally sold as loose sheets) shows the garden at Chiswick belonging to Richard Boyle, Earl of Burlington. It was the monument of the garden as theorized by the Palladian circle, who were the advocates of Neoclassicism conceived as a form of national modernization and new relations with Europe and its history.

Charles Bridgeman (who died in 1738, the designer of the similar extraordinary garden at Stowe, which was illustrated in a printed guide for visitors in 1732) and William Kent (ca. 1685-1748), the friends of the poet Alexander Pope (1688-1744), were the leading lights of Burlington's artistic circle. They worked on this garden until about 1720. Robert Castell was another member who stimulated renewed interest in Roman gardens through his Neoclassic and imaginative reconstruction of Pliny's gardens in 1728. The passion for bringing antiquity back to life was the spark for this model of a fantastic garden with all its necessary architectonic complements. The *culture of complexity*, seen in the elaboration of never-ending geometries that formed the frame of reference for designing new gardens, leads back to Switzer and Langley's concurrent research. But these studies were filtered through what had become a strongly naturalistic, conceptual and propositive component that was the matrix for landscape gardening. Here too, the intricate patchwork was not the result of an eclectic system, but the carefully reasoned range of all the possible geometries for building gardens for any kind of future where the serpentine would always be the main feature. An examination of this cultural project reveals the organic relationship between Palladianism (which was nothing less than preromantic Neoclassicism) and the no-longer formal garden. Ever since then the miniature classical buildings, including a Manneristic grotto shown here analytically as if the print was a catalog, were to interact with every landscape garden.

*Peter Willis, *Charles Bridgeman and the English Landscape Garden*, London 1977; John Dixon Hunt, *William Kent, Landscape Garden Designer*, London 1987.

PLATE 106

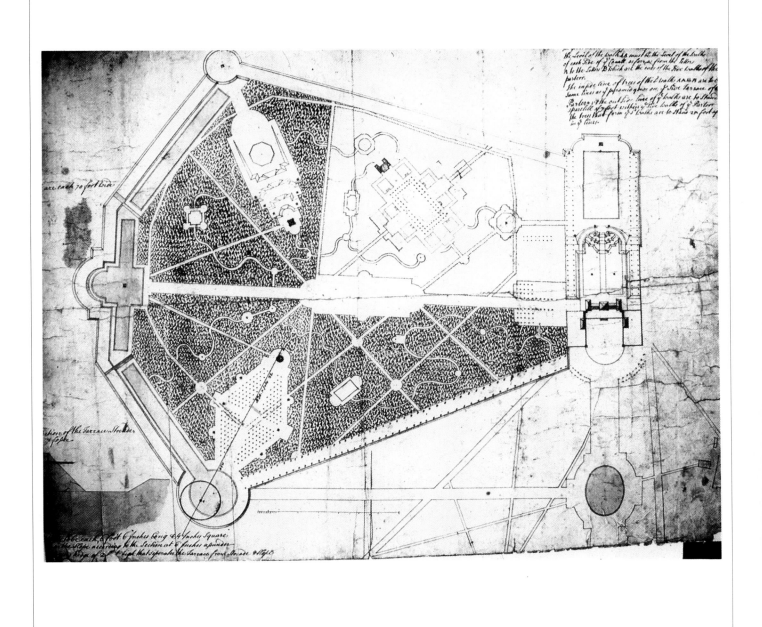

This engraving, going back to about 1730, was a blueprint for building the garden at Farley. It is attributed to Charles Bridgeman, the most fashionable garden designer in England at the time of the destruction of the geometrical and obsessive fundamentals of the French formal garden. Bridgeman started his work under the theoretical guidance of William Kent who had first perceived the urgent need for a new aesthetics.

"But the capital stroke, the leading step to all that has followed (I believe the first thought was Bridgeman's) the destruction of walls for boundaries, and the invention of fosses... an attempt then deemed so astonishing, that the common people called them Ha! Ha's! to express their surprise at finding a sudden and unperceived check to their walk." These words of Horace Walpole, written in 1784, placed Bridgeman among the founding fathers of the modern garden. It was this invention that, in Walpole's opinion, was to make Kent leap the fence and see that all nature was a garden. In 1739, a year after Bridgeman's death, his daughter Sarah described her father's masterpiece in the guidebook *A General Plan of the Woods, Park and Gardens of Stowe... with Several Perspective Views in the Gardens,* which also provided a document of his extraordinary cultural and artistic career. This drawing reveals the structure of a process of design that was to lead, as at Stowe, to the formation of the garden of complexities. It was the anthropological and aesthetic destruction of the previous formal canons, and was full of possibilities that were not all realized. The great eighteenth-century axiality and the seventeenth-century mathematical weaving of walks through the wood were kept because they were objectively beneficial in any garden of reason. This intuition in design was the origin of all possible gardens governed by the disturbing serpentine, the emblem of the new aesthetic gestation.

PLATE 107

Prospectus Cameratę Vineę in Hortis Gubernatoris Pondicherii in Indis Orientalibus ad oram Coromandelis
Dd 4.

This memorable eighteenth-century engraving with a contemporary watercolor finish shows a vast pergola of grapevines that is an infinite shady walk. The pergola was the central part of the garden of the residence of the Governor of the East Indies. It was an example, in architectural terms as well, of European exotica in the Eastern lands that were yielding to the economic, cultural, and administrative dictates of Europe.

From the point of view of communication techniques, the pergola, the main feature of the print, seems gigantic compared with what might be expected because of the deliberate false impression of the perspective that was often used in the eighteenth century to emphasize in close-ups the grandeur and wonders of gardens. On the other hand, the same perspective of the pergola, with variations as regards the sides, was to be used to illustrate many other gardens, this time European ones. The pergola is inserted in the part of the garden that is not symmetrical but arranged in a regular pattern of beds, fenced gardens, and tall trees. The ambiguous character of the pergola, here with its late seventeenth-century basket-handle arched vault, is fascinating. From the distant past of the European classical age to the time of its Renaissance revival, pergolas were architectonic ornaments designed for the regulated growth of plants that would then simulate a plant construction. This was not, however, to be taken simply as a kind of temporal shortcut with respect to the creation of green architectures made from plants alone. The architectonic supporting structure for the intertwining plants was in itself a symbol of the specific concept of the relationship between man and nature. It was a relationship in which the human dimension was artfully concealed in the illusion of a mathematical curiosity of nature.

PLATE 108

At Chiswick, the tiny Neoclassical or Palladian buildings were harmonious, almost musical accents in a succession of panoramic focal points, as if they were the subjects of contemporary landscape paintings. In this garden, however, they could express alternative semantic connotations, as was the case of the geometrical arrangement of pots of orange trees set out in front of the little temple and around a pool dominated by an obelisk.

The design configuration of this little temple in the garden, which was natural with respect to the aesthetics of the time, implied a large green parterre, wings formed of tall trees, and a dual relationship with the obelisk. The little temple was situated on the perspective axis linking it with the central position of the pool. It was the focal point of the scene and its general semantic message concerning the aesthetic relationship between nature and culture. In Pieter Andreas Rysbrack's painting of about 1730, ten years after Bridgeman and Kent had finished building Burlington's garden, the disturbing colorful presence (in a garden where flowers had been banished) of the system of pots for cultivating oranges indicated something semantically different from the aesthetic categories that had established the original garden. The three circular rows of pots laid out in a regular, rational, and enlightened sequence destroyed the earlier, pre-romantic aspect of the image, that of architectural constructions placed by themselves in an artifical environment designed to seem natural. The human intervention in the cultivation (that was so complex as to make a scene like this possible only in summer since the pots had to be kept in greenhouses during the cold) announced anthropic predominance which would have certainly pleased the producer or observer. Without the pots, the scene would have revealed its artificial character, which was to be a perfect reproduction of nature, where the presence of man was tacit, his work hidden by the magic of the naturalistic result.

PLATE 109

A canal, the fruit of human efforts to achieve rational navigation, is certainly not a naturally winding stream to which further man-made curves can be added according to the whys and wherefores of landscape design. The relationship between this middle class house and the Dutch canal in front of it raises the problem of the impracticability of applying traditional landscape theories to certain geographically static environments.

Herr Boendermaker's little house and garden (this is the central part, full of symmetries) is seen here from the road running along the other side of the canal. Its axial character could be perceived only in the moment when the symmetrical axis was at right-angles to a passing carriage or boat. This was, therefore, a glaring mistake in landscape art, due to questions of status symbols, because the opening onto the canal was decided more in order to be seen than for the aesthetic contemplation of the outside world. The lower picture, whose view includes the whole extension of the garden along the canal, is proof of this. Leaving out the central part, the garden exhibits correctly its real design to viewers along the canal. It is a *hortus conclusus* whose outer walls, which can be seen from the public water- and carriageways, reflect a complex eighteenth-century type of configuration including belvederes at the far ends. The rhythmic succession of interdependent architectonic structures for supporting climbing plants, brickwork gazebos and furnishings, and barrel-vaulted *berceaux*, winds on to the opening of the small parterre in front of the villa which can only be seen from a side view from a boat or carriage, thus contradicting the axial layout of its architectonic project.

*Henry Van Oosten, The Dutch Gardener, London 1710; A. Rademaker, L'Arcadie Hollandoise, Amsterdam 1730.

PLATE 110

The English garden was adopted throughout the world, bringing with it all its heritage of metaphors. It was as if the garden was a product of mass consumption, with strong semantic connotations, exported from an economically advanced nation and imposed both practically and with its symbolic qualities on other countries destined to be colonialized culturally and economically. Its presence in Russia, as this print confirms, reached levels of surrealism.

Tsarskoye Selo was in the European area of the great Czarist Russia, which became European through the determination of Peter the Great, who founded St. Petersburg in 1702 in order to open a window onto Europe. This was the official name of the site which, thanks to the work of European architects, town planners, and technicians, was to become the village of the Czars, later renamed Pushkin. The first layout dedicated to Peter's second wife, Catherine, was the work of Carlo Rastrelli, the Italian architect of the Baroque style. He designed a huge palace with a vast formal garden in front of it. But Catherine the Great (1762-1796), who spread her own version of the Age of Enlightenment in Russia, was the empress responsible for the complex Neoclassic, eclectic, and exotic as well as romantic naturalistic composition of Tsarskoye Selo. The catalog of the Jekaterininskij Park included the gallery designed by Charles Cameron, the Scottish architect, a hermitage, column, naval pavilion, Rococo grotto, Turkish bath, pyramid, marble bridge, fountain, concert hall, *gran capriccio* or arcade with a Chinese pavilion, Chinese pavilion, Chinese village, obelisk, Chinese theater, and arsenal or Neo-gothic curiosity. This late eighteenth-century lithograph shows how it was possible to *translate* a Russian landscape in northern Europe into perfect English that amazed observers even on closer examination. It was proof of the persuasive capacities of the naturalistic garden.

PLATE 111

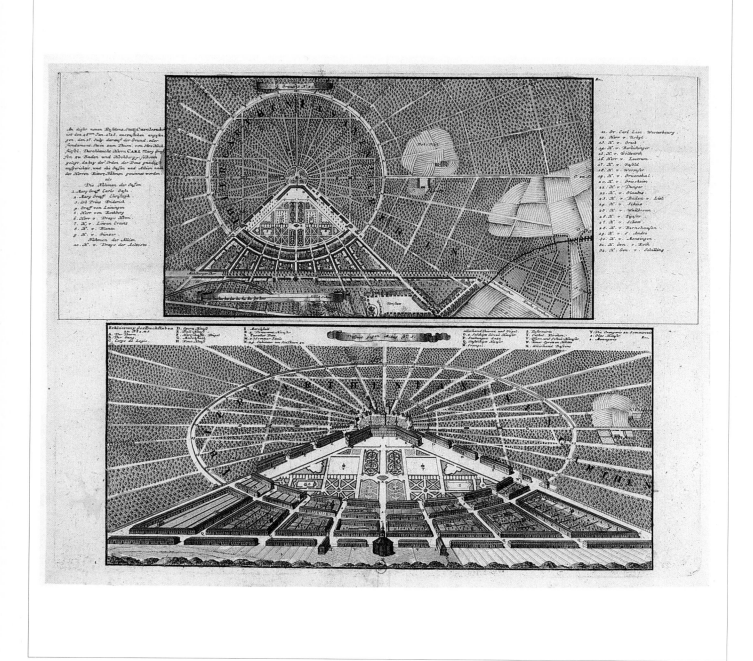

These two prints, a plan and a bird's-eye view, describe the relationship between the city of Karlsruhe and the Hardtwald, the grand duke's castle. The latter was the heart of a great circle and system of sunburst rays that extended into the infinite distance as a metaphor of the potential government of the world from this center of power. The complex urbanistic, architectonic, scenic, and symbolic product was clearly revealed in these German engravings of 1715.

The little city and its tie with the urbanized territory surrounding it converge on the centrality of the castle (in particular, on its Bleiturm, the earliest part of the complex structure), whose presence seems to attract and generate the various directions. All European eighteenth-century culture required rich formal garden based on the symmetrical interdependency of the great embroidered parterres. This one lay between the circular sector of the built-up area connected to the great ring road and the castle. Behind the castle another circular crown of little buildings and pavilions defined the core of the sunburst rays that extended beyond the huge circle (which also engirdled a more delicate square). The rays of the avenues divided the thick forest into wedge shapes, making it possible to cross it in every direction according to the original seventeenth-century rules for royal hunting grounds. The metaphor of the centrality of power is expressed didactically by a geometrical design, the only one possible for this kind of environment and for the political culture that was dominant. The absolutism implicit here was of a mechanistic nature and, exactly for this reason, it was so elemental as to present itself, as these pictures show, in the form of an extraordinary planned scenic poem. It was, perhaps, the most organic relationship in Europe between a city and its natural environment, and alluded figuratively to a considerably different future for cities which should always be *garden cities*, as the island of Cythera in *Hypnerotomachia Poliphili* implicitly suggested.

PLATE 112

In 1728, Batty Langley (1696-1751) published his book, *New Principles of Gardening: Or, The Laying out and Planting Parterres, Groves, Wildernesses, Labyrinths, Avenues, Parks, &c.*, in London. The title included all the fashionable features of the new English garden, so the frontispiece became a kind of prominent menu to stimulate the appetites of readers. This form of didactic presentation was to become a characteristic of English books on gardens.

This engraving was one of a series of six inserted in the first part of the book on the principles of gardening, before the section on kitchen gardens. It shows a garden divided into four sectors by two large tree-lined avenues that intersect around a circular pool. There are four statues near the pool, placed in semicircular niches scooped out of the green mass. Each one marks the beginning of a square. From a gardener's point of view, the print offers a precise description of the scene. There is a grove of evergreens, an open plain of grass, the orangery, a flower garden, a fruit garden, an aromatic herb garden such as camomile, etc., a hop garden, and a physick garden. But the real semantic quality of this picture, like the other five, is concentrated in the plurality of geometrical patterns present in this model garden, and is therefore coexistent from the aesthetic point of view. Rather than being a souvenir of the ancient principle of symmetry, the great crossed axes seem to be the coordinates for setting out every possible variety of pattern to be drawn on, without any prejudice, according to need. Sunburst rays interrupted by sinusoidal figures, circular and rectangular mazes, a square completely taken up by a serpentine, fit together, quite casually, as if they were pieces of a puzzle. The whole design has been built in a thick wood with the take-away technique, and embellished with statues and fountains and the alternation of the tiny specialistic gardens. The structural chaos is, in truth, the mimetic mask of a precise government of reason over all the innumerable possibilities of choice offered by human creativeness.

PLATE 113

In 1779, Louis Carrogis, known as Carmontelle, published in Paris this engraving of the "Jardin de Monceau près de Paris, appartenant S. A. S. Mgr le duc de Chartres," which was one of a series of 17 plates, each with a plan and a short text. This print was the most eloquent for both the analytical description of an important part of the garden, the Temple of Mars, and the complex composition of the symbolic network.

For the Duke of Chartres, the future Philippe Egalité, a passionate anglophile, Carmontelle (who took on the project in 1773) planned to make the garden at Monceau a place where everything was to stimulate gaiety. It was not to be just an ordinary English garden. It was to incorporate gardens of all times and all places in one single park. This was why Monceau became the favorite haunt of landscape painters who portrayed its typical scenes, from the lake arranged for *naumachiae* to the Egyptian pyramid. These scenes were designed with man-made furnishings that were arranged in such a way as to give the impression, at a certain distance, of enlarging every part of the garden. "If a picturesque garden can be turned into a place of illusion, why not do it?" were the words of the author. The 17 scenes

illustrating his garden should be studied to be able to understand the spirit of Carmontelle's work, which he himself considered unconventional and ethical. One of these picturesque scenes is that of the fake ruins of a hypothetical Temple of Mars, lying in a reasoned disorder of unrestrained vegetation. Among the various three-dimensional figurations necessary for practising the aesthetics of ruins, this one might not immediately appear to be one of the most significant. But the mesh of symbols must be untangled to extract the fake dead tree planted in the center of the scene. It becomes the main feature not just because of its bizarreness, but for the union between culture and nature.

*Ville de Paris, ed., Grandes et petites heures du Parc Monceau, catalog of the exhibition held at Musée Cernuschi, Paris 1981.

PLATE 114

In the decade before the revolution, J. F. Bélanger, the French architect who had
spent many years in England, and Thomas Blaikie, a Scotsman who had been
active in Germany spreading the English style of garden, together created this
park called Bagatelle. It soon became a regular stop on any journey planned to
contemplate plants, since it contained a large selection laid out
according to the principles of landscape gardening.

Its exceptional botanical collection and its scenic
attractions, which included little buildings and
romantic pavilions, contributed to making this
garden very famous. But was it possible to visit
Bagatelle without actually going there? Entrepre-
neurial inventiveness typical of eighteenth-century France came up with a reply to this
question. On the basis of drawings by Pierre-
Antoine Mongin, the "Arthur et Robert" manu-
facturers produced a series of large strips of
papier peint of an illusory and naturalistic character. With the romantic technique of landscape
painting and the effectiveness of *trompe l'oeil*, a
large hall was transformed into a multidirectional *belvedere* because the scenery of the Bagatelle park was visible in every direction in such a
credible dioramic form as to give the impression
of being in the middle of that extraordinary pan-

orama. And the *panorama*, an English term
coined in 1799, was the great scientific and epistemological (in the sense of knowing everything
about one's self) entertainment of those years. In
1787, the painter Robert Barker had patented his
panoramic view which he defined as "nature at a
glance". Neither the old landscape of a small
painting nor the antiquarian curiosity of the
trompe l'oeil were sufficient anymore. With the
papier peint, both the very new panorama and the
fascinating romantic garden entered people's
homes. Together they expressed a better reality
than reality itself because they proved that it was
possible to master the knowledge of the environment and that man was capable of modifying it
as well.

*Françoise Teynac, Pierre Nolot, Jean-Denis Vivien, *Le Monde du papier peint*, Paris
1981.

PLATE 115

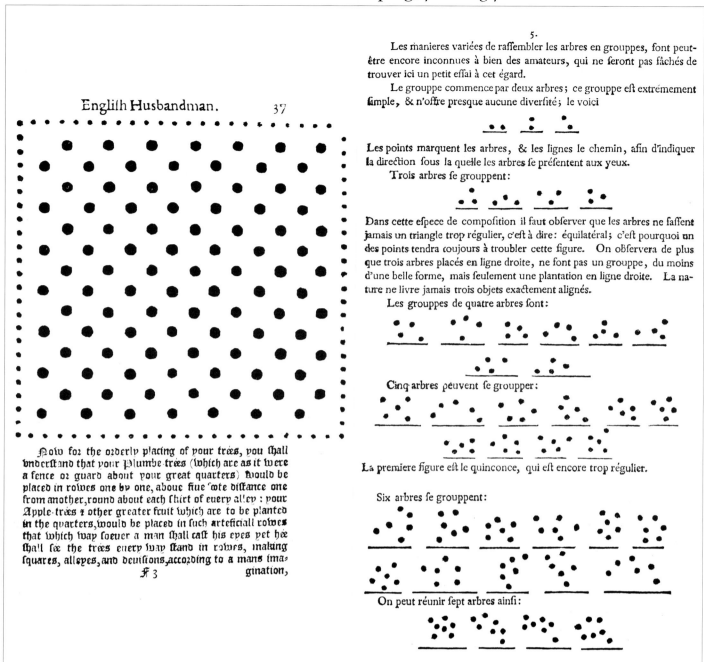

The opposition of nature and culture in the development of gardening tended to be treated technically and culturally through complex devices. These patterns for planting a group of trees in a garden illustrate how those artifices changed in time according to changes in taste and variations in aesthetic principles.

At the top there is the mathematical arrangement known as a *quincunx*, the agricultural and landscape formula handed down from classical antiquity and Roman treatises that guaranteed a rational form of cultivation, if the distance between the trees was regulated according to their growth and species, and if the location was likewise correct. This principle lasted centuries, and the diagram above comes from Gervase Markham's book, *The English Husbandman*, published in London in 1613. In the third volume of another treatise that came out in German in 1780 and in French in 1781, which classified the techniques and the taste of the new landscape garden in what was also a philosophical category called the *art of gardening*, Christian Cay Lorenz Hirschfeld imposed new norms in planting: regular irregularity. The examples for forming groups of trees involve two, three, four, five, six, and seven plants placed in a pattern of interdependency and alternation that aimed at imitating the natural form in contrast to the obviously man-made quincuncial checkerboards. This arrangement was confirmed by the abundant experiments that had been carried out by English gardeners in building landscape gardens. It was, in reality, a ratification of what was by then a widespread and endorsed practice, and the codifier was sure that his rules were scientifically exact and exhaustive. But this was not to be the case for others soon after.

PLATE 116

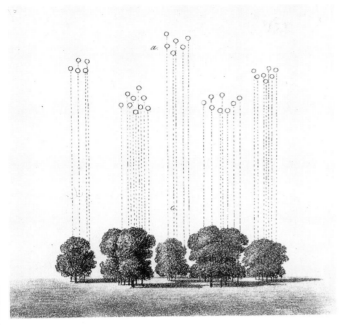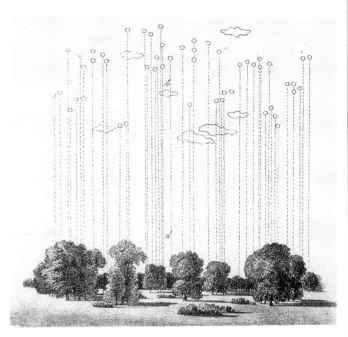

Herman Fürst von Pückler-Muskau was another German who wanted to theorize and codify the aesthetic and technical principles of the new garden, unlike English gardeners who preferred working, letting the Germans do all the theorizing about what they were doing. Pückler-Muskau contributed to the debate on the scenic arrangement of trees and contradicted Hirschfeld.

Prince Pückler-Muskau (1785-1871) was a friend of Heinrich Heine and corresponded with Johann Wolfgang von Goethe. He expressed the results of his studies of English gardens and his own personal experiments in the parks of Moskau and Braintz in a scientific and didactic treatise, *Andeutungen über Landschaftsgärtnerei*, published in Stuttgart in 1834 and soon translated into French and English. These are three illustrations from the book. The large panoramic scene is proof of the virtue of the principles that the noble dilettante in the art of gardening had elaborated and expounded in precise rules. This detail of the landscape in his park at Moskau does seem natural. And it was exactly the lack of a real natural quality that Pückler-Muskau attributed to the first norms of the treatises and to the

consequent layouts of landscape gardens. The two smaller diagrams (shown intelligently as a plan and a perspective view) present alternative solutions for grouping trees. The first shows a poor arrangement with unnatural looking results due to the insuperable immaturity of a naturalistic concept. The second, which goes further into the question, shows a more successful grouping with trees planted according to nature, that is to say, in a philological imitation of those growing spontaneously. The debate over the concept of *natural* in regard to the artificial reconstruction of the plant world in the garden was the focal point of the development of the idea of the garden in Europe between the end of the eighteenth century and the beginning of the nineteenth.

PLATE 117

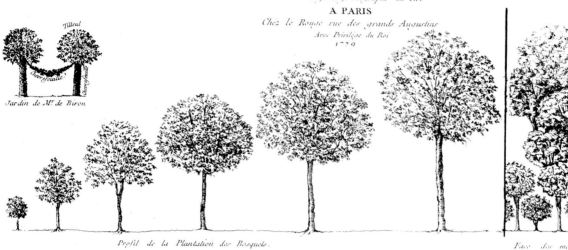

TABLEAU

De la Plantation générale de tous les Arbres, Arbrisseaux et Sousarbrisseaux existants en France qui supportent nos Hivers, rangés sur Six Lignes en Amphitheatre pour designer la Hauteur de leur accroissement naturel; placés de façon qu'on y trouve la difference des figures de leurs feuilles, leurs couleurs, Scavoir Verd-Foncé, Verd clair, Verd de Mer, ou blanché dessous, les toujours verds; Ces differentes nuances sont opposées— autant qu'il est possible. aussi les jardins modernes demandent ils que tout y soit varié

DEDIÉ ET PRESENTÉ
a M. le Comte de la Billardrie d'Angiviller
Directeur et Ordoñateur Général des Batimens du Roi Jardins arts Académies et Manufactures Royales
par Richard jardinier de la Reine
et le Rouge Ingr Geographe du Roi
A PARIS
Chez le Rouge rue des grands Augustins
Avec Privilège du Roi
1779

Tilleul

Jardin de Mr de Biron

Profil de la Plantation des Bosquets.

Face des mêmes Bosquets.

The seventh notebook by Georges Louis Le Rouge printed in 1799 was a complex *tableau* that offered systematic tables of all the plants in France to the designers of the new garden that the author himself called *anglo-chinois* in the title of his complete work. Similar catalogs were never exclusively botanical because the aim was to create a landscape, and the plant world was observed and described from this point of view.

Apart from the long inscription, there are two specific illustrations strictly tied to the idea of the garden to be seen in this frontispiece of the tables that formed the *tableau*. The first (a picture of the real arrangement of plants in M. de Brion's garden) displays the micro-system of two limes, side by side, used as supports for regulating the growth of a climbing honeysuckle that creates a graceful festoon between the trees. It is an image deeply rooted in the Renaissance in origin and taste, while utilizing eighteenth-century elegance. The second is implicitly critical of a conception of the garden taken as a series of picturesque scenes to be seen and contemplated from only one standpoint, as if they were the three-dimensional copies of landscape paintings hanging on the walls at home. The side view of the planting arrangement of a grove is placed next to the somewhat schematic front view to show that different standpoints, which are naturally innumerable, offer different scenes. This was an opinion that contradicted what had been established and advocated by much landscape theory. In these tables, the author puts forward the innovative idea, perhaps unconsciously, that a route in a garden could go beyond the role assigned it by the designer, and that every plant morphology had the right to display itself and to be appreciated from any standpoint whatsoever.

PLATE 118

Ger Dekkers, a Dutch artist, is one of several modern artists who work in the category and cultural dimension of concepts. He uses the serial repetition of photographic images. This sequence comes from the catalog of his exhibition called "Landschapswaarneming," held at the Haags Gemeentemuseum in the winter of 1974 and spring of 1975. The theme of the exhibition was the perception of the landscape.

The title of these two series of five photographs is descriptive: "Three trees near Windesheim." The subjects are three deciduous trees in the juxtaposition of their summer and winter appearances, one of the continual biological mutations that, together with growth, characterize the plant world. The sense of these photographs lies in proving scientifically and poetically that the knowledge of our landscape is infinite because there are an infinite number of standpoints from which an aesthetically and sensitively active interdependent relationship with it can be established. The three trees, two in front and one to the back left, seen in the two symmetrical series with and without leaves, are the permanent main features of a scene which rotates on its own axis offering the visual perception of the different relations between the three elements. Thus in the second couple of photos the three trees have become two; in the third, three, but with the smallest one in the center; in the fourth they have gone back to two again; and in the fifth which is symmetrical with respect to the first, they are three with the third one at a certain distance in the perspective view. Similar conceptual works do not have and do not seem to want to have any practical purpose, but they are a poetic stimulus to acquiring different and deeper knowledge of our reality. They provide a new maieutic form designed to achieve permanent aesthetic education. Through photographic sequentiality, Ger Dekkers intends to instill in observers a more rich and complex conception of landscape.

PLATE 119

Edouard André was the nineteenth-century, late critic (the battle had already been fought, won, and forgotten) of the ingenuousness of the early examples of the naturalistic devices of English eighteenth-century landscape gardening. In his book, *L'art des jardins, traité général de la composition des parcs et jardins*, printed in Paris in 1879, he engaged in a quarrel with Lancelot Capability Brown as if he was a contemporary.

These two didactically exhaustive illustrations rekindled at a much later date the debate with the landscape garden's founding fathers, demonstrating with the same arguments used in a similar quarrel over a century before that their garden was not really natural. The picture at the top shows a landscape scene that André defined as *artificial* (in the sense, obviously, of the man-made reconstruction of a natural scene that is not sufficiently natural). The trees with their supports are too straight. The use of cows to crop the grass has led to the foliage growing high up (at the height of the heads of the animals). There are no shrubs at ground level.

The same scene has been made natural in the second picture. The trees are no longer straight: this is how they grow naturally. The foliage grows irregularly, as it does in nature, and bushes grow on the ground as they do naturally. The right number of cows for keeping the grass as short as a lawn have disappeared. In their place there are a few deer that are much more graceful and certainly less capable of standardizing in an unnatural way the plant world that surrounds them. This was the technical and cultural side of an important part of a debate, which seemed to aim at the reproduction of the natural model by means of natural materials.

PLATE 120

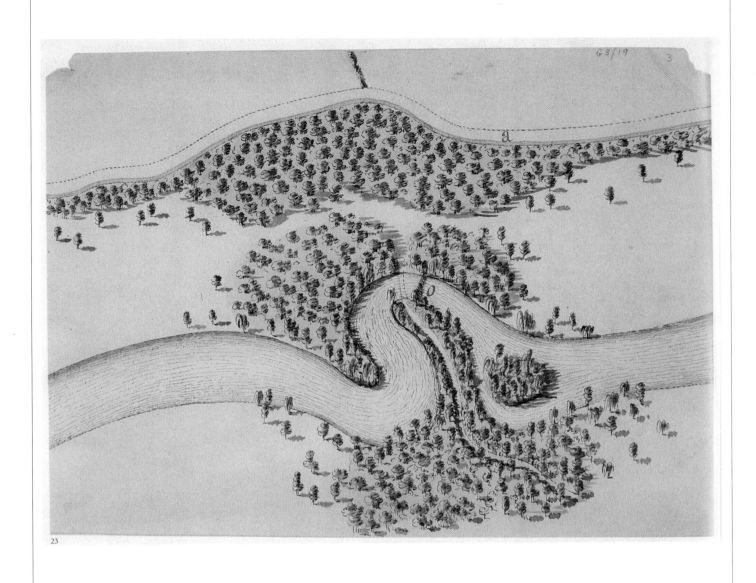

The great English landscape gardener Lancelot Brown (1716-1783), one of the fathers of the formulation and spreading of landscape gardening, had a habit of replying to questions about the underlying problems and difficulties in modifying a site with the words: it has capabilities. This is why he was nicknamed and known to all as Capability Brown. His name, with its semantic significance, is almost a connotation of this epoch of the aesthetic transformation of nature.

This drawing of his, dated about 1764, is a sketch for the landscape design of the trees around a loop in a river. The morphological structures of his idea of a *natural landscape* to be reconstructed artificially following the conceptual model of a specific kind of scenery (the most typical English agricultural countryside) are evident. The great open meadows, or pastureland, are progressively occupied at first by specimen trees, then by groups, and then by a thick, compact wood crossed by a meandering river created by considerable earthworks. All these ingredients formed a natural landscape, which was the constituent factor of every imaginable garden of the time. According to William Kent's pupil, this type of landscape with its structure and the assembley of its grammatical parts was to transform, if not the world, then at least the whole of England, so that there would no longer be any difference between gardens and the agricultural countryside. A universal rule produced a smooth continuity characterized by the rigorous lack of any geometrical form unless it imitated nature a lack and of those architectonic ornaments dear to certain pretentiously cultural gardens. But a consequence of his professional success and his great fame was that Brown ended up the center of a controversy on the significance and the model of nature to be referred to when designing a garden.

*Dorothy Stroud, *Capability Brown*, London 1950; Edward Hyams, *Capability Brown and Humphry Repton*, London 1971; David C. Stuart, *Georgian Gardens*, London 1979; David Jacques, *Georgian Gardens. The Reign of Nature*, London 1983.

PLATE 121

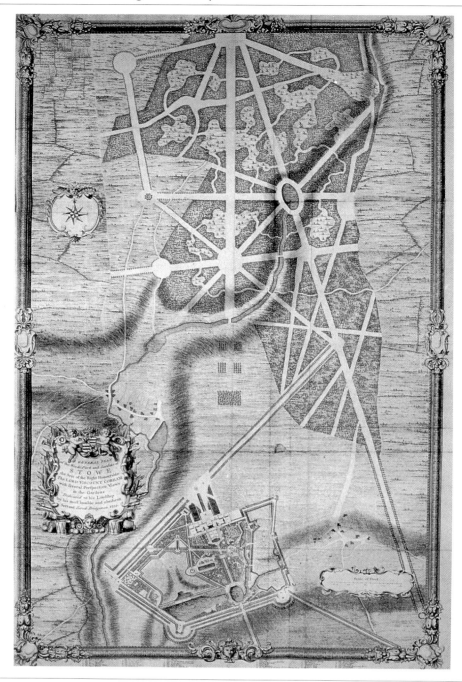

Charles Bridgeman designed the layout of the famous garden at Stowe. This table comes from the book, *A General Plan of the Woods, Park and Gardens of Stowe... with Several Perspective Views in the Gardens*, written by his daughter Sarah in 1739, a year after his death, to tell the story of the masterpiece. This was not the first book to deal with George West's garden. In 1732 a guidebook, *Stowe: the Garden*, had been published, which shows the success of the first entirely landscaped garden that was the haunt of many enthusiastic visitors.

This general view of the Stowe estate, engraved by J. Rigaud for Sarah Bridgeman's book, shows the original general layout around the house, previous to Kent's project, with the proposals Bridgeman made for the garden and for the vast extension of the wooded park belonging to Lord Cobham, an ardent dilettante of the new English garden who enlarged the garden from 28 to 500 acres. The layout suggested by these projects, which aimed at creating a naturalistic scene without completely succeeding, still has a classical seventeenth-century air to it, both in the garden and in the structure of the avenues leading in various directions through the wood which converge and form complicated triangular and starlike geometrical figures. Inside that structure, a naturalistic serpentine weaves through the wood, rejecting (in the plant world) any reference to obvious human intervention in order to achieve markedly scenic effects. The garden around the house perhaps seems exaggeratedly geometric in the drawing. However, the composition was deeply imbued with the interlacing of cultural as well as formal references to the past that were full of new and up-to-date ideas, with evident scenic anticipations that were to become a part of the framework of landscape gardening. Its fundamental element was the destruction of enclosures that were substituted by ha-has.

*William Gilpin, *A Dialogue upon the Gardens of the Right Honourable the Lord Viscount Cobham, at Stowe in Buckinghamshire*, London 1747.

PLATE 122

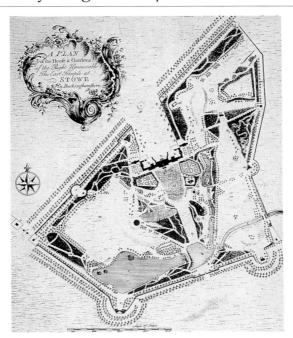

These two pictures, evidence of the changes in taste, aesthetic values, and the naturalistic conception of a garden, show how the garden around the house at Stowe was modified in stages by William Kent and Capability Brown, two designers of the landscape garden school, in a continual *Kunstwollen* that aimed at imitating nature through the construction of artificial botanical scenery.

The battle that took place in this garden, within its intricate system of architectural structures, little temples and pavilions, was of an aesthetic nature. The first project designed by William Kent, the top picture, might seem modest, but it was epistemologically fundamental for the naturalistic aesthetics. Kent eliminated or reduced or softened almost all the straight lines marked by plant material and conserved by Bridgeman. This can be observed in a comparison of the two figures. The external perimeters, if not the inner ones, maintained their previous linearity. His intervention was instead decisive, and significant for this reason, on the water layout. While Kent could still accept a straight tree-lined avenue, a pool could only have a curved border to it, obviously based on the serpentine. The great octagonal pool on an axis with the house and the vast triangular sheet of water thus became natural lakes and lost their earlier semantic value. Then it was the turn of Capability Brown, and everything that Kent had done was taken to extremes. The picture below comes from Nicolas Vergnaud's book, *L'art de créer les jardins*, which was published in Paris in 1835. It illustrated Brown's work at Stowe. Perhaps not everything was changed, but with careful critical research, anything that showed signs of geometrical regularity was eliminated. The resulting composition seemed to be softly and organically natural, or so it was thought at the time.

PLATE 123

Humphry Repton, who was born in 1725 and died in 1818, could have attributed his longevity to his love of gardens. Repton coined the term landscape gardening, which then denoted the English style garden, a garden which dissolved into the infinite distance of the landscape, which was in turn aesthetically governed by man as these two pictures demonstrate. This was the *before* and *after* technique: the first print showed the existing scene that could be landscaped; the second, the possible result if the project was carried out.

In the second half of the eighteenth century, Horace Walpole proposed the first history of the landscape garden and declared William Kent its father because he had been capable of leaping the fence formed by every enclosure around a garden and seeing that all Nature was a garden. Humphry Repton showed that he had understood this new concept of the garden in all his projects. The goal was always an aesthetic one: to transform the landscape into a garden. The technique of the *before* and *after* perspectives (which he used to present the projects to his clients in the so-called *Red Books*) helps to understand the significance of the proposed changes. The top drawing shows a hillside that is partly cultivated with regular fields. The one below is the planned transformation, quite indifferent to agricultural productivity, which is capable of guaranteeing a real landscape garden or new overall landscape.

Humphry Repton chose books to spread this new culture: his design method, which he had considered as a visual support for the client, became a message for everyone. Apart from the dimensions of the giant landscape, this method also analysed the man-made structures capable of communicating with their linguistic and architectonic qualities, the spirit of the landscape poetics, as is the case of the little building. Repton's long professional life led him into a dispute with the advocates of the *picturesque garden*. But he showed that he too was capable of expressing the new aesthetics which proposed to make the natural rarity the main feature of a garden, and which brought flowers back into the garden after centuries of exile.

*Humphry Repton, *Sketches and Hints on Landscape Gardening*, London 1795; Humphry Repton, *Observations on the Theory and Practice of Landscape Gardening*, London 1803; Dorothy Stroud, *Humphry Repton*, London 1962.

PLATE 124

The twin series of before and after drawings is applied here to two different situations. The first is the landscape to be seen from a new house. The elimination of the pit and the quarriers' cottages will suffice for creating an excellent landscape scene for the owners and guests of the English country house (the landscape has priority). The second shows that a simple architectural *maquillage* with wood and stucco can transform semantically an austere Georgian building in a garden into a romantic Neoclassic temple.

The romantic spirit was the essence of the landscape garden. It proposed with its high sensibility to be the dialectic and anthropologically necessary complement to the rigid reiteration of Neoclassic architecture. This was lucky for the landscape garden as well as for Neoclassic architecture. Perfection in the practical expression of a taste, which was considered indispensable for obtaining the proposed objective, demanded a rejection of compromise. If all the landscape became a garden, at least as far as the eye could see, then any obstacle to forming the optimum scene had to be eliminated without any consideration for the non-aesthetic categories, even if they were of economic and productive importance, as these examples show. The case of the little building in the park is very interesting.

Here Repton considered the architecture as a form of communication of sentiments, obviously, more than of architectonic styles. At the end of the eighteenth century a sober and functional building, a model of considerable qualities, underwent a semantic metamorphosis. A face-lift was enough to transform the image, which now states in architectonic terms the romantic sentiments practiced by all. Not much later the Victorian era was to contest this. General puritanism infected both styles and materials. The wood and stucco used to decorate the buildings in Regent Street and this rennovated little temple were to be considered as unacceptable fakes, and the new architecture was to proclaim the *truth* in the use of materials, within the general falsity of eclectic historicism.

PLATE 125

Bath was a town in Avon that was developed thanks to the complicity of financiers, architects (in this case John Wood the Elder, 1704-1754, and his son John the Younger, 1728-1781), and doctors who ordered their wealthy London patients to take the waters. This therapeutic trend sparked off a specific type of tourism, whose goals were metaphysical pseudo-towns from the point of view of urban sociology lived in occasionally only by the rich and their servants.

In the early decades of the eighteenth century, new relations between the city and the plant world were experimented with in Bath. It became an urban prototype that served as a genetic reference for other English cities that later on felt the need to expand in a suitable manner. Circus, square, crescent, and terrace were the terms used to define the new elegant eighteenth-century and Neoclassic urban spaces. The high technology of the repetitive Neoclassic architecture needed to be compensated, like the garden, by complementary interventions of great sensibility. For example, in the case of the garden in front of a house, methods of landscape gardening were utilized, whereas in a city, open spaces decorated with plants were introduced. This was the origin of urban green space, which was designed specifically here to form new urban landscapes where the plant world was at long last co-protagonist. These prints show the Royal Crescent (above) designed by John Wood the Younger and the Circus (below), by John Wood the Elder. The Circus's round garden has been enclosed by clearly visible railings. Only those who had the key to the garden, the owners or tenants of the houses in the Circus, could go inside it. This greenery was therefore part of the urban landscape but it was not open to the public, an ingenious invention of the English landscape school. The garden in the neighbouring Crescent was a half-moon organized in the same way. Beyond it there was a large public garden whose landscape merged with the Crescent. The fascination of Bath spread quickly on the Continent.

*Vincenzo Marulli, Su l'architettura e su la nettezza delle città, Firenze 1808.

PLATE 126

At the headword *English gardens* in his *Dictionnaire des idées reçues*, Gustave Flaubert wrote: "More natural than French gardens". The history of the success of *romantic* gardens is characterized by an infinite succession of banalities perpetrated first and foremost by the disciples of the new aesthetic religion. These two illustrations, coming from what was a serious attempt at spreading information, have turned into iconographic clichés.

These prints come from a book on the art of English gardens published in 1801 by Ercole Silva, a nobleman and dilettante in the new art of gardening. The first is a view of the Villa Belgiojoso in Milan that is practically the same today. The second is an imaginary view of the author's own garden near Milan whose original settecentesque formal layout was completely transformed. It is interesting to note that with respect to the syntax and grammar of the new garden (which the author had borrowed from Hirschfeld's treatise) these images communicate the most obvious stylistic features, those capable of turning a careless observer into a self-taught enthusiast convinced of his own sudden creative capacities. This was to be the case of many a successful European manual, especially those containing immediate and cogent pictures. Literary works also provided reasoned examples of this situation set in tragic or comic circumstances. In his book *Die Wahlverwandtschaften* dated 1809, Johann Wolfgang von Goethe demonstrates ironically that in the emergence of the *elective affinities* of the time, the garden played the role of go-between, especially the romantic garden like this one. *Bouvard et Pécuchet* by Gustave Flaubert (1874 was the year of the partial draft; it was published posthumously in 1881) was a book that ran through every possible kind of dilettantism. In it his two main characters are fascinated by a private garden that could be looked after by its enthusiastic owner and amateur gardener by means of one of the most well-known short manuals of the time, "L'architecte des jardins" by Pierre Boitard. The final version of this handbook came out in 1834 and it was reprinted in six editions until 1852.

PLATE 127

An aesthetic war concerning the relationship between man and nature, the predominant element of the landscape garden, broke out in England in the later half of the eighteenth century. The subject of this heated debate was the landscape garden, or rather the garden that was the result of insufficient theoretical research according to the innovators. The ultimate object of landscape gardening was not the achievement of natural beauty but the construction of picturesque beauty.

Like romantic aesthetics, of which it was a part, the theory of the picturesque garden (but also of all the picturesque territory) was based on exaggerated concepts which were expressed in the appreciation and contemplation of exaggerated landscapes. The founders and activists of this rebellion were three young intellectuals: William Sawrey Gilpin (1724-1804), Uvedale Price (1747-1829), and Richard Payne Knight (1750-1824), who published essays on aesthetics and extremely effective models of projects by utilizing the before- and-after technique of communication, a method often used by landscape gardeners for presenting views of their proposals. This is one of the first models showing an alternative between the banality of nature and the sublimeness of the

picturesque, taken from Gilpin's book published in 1792. The contrast lies in the softness of the sinuous lines of a vast naturalistic landscape (the garden was too small for similar striking aesthetic visions) and the aggressive image of a complex and savage environment capable of provoking new and strong emotions. If nature did not provide them, then they could be built, when the aesthetic foundations were solid. This aesthetic debate was to burst violently into gardening as well.

*William Gilpin, *Three Essays: On Picturesque Beauty; On Picturesque Travel; and On Sketching Landscape; to Which is Added a Poem, On Landscape Painting*, London 1794; Richard Payne Knight, *The Landscape, a Didactic Poem*, London 1794; Uvedale Price, *An Essay on the Picturesque*, London 1794; Walter John Hipple Jr., *The Beautiful, the Sublime, & the Picturesque in Eighteenth-Century British Aesthetic Theory*, Carbondale 1957.

PLATE 128

These two engravings by Thomas Hearne are critical and propositional illustrations inserted in *The Landscape, a Didactic Poem,* by Richard Payne Knight, printed in London in 1794. The first print aims at deriding the naturalistic methods of Capability Brown to be found all over England at the time. The second is a concisely illustrated proposal-cum-manifesto for the possible near future: a natural, artistically designed environment.

The concept of *picturesque*, which was strongly characterized from the semantic point of view, with a matrix parallel to *landscape* (the word that defined a painting of natural scenery) enjoyed a long-lasting, unexpected, widespread success. When Roland Barthes analysed after the last war the instruments of mass tourism, he wrote that, for example, "the Guide Bleu does not know any landscape apart from the picturesque form." When the aesthetic debate on the picturesque garden raged in England at the end of the eighteenth century, its main target, the famous and fortunate Capability Brown, was already dead (1783). Old Humphry Repton (1725-1818), Brown's disciple, ended up at the heart of the storm because he had used the master's archives and had invented the term *landscape gardener*. This well-known, successful, and busy seventy-year-old took part in the *querelle* (which looked rather like a squabble among professionals) with various essays including the handwritten notes of his "Red Books" dedicated to clients to show that he had already absorbed and practiced the aesthetics of the picturesque in his gardens. While in the rest of Europe the old aesthetic theory of the first landscape gardening was still being spread, Repton wrote an impassioned "Letter to Price" who replied with a "Letter to Repton." These two culturally and anthropologically contrasting pictures provide exceptional and eloquent evidence of the battle between the landscape and the picturesque garden.

PLATE 129

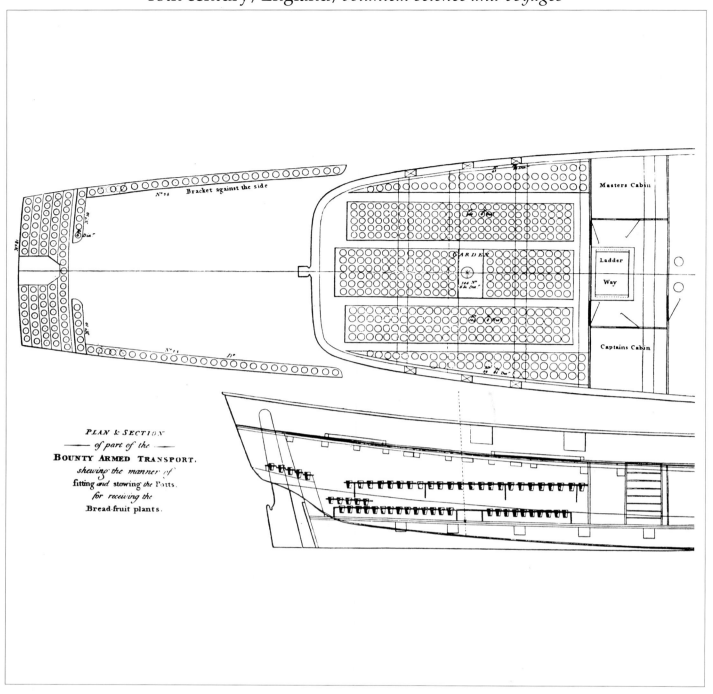

PLAN & SECTION
—— *of part of the* ——
BOUNTY ARMED TRANSPORT.
shewing the manner of
fitting and stowing the Potts.
for receiving the
Bread-fruit plants.

The plan and section of the stern of the Bounty, the eighteenth-century vessel equipped to transport breadfruit trees to England, take us back to the mass of literary and cinematographic documentation of its adventures rooted in our social heritage. In the history of the human modification of the planet, the transport of plants is an inherent part of the history of botany and of the use of plants for creating exotically lovelier gardens.

European nations had organized with calm regularity from bygone times the migration of plants from the Middle and Far East for their farms and their gardens. But the discovery of the Americas and the exploration of the immense Indian and Pacific Oceans stimulated and promoted scientific expeditions, arduous journeys for practical ends, raids of adventurers and plant hunters across land and sea. The voyage of the Bounty was one of the latter. It set sail from Tahiti for Jamaica in 1789 under the captaincy of lieutenant William Bligh with more than a thousand breadfruit trees (planted as cuttings) and a few other indigenous plants on board, laid out in 837 pots, boxes, and tubes. But the Bounty never reached its destination. Jamaica can be considered an emblem of a certain phase in the transport of plants from the Pacific to the Atlantic, as this and the other Caribbean islands served as intensive plantations of heterochthonous plants before they were transferred to Europe. Scientific curiosity regarding plants, practical utility for the alimentation of the overpopulated old continent, and aesthetic needs to add exotic touches to the gardener's European garden in the service of the nursery business, all converged in the explosion of botanical voyages that took place in Europe from the start of the sixteenth century.

*Tyler Whittle, *The Plant Hunters*, London 1970; Edward Hyams, *Plants in the Service of Man*, London 1971; Edward Hyams, *Animals in the Service of Man*, London 1972; Redcliffe N. Salaman, *The History and Social Influence of the Potato*, Cambridge 1985; Alfred W. Crosby, *Ecological Imperialism: the Biological Expansion of Europe 900-1900*, Cambridge 1986.

PLATE 130

Nathanial Bagshaw Ward (1791-1868), the botanist and amateur inventor from London, designed the container for transporting certain species over long distances. It was called the Wardian case after him. This print dated 1829 shows one kind of terrarium. The little plants inside the sealed glass container with the soil and air necessary for maintaining life only needed daylight in order to carry out their chlorophyllous processes.

The passion for transporting plants reached such levels that in 1833 *The Gardener's Magazine* congratulated the captain of a merchant vessel who had succeeded in keeping alive eight azaleas out of a total of twenty-nine on a voyage from Canton to London. John Claudius Loudon made a study of these botanical expeditions and drew up an accurate quantitative balance. At the beginning of the nineteenth century, thirteen thousand one hundred and forty plants were cultivated in the British Isles, of which only one thousand four hundred were indigenous. The botanical and medical worlds used the portable greenhouse invented by Ward in 1827 to enrich their collections and to try out new experiments and cultivations. In eclectic and curious Victorian England, scientific instruments were immediately considered of great utility for completing the geography of exotica in the garden. The Wardian case was a practical and conceptual bridge between the past experience of the glasshouse and the new concept of decoration and ornamentation of the home. Little cases usually stood on tables, but very often complex pieces of furniture supported glass-faced, minute Neo-Gothic temples. At the time of the Great Exhibition of 1851, every drawing room in London (and in a short while, all over the country) had to have a Wardian case in the shape of the Crystal Palace, the extraordinary glasshouse-pavilion that hosted and was a symbol of the great universal exhibition. This was the start of the triumphal march of Wardian cases into the limitless realm of vulgarity. All the same, apart from a touch of dubious taste, the terrarium brought a form of plant life (ferns and mosses) into the home. It was an important reaction to the old and unique presence of cut flowers and the occasional potted plant.

*Roger Ground, *Bottle Gardens*, London 1976.

PLATE 131

Flowers had been ridiculously excluded from European gardens for centuries. During the period of the French formal garden and the landscape garden, dimensions became scenographic due to the composition of man-made landscapes. The continual movement of colors and forms would, perhaps, have upset the rigidity or soft curves of figures designed to be seen as changeless.

Flowers, and wild flowers too, were, however, not the main, but an indispensable ingredient of the new picturesque aesthetics. They signified an intricate presence that varied over time in the global system of plant life. With the support of this theoretical principle, flowers came back to all kinds of gardens in such an arrogant and impetuous way as to make a suspicion of a return to formal gardens (though under a new guise) seem plausible. William Robinson took on the task of teaching how to enjoy the beauty of a flower independently of its being kept in a pot or a bed. In this watercolor, which immortalizes a flower garden, Humphry Repton, the old landscape gardener who had never utilized flowers and who was at the center of the debate with the advocates of picturesque gardens, showed that he was second to none in the capacity to bring flowers back into the garden. This picture shows the rosary at Ashridge Park in Hertfordshire, which was built in the first few decades of the nineteenth century. It was organized structurally as a circular system of arches for regulating the climbing roses which were visible from a pavilion that also acted as a support for more roses. There was a pool in the center surrounded by rose beds arranged like the petals of a flower. All this was new and very different from the image of the ancient European rose gardens, designed with espaliers in the *hortus conclusus* or allowed to grow naturally as large shrubs when the old roses were rampant.

PLATE 132

With poetic and tautological eloquence, Gertrude Stein defined a rose in the following terms: "Rose is a rose is a rose." These are four of the extraordinary portraits of 170 roses which were drawn and painted in watercolors and then engraved and printed with a glaze technique by Pierre-Joseph Redouté (a Belgian artist, 1759-1840), the Raphael of flowers. The pictures in his book, *Les roses*, have been used all over the world in innumerable ways for all kinds of floral decorations.

Redouté was inspired by the Empress Josephine (to whom the book was partly dedicated) and by her gardens at the Malmaison, where there was an infinite collection of roses. Curiously enough, imports of roses during the years of the blockade against Napoleonic France were only possible thanks to the naturalistic sympathies of the English for the Empress. Redouté had begun to work for Josephine in 1798, and he reached the peak of his career with this work. Its technical merits lay in the combination of precise and calligraphic botanical and scientific representation with the stylization and elegance of the new romantic approach of the picturesque school. Redouté was the last great maestro to add to the *Vélins de Roi*, the well-known French collection of plant illustrations. The passion for roses was absolute. Numerous publications prove this: in France, for example, a periodical on roses, *Journal des roses*, was published between 1877 and 1914. Among many famous gardeners who also published works on roses, the great Ann Ellen Willmott (1858-1934) wrote an enormous book, *Genus Rosa* between 1910 and 1914. It was a generous and extraordinary intrusion of gardening culture into the world of botanical science which had always been prejudiced against amateurs and was in this case too. With its old-fashioned charms, the rose is also full of infinite symbolic qualities. Eithne Wilkins has documented innumerable cases in her book, *The Rose Garden Game*, which was published in London in 1969. Mirella Levi D'Ancona has analysed twenty-six explicit examples in Italian Renaissance paintings.

*William Blunt, *The Art of Botanical Illustration*, London 1950; Allen Paterson, *The History of the Rose*, London 1983; Gerd Heinz-Mohr and Volker Sommer, *Die Rose*, Munich 1989.

PLATE 133

The nineteenth-century towns of the middle classes that were experiencing industrialization and the phenomena of modern town planning sprawled out in new, concentric, and never-ending suburbs. Here space was not infinite, as the theory of landscape gardening advocated and required. Consequently, small suburban gardens, which were a possibility for the *petit bourgeoisie*, and later on for the lower classes as well, tended toward the picturesque style.

John Claudius Loudon (1783-1843), gardener, theoretician of the art of gardening, as well as critic and popularizer of Repton's works, designed the little garden in this illustration from his specialistic book, *The Suburban Gardener and Villa Companion*, published in London in 1838. The picture shows the little garden next to a small house and beyond it an unlikely wood that hides neighboring buildings. The garden is furnished with ornaments of a size suited to this site, and with a few potted trees. The parterre-lawn is surrounded by a complicated border comprising shrubbery, with its small trees and flowering bushes, and the arches for cultivating climbers. This is the miniature world of family femininity, a place to express the love of children. It is not the scenography for private entertainment. The actual size of the garden, a logical consequence of the financial and sociological means of the owner, necessitates a notable epistemological regression. The design and shape of the garden clearly indicate a return to the ancient *hortus conclusus*, but one that is much more limited and private than the original. In line with that specific tradition, this style revives and emphasizes the relationship between man and the single plant—in particular, the flowering plant—with the result that every garden imitating it became a flower garden.

PLATE 134

At the end of the thirteenth century, a member of a Milanese religious order, the *Ordine degli Umiliati*, who was famous for his compilation of the first scientific and statistic medieval description of a city in 1288, *De magnalibus Mediolani*, proposed a new aesthetic theory based on ethic and moral as well as metaphorical values in opposition to the fantastic and rhetorical *laudes civitatis*. The new theory was expounded in *Disputatio rosae cum viola*, the debate between the rose and the violet, where he sided with the humble violet.

A study of the text reveals the symbolic background of the two flowers and a kind of intrinsic misogyny in the monk's preference. It is interesting to note how the choice swung toward an ordinary, popular flower that grew in ditches and could be enjoyed without the interference of expensive cultivation. Common sense declared it more useful than the rose. The aesthetics of weeds were never to have a theoretical champion, even though every kind of wild garden starting from the picturesque one at the end of the eighteenth century contained, implicitly, large numbers of weeds. These two exceptional pictures come from a nineteenth-century French treatise on the art of gardening by Edouard André. The first describes how plants decorate the old walls of some moorings; the second shows how bindweed covers a roof in Port Said. Both of them are illustrations from the paragraph on rock plants in the chapter on floral decoration. The author asserts that there are a multitude of them and that for a certain class of plant lovers, their fascination equals that of orchids. This positivist interest in everything, and therefore also in the microfloral world (such as the tiny ferns in Wardian cases and all that could be observed in detail with magnifying glasses and microscopes), brought the aesthetic theory of gardens to the brink of another epistemological revolution. But its many possibilities were not developed.

PLATE 135

This illustration of the flower garden at Hoole House, the famous estate of Lady Broughton, was published in the fourteenth issue in 1837 of *The Gardeners' Magazine*, the first periodical run by John Claudius Loudon and published in London since 1826. The Savoy Alps and the valley of Chamonix were reconstructed here according to the canons of picturesque aesthetics. Flowers, too, had their own specific large space.

In his introduction, Loudon praised the perfection of the circular beds whose round microcosm was certainly less hostile than flowers packed into geometric or fancy patterns. From the practical point of view, changeable flower gardens as Loudon had defined them in 1822 in his *Encyclopedia of Gardening* could easily transform the landscape with the rotation of bedding plants, taken in pots from greenhouses or nurseries and planted when they were due to flower. With this picturesque approach to flower gardens, the emphasis was solely on flowers. The beauty of a shrub or perennial plant when not in flower had not yet been discovered. Flowers were soon to be made prisoners in very different and more formal beds with such decorative functions that they lost the identity that had taken so much effort to establish in the early decades of the century. This was the period of the return of the formal garden in England and then consequently all over Europe. But a few years later, with William Robinson at their head, flowers were to *leap the fence* around every bed to grow freely and naturally. In the right foreground of this picture there is another fetter placed in good faith by the gardener: the architectural support for climbing plants, a recollection and active homage to infinite pasts and some near futures.

*Melanie Louise Simo, *Loudon and the Landscape, from Country Seat to Metropolis 1783-1843*, London 1988.

PLATE 136

These three drawings show proposals, suggested by Herman Fürst von Pückler-Muskau in 1834 in his treatise on the art of gardening, for building, just with strong wire, eye-catching, elegant, and bizarre treillages to grow plants on. It was the absurd perfection of an elegance of taste that was unaware, as yet, of being kitsch.

This fashion was so widespread that the author's instructions assume tones of normality: "For climbing plants various trellises are made of strong wire, which in themselves are quite pretty things, and which allow the plants to cling freely on all sides. In England one can find them ready-made and of neat workmanship, whether as gates, arches, overhead trellis, broken pillars, or little obelisks; here, however, they must be made by capable smiths from drawings." Drawing on his own experience, Prince Pückler-Muskau suggested the species to use to climb up these supporting structures. *Wisteria sinensis* is suited for the umbrella with its pale blue bunches hanging from the trelliswork. *Cobea scandens* should grow on the arch, and various kinds of clematis on the semicircular fan. This is certainly not the reappearance of the spirit of Renaissance, seventeenth-, or eighteenth-century treillages. These are products of the climate of the first few decades of the nineteenth century: that of political and, to a certain extent, of cultural restoration. It revealed the urgent need to hide shapes that were pleasing to the eye, as was to be the case of women's bodies, squeezed into wasp-waisted corsets, or even food. Consider the inventiveness with which, in order to achieve a charming decoration, the great maestro of the European cuisine, Marie-Antonin Carême, cook of kings and king of cooks, the founder of *haute cuisine*, disguised the natural appearance of the food he prepared for his guests.

PLATE 137

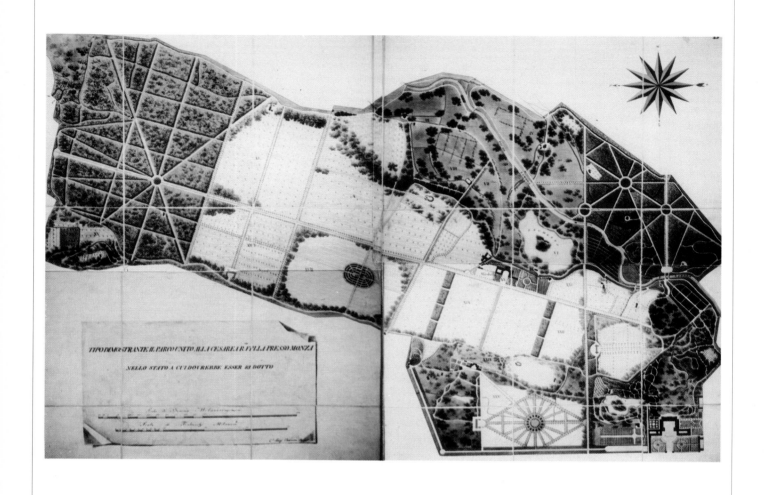

This watercolored print by Luigi Canonica (1762-1844), dated about 1808, kept in the Austrian National Library in Vienna, is one of the drawings from the project for the Royal Park of Monza, near Milan. The park measured nearly one and half thousand acres and was perhaps one of the largest to be created in Europe at that time. It was built on instructions from Napoleon, then King of Italy, and work started in 1805. The following year the park was already enclosed by a large wall running fourteen kilometers around it.

Italian historical events and obsolescence due to illicit utilization of its areas have obliterated the innovatory significance of this extraordinary European monument of the history of the garden and of the development of its *idea*. From the morphological point of view, the park contains the whole of the history of gardens: from the Renaissance and formal garden around the Royal Palace designed by Piermarini, the seventeenth-century mathematical layout of the groves, and the settecentesque axes, to the curving walks and meadows typical of landscape gardens, the romantic architectonic connotations, and the highly picturesque aspects emphasized by tortuous streams. But today, perhaps, it means something else. Napoleon ordered that every *lycée* in the Kingdom of Italy was to set up an educational botanical garden (because this was the best book for studying botany), and the

general layout of the Royal Park at Monza was to be used as the standard cultural reference. It was not really the garden of a royal palace with the relative extension of the park where the king went hunting. On the contrary, Napoleon, forward-looking as ever, proposed to experiment with the *idea of progress*. The Royal Park was considered in the logic of public utility as an immense menagerie for the domestication, breeding, and reproduction of animals and plants. From the botanical point of view, the park was "a Royal nursery for the conservation of fruits, trees, shrubs and indigenous and exotic plants necessary for the plantations along paths and avenues for embellishing the public gardens of the Kingdom."

*Maristella La Rosa, L'albero della libertà. Orti botanici e agrari: uno spazio per sperimentare, in Momenti dell'et napoleonica nelle carte dell'Archivio di Stato di Milano, Milan 1987.

PLATE 138

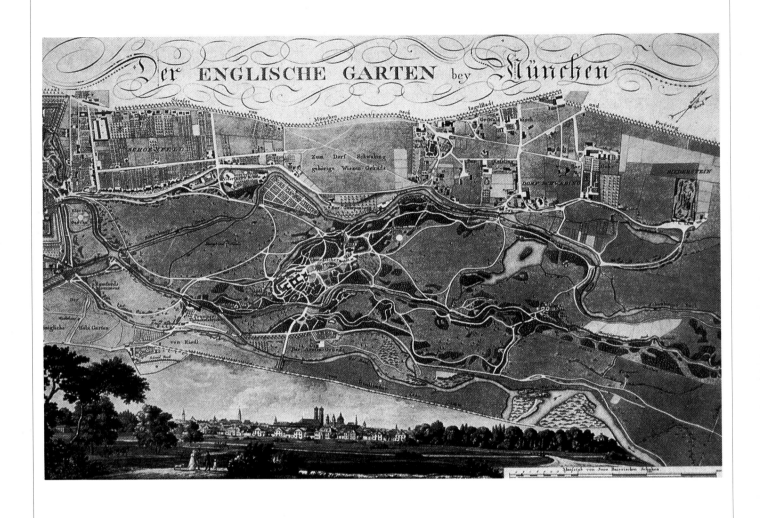

At the end of the eighteenth century, a new nine-hundred-acre public garden was built in Munich, the capital of Bavaria. It was immediately known as *Der Englische Garten* for its design, which included a towering Chinese pagoda built in 1791. It was probably the largest stylistic garden in Europe and the oldest public garden in Germany built when the first examples of English landscape gardens were limited to small private estates.

The park was designed by Friedrich L. von Sckell (1750-1823), the landscape gardener, a firm follower of the theories and works of Capability Brown and Humphry Repton. No limits were placed on the formation of a vast overall landscape composition. The physical and psychological size of what was a public garden, the extension of its irregular network open to all and sundry, were so great as to impose it on the city not just as a curiosity or the simple experimentation of a new taste that was difficult to generalize, but as a fundamental aspect of the urban structure, of the very *forma urbis*. Von Sckell described the theory behind his project, which had borrowed from English culture but was then translated into a German version that put landscape principles on a par with the new picturesque ones. "It's nature which serves new gardens as an example. Its various images can also decorate our gardens, but without thus imposing the slightest obligation to make a hasty imitation. These images of nature must be composed with taste in such a way as to appear entirely blended; enriched with exotic trees, shrubs and flowers, they will form a garden in which nature appears dressed in its Sunday best." Today this public garden in Munich has changed not just biologically, and its pagoda has been rebuilt after a fire. But it still provokes amazement for the grandeur of its conception, especially when compared to the size of the city at that time.

PLATE 139

This Neoclassic *Arena*, reminiscent of a distant past, was the stone replacement of an earlier wooden one. It was built in Napoleonic Milan, to the side of the Place of Arms (seen on the left of this print) and at a tangent to the network of tree-lined streets.

The stone Arena, seating more than thirty thousand people out of a total urban population of little more than one hundred thousand, was decided upon as if to seal Milan's newly acquired role as capital of the Kingdom of Italy, whose king was Napoleon Bonaparte. Built in 1806 with a strongly Neoclassic design by Luigi Canonica, a Swiss architect who lived in Milan, it became the setting for holidays in the classical tradition that had been reintroduced in the Jacobin and republican age. It was a perfect structure of public utility inside a complex system of public urban green-space (the Place of Arms could be included when it was not being used for displays or drilling). Canonica's touch of genius was his capacity to amalgamate symbolically the physical presence of this construction with the botanical urban landscape around it. As *il Filarete* had suggested for fifteenth-century Milan, an oval hanging garden composed of two rows of trees crowned the Arena and could be seen from the city and the surrounding neighborhood. Late nineteenth-century foolishness brought about the destruction of this magical scene, upsetting its context by planting huge trees too close to the building that hid the extraordinary crown. The watercolor testifies to the importance of this stone and plant construction in the life of the city. A mock naval battle is going on inside the Arena as an homage to the public games of classical antiquity. Many other events were held there, including traditional festivals, fireworks, equestrian parades, displays of gymnastics, and even mass banquets.

PLATE 140

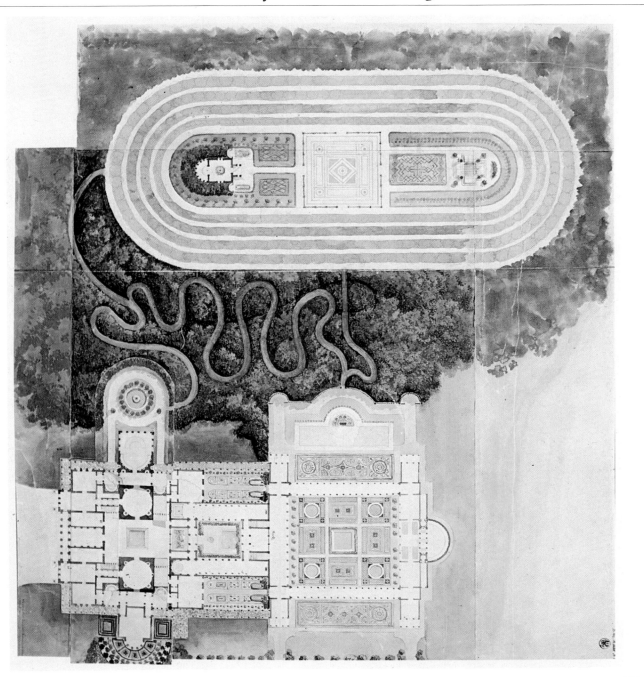

This splendid design by Karl Friedrich Schinkel (1781-1841) dates back to the 1830s. It reflects the dynamism of the alternation of his classical and romantic principles. This is the plan of an old-fashioned villa set in a large park with a hippodrome and woodland behind it.

All Schinkel's projects, whether drawn, engraved, or simulated in realistic paintings of landscapes, are set in specific dioramas where the plant life is the most important element. Even in urban environments his perspectives tend to combine the rigidity of the buildings with the free forms of the plant world. The ability of a great artist lies also in communicating semantic qualities with only a few prominent signs. The task here is carried out by the ancient serpentine which is teeming with romantic significance. Formal gardens cover the large patio and surround the old-fashioned villa. Others can be seen inside the race course of the enormous hippodrome. Between the two structures, there is a more detailed and thicker wood than the second lightly sketched one beyond the hippodrome. The wood is the real garden, or rather it becomes so with the curving path of the expressive serpentine, which magically turns the mass of plants into a place that is romantic beyond all imagination. It is not just the means for connecting the two architectonic figures, but is a space in its own right, designed for the sentimental contemplation of this wilderness. Rarely in the history of the ecology of images has a figure expressed so much and in such an unequivocal way.

PLATE 141

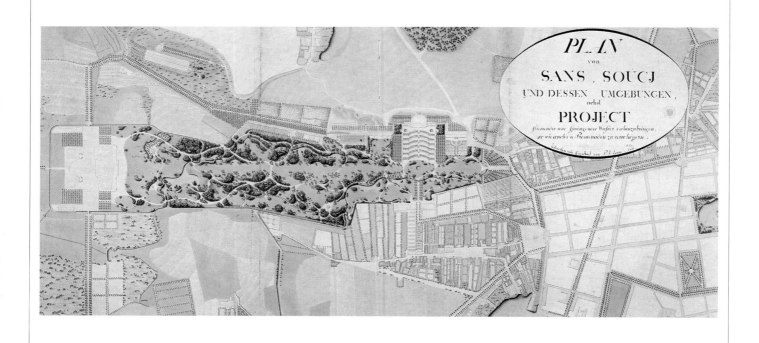

Peter Joseph Lenné (1789-1866) was one of the most important and famous German botanists and garden designers in the age of landscape gardening. He studied at the well-known Jardin Botanique in Paris and later worked in Prussia. He was responsible for the greater part of the modernization of the park of Sans-souci, the sumptuous residence built by Frederick the Great near Potsdam. Work on it started in 1745, and it soon became the place where the soldier-king could rest, free from cares, between one war and the next, and where he died

The recollection of the Italian garden of the Renaissance in this great park led to its being called "an Italy in the marchland of Brandenburg." But the botanical curiosity that its modernizer had cultivated in Paris and the general idea of English landscape gardens were also present. The Sicilian garden, the orangery, the botanical garden, and the Nordic garden, all planted with endemic species, showed how Lenné was interested in applying a new concept of modernness to the nineteenth-century garden. The great park of Sans-souci that Lenné had redesigned completely, while preserving a series of architectural pavilions, measured roughly seven hundred and forty acres and contained four hundred species of exotic trees and shrubs. Its configuration made it a kind of condensed version of the history and cultural geography of gardens. The castle of Sans-souci was a jewel of the German Rococo style. It was built between 1745 and 1748 under the watchful eye of Frederick II, on the basis of a project by Georg Wenzeslaus von Knobelsdorff (1699-1753), who also designed other buildings on the estate, including some *chinoiseries*. Lenné worked in this historical context. This is one of his own signed drawings, dated 1816, from the long series of designs he made for modernizing the park. It was a statement of the victory of landscape gardening over the whole area, with the emergence of winding paths and waterways leading into the indispensable lakes.

*Harri Günther, Peter Joseph Lenné, Garten, Parke, Landschaften, Stuttgart 1985.

PLATE 142

Lenné's theoretical and practical development could be termed a move from romantic aspirations to a compromise with nineteenth-century common sense, starting from the project (opposite) designed when he was twenty-seven and ending with this record of the park of Sans-souci in 1836 when he was forty-seven. The great central axis, with its regular rows of trees, that modifies the semantic significance of the first project, had been designed by Lenné in 1828.

The extensions to Charlottenhof and the great hippodrome framed by a pattern of plants (1835) stand out in this plan. The ideological and aesthetic variation was explicit from the morphological point of view. It was the terminus of a twenty-year journey through projects, interventions, and afterthoughts. The main target of innovation was around the castle. In the first drawing it was characterized by the English style garden that went right up to the front of the building and was limited at the sides by simple groves. In the second project the manner house has been totally surrounded by formal gardens that seem to put the clock back a century. Of the much discussed romantic garden of 1816, where water was semantically prominent, the winding waterway is still there, but the curvy, almost-natural lake in front of the castle, which had been inserted as an essential and central view, has been placed to one side. It is now in the propulsive center of the new expansion of the romantic garden. The new garden spreads as far as the geometrical layout (achieved by plants as well) of the hippodrome and other buildings. The long tree-lined avenue is not, as it was in seventeenth- and eighteenth-century layouts, the place where the whole vastness of a park could be perceived at its crossroads. It serves here to repair the dichotomy between the straight line that is fundamental for the formal garden around the castle and the earlier romantic garden, inappropriately split up in a way that defies its significance.

PLATE 143

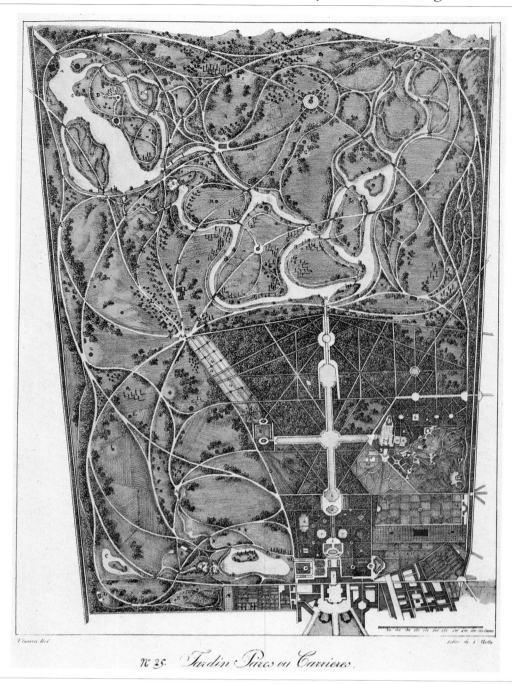

N° 35. *Jardin Parcs ou Carrieres.*

The emphasis on bizarre propositions as well as the circulation of normal kinds of models led to considering a folly as a non-dimensional and ahistoric category to be pursued, in the Romantic age, as if it was a precise dictation of reason. This was the case with Gabriel Thouin, the French landscape gardener who expressed his ideas in *Plans raisonnés de toutes les espèces de jardins*, which was printed in Paris in 1820.

The book, with its fifty-seven pages and fifty-seven color lithographs was published by means of an advance subscription paid by customers in 1819. It was a great success and was reprinted in 1823 and 1828 (the last edition added one page and two plates). Thouin, who was now an old man, had been the king's gardener at Versailles in the 1770s. His attitude to the modern garden had the same founding slant as that of the visionary architects of the late Enlightenment who were the driving force of the revolutionary years. In this plan, the old gardener who had tended the formal gardens at Versailles as well as the romantic ones around the Petit Trianon launched his dream (which was banal rather than outstanding) of the multiple extension of the Sun King's great garden and park and its transformation into a landscape garden. It was an absurd project because the morphology of the park could never have been perceived in an area of this size. The drawing is out of scale. It could have been one of many projects for a small, certainly elegant, and fashionable garden with sinuous forms characterized by an increasingly nineteenth-century fluidity. The color lithograph is symbolical. Its origins are aesthetic, but the semantic purport of the two shapes implies the overlapping of the old by the new.

PLATE 144

Thouin Del.   Lith. de C. Motte.

n.º 53 - Fabriques pour l'ornement des jardins.

Gabriel Thouin's curious book is both a systematic and an imaginative proposition. It classifies real or possible gardens of the cultural environment and gives examples of them with plans and iconic illustrations. Thouin's repertory includes different productive types and models for different public and private uses, and an alternation of styles, especially Chinese and English ones. As this page of garden ornaments suggests, they look as if they were ready for use.

The various kinds of models of gardens brought together in the book offer the entire range of cultural possibilities open to the choice of the consumer. The same is true of these buildings. They seem to be the reasoned collection of all the types and all the styles used a century earlier in order to embellish a garden with the necessary and certainly useful curiosities and follies when the scene to be contemplated had to be picturesque. This was the origin of the semantic value of each of these architectonic types. When the garden was still of a naturalistic kind, the buildings (and there were fewer of them) were mostly Classical (better still if they were solely Palladian) with occasional examples of exotica. The scenes were deliberately pictorial, never picturesque: the garden was arranged as a succession of paintings. Now everything was pronounced emphatically, from the architectural constructions to the models for fake ruins and *chinoiseries*, from Neo-Gothic to Classical styles, from useful or decorative buildings to fountains and boats that were to glide charmingly over the various lakes. The fundamental idea behind this way of thinking was the possible classification of everything that was considered as acceptable in the garden. Within the range of that totality, anyone could choose according to his personal taste.

PLATE 145

FRONTISPICE.

Plans des plus beaux Jardins pittoresques de France, d'Angleterre et d'Allemagne.

Jean-Charles Krafft, who called himself an architect and designer, published in 1808 a series of prints entitled *Plans des plus beaux jardins pittoresques de France, d'Angleterre et d'Allemagne, et des edifices, monuments, fabriques, etc. qui concourrent a leur embellissement, dans tous les genres d'architecture, tels que chinois, egyptien, anglois, arabe, moresque, etc... Dediés aux architectes et aux amateurs.* These were later bound and sold in two volumes in 1809 and 1810.

Krafft had already published in Paris at the beginning of the century two volumes on architecture and on the new English gardens. He launched this new publishing project in response to the ever growing interest in the English landscape garden, the source of all romantic gardens, in spite of the commercial blockades that intervened at times between Georgian England and Napoleonic France. Krafft's book was designed for a vast public (architects and amateurs) and was sold in a trilingual edition (French, English, and German). It was an exhaustive collection of types and models, a sort of complete encyclopedia containing about two hundred pictures, and their relative descriptions, of everything that had been done in European gardens for more than a century. While it could be read as scientific documentation, its real aim was to offer a vast range of possibilities for those who searched for models of decorative ornaments to create or embellish a garden where the exotic nature of this never-ending eclectic theory was so important that Krafft used it in the title of his work, as a means of attracting the general attention of his future readers. As a symbol and declaration of intent, the frontispiece of the first volume showed the innumerable possibilities of improving a garden with either a Neo-Gothic or a Chinese or a Moorish building, presented here in a miscellaneous fashion, which would have been legitimate and appropriate in any garden.

PLATE 146

One kind of exoticism which was not expressed specifically as a revival was that of European Islamic gardens. These had characterized Spanish landscapes from the eighth century to the time of the *reconquista*. When the very Catholic kings of Spain occupied Seville and Granada, the great capital of Muslim Spain, the expulsion of a civilization did not completely cancel what were solely the architectonic traces of its gardens.

Alcazar de la Alhambra, in Granada, is the most important architectonic container of precious gardens built between the thirteenth and fourteenth century by the Spanish Moors. Considerable research in the field of botanical archaeology has made the reconstruction of even a plant map of that ancient splendour possible. A romantic American and extraordinary story writer, Washington Irving (1783-1853), who was then secretary to the American Legation, brought about the rediscovery of the fascination of these archaeological remains when he wrote his books, *The Conquest of Granada* in 1829 and *The Alhambra* in 1832, known all over the world as the tales from Alhambra. These four pictures come from a nineteenth-century edition of the tales. They are highly significant, not just for what was then a possible revival, but for their structural and ahistorical content. The illustrations show the old buildings still intact and the patios where the plants were cultivated. The star of the gardens, in this drought-free part of southern Europe, was their vital nourishment, water, in a role different from that which it had played in the ancient Moors homelands. Water as the precious source of life was part of the social heritage of that race, which knew of its rarity and fertility thanks to rivulets flowing in oases in the desert. With this same ancient anthropological and cultural attitude, the Arabs organized their gardens in European Sicily and Spain. The pictures show how that "extraordinary liquid" was channeled in minute and elegant streams. It was not the quantity but merely its presence that gave the water in the garden all its significance.

PLATE 147

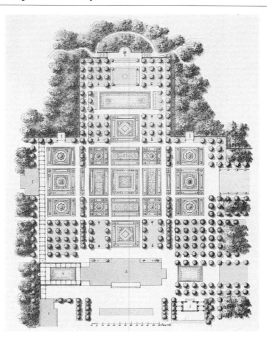

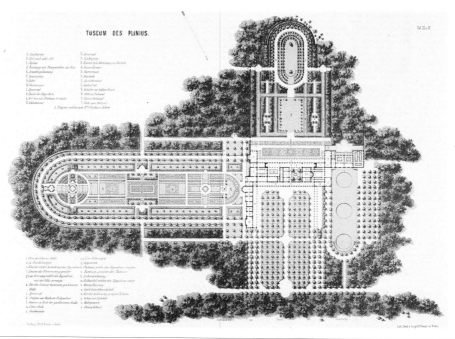

Unlike nineteenth-century cities, which admitted various styles of buildings, architecture refused to be totally and utterly eclectic and to include only the best of every style in order to achieve abstract perfection. In the same way, the garden also rapidly rejected the synchronic stylistic goal that was an eager attempt to use the history of its styles as a fundamental principle.

This was true of much of the late romantic experience of European historicism, even though it clashed with the cultural achievements accumulated, not just in technical terms, over two centuries of experiments and theoretical and aesthetic elaboration. But historical classification, with its implicit program of ever-growing revivials, was fascinating. It influenced the garden as well. This can be seen in these four drawings by Gustav Meyer (1816-1877), which he presented as forms of credible historical and stylistic models to be marked and learned by everyone, whether technicians or connoisseurs, for their improbable reintroduction. The publishing and professional goal of the author was that of displaying knowl-edge and erudition of a philological and accademic kind as well. The book started with some essays on the reconstruction of Arabian gardens, followed by other (real or interpreted) historical examples including these four, and it ended with the author's own modest projects for small landscape gardens, almost as if the historical approach served as a form of authentication. This page shows Meyer's proposals for model Greek and Roman gardens, the latter being interpreted as an assembly of many eighteenth- and nineteenth-century formulas that were the graphical translation of literary descriptions. Interest in historical gardens was basically limited to its probable forms.

*Gustav Meyer, Lehrbuch der Schönen Gartenkunst, Berlin 1860.

PLATE 148

In the eighteenth century there was a tendency to look to models from other cultures and other periods, especially to Chinese ones, in an ambiguous way, more as a need for an exotic and historical backing for spreading the new aesthetics of landscape gardening than as a desire for philological knowledge. But as far as the culture of historicism was concerned, history was an infinite book whose pages could be brought back to life according to the likes and dislikes of contemporary taste.

These two drawings by Gustav Meyer are more romantic than the first two. Their referents are to be found in aesthetic universes, the Gothic and Chinese worlds which nourished many expressions of Romanticism, especially the one involving gardens. The Gothic model is obviously an improbable revival. What does it indicate, then? First and foremost, the author's capacity to dominate this style (as well as all the others) not through the scale and size of the garden, which is not even touched on in the few historical pictures and miniatures available, but by resorting to a Gothic-style calligraphy that can be seen in the mass of Neo-Gothic decorations and ornaments. The singular character of this style was often concentrated in the effectiveness of the ornamental designs, here to be seen in the flower beds and in the highly unlikely symmetry of the central part of the garden. The fourth drawing, like the Roman one showing one of Pliny's villas, is not presented as an example of an ancient style, but as a document of the Forbidden City in Peking, taken from earlier publications. The reference to Chinese culture (which had been used and abused for a long time) to improve the origins of the European landscape garden can be seen here in the predominance of the sinusoidal network of walks and in the emphasis on the relationship between parterre and groves with occasional specimen trees. A novicelike landscape gardener would have carefully laid out the garden in this way in the second half of the eighteenth century.

PLATE 149

John Claudius Loudon took part in the widespread movement in favor of the new aesthetic theory of the picturesque garden and against the landscape garden, which was considered insufficiently natural. Based on the complete integration of the architectural and environmental projects, and put into practice in an eclectic manner but with remarkable semantic eloquence, Loudon's way of redesigning the world was, in reality, a step beyond the landscape model.
In the 1830s it was known as *gardenesque.*

Gardenesque meant knowing how to work (perhaps with the techniques used by Repton, whose complete works had been published by Loudon) in a large park or small garden and to arrange the flowers into a composition of herbacious borders or in formal flower beds. It was a kind of continual all-embracing eclecticism based not only on common sense but also on the intelligence and skills of the gardener. *Gardenesque* really meant a style calculated to bring out the arts of the gardener. These two pictures, utilizing the before-and-after method of salesmanship, were ahead of the new trend; they express it to a certain extent, although Loudon had not yet completely formulated it at the time of their publication. They come from the book, *A Treatise on Forming, Improving, and Managing Country Residences... so as to Combine Architectural Fineness with Picturesque*

Effect, printed in London in 1806. The combination of architectural fineness and picturesque effect is clearly illustrated here. A simple house, Barnbarrow, placed in a landscape designed in the manner of Brown or early Repton, has been transformed architectonically as well as scenically in such an overwhelming way that the house was nick-named Barnbarroch. The sequence of the two pictures fully expresses the ideology that alimented the violent cultural debate between landscape and picturesque gardens, which was extended obviously to every branch of the fine arts and not limited to gardening. They were designed to highlight the specific character of the two alternative styles: everything was natural and normal in the first, while everything was exceptional and picturesque and, of course, expressed emphatically in the second.

PLATE 150

Natural, picturesque and gardenesque, gardenesque planting and irregular style are the old and new terms for defining the many theoretical and practical activities of John Claudius Loudon, a follower of the eclectic method. These three drawings come from *A Treatise on Forming, Improving and Managing Country Residences...*, an encyclopedia of everything a gardener should know, where Loudon again debated the theme of the comparison between *naturalistic* and *picturesque* in a successfully didactic manner.

The three pictures illustrate the passage from the serpentine style (typical of Lancelot Capability Brown's landscape garden and the first projects by Humphry Repton) to the irregular style characteristic of picturesque gardens advocated by William Gilpin, Uvedale Price and Payne Knight in opposition to the still active Repton. The realistic scene at the top shows the gentle ambiance of a meandering river in a suitable setting with alternating meadows and groves and occasional specimen trees. By using an ingenious method of superimposing one drawing on another, the central plan shows the present and the future situation. The bottom table represents the renewed landscape seen from the same standpoint and demonstrates how the tranquil immobility of the former can acquire, with not much effort, semantically antithetic quality consistent with the requirements of the new taste. The didactic capacity of the before-and-after method is at its best here in explaining the opposition of the two aesthetic conceptions of the figuration of nature. Those who had asserted that a natural landscape, or one organized artificially by man to appear natural, had a function of stimulating sentiments, could not deny that in this triad of illustrations the sentiments provoked by the picturesque scene were certainly more intense than those deriving from the naturalistic scene. If it had been a question of the quantity of sentiments, the picturesque style would have swept the board forever.

*Tom Turner, *English Garden Design, History and Styles since 1650*, Woodbridge 1986.

PLATE 151

Constant Bourgeois del.   Felipe Cardano aqua forti.   Perdoux sculp.

Maison bourgeoise changée en une Habitation agréable.

Constant Bourgeois del.   Felipe Cardano aqua forti.   Perdoux sculp.

Maison bourgeoise changée en une Habitation agréable.

While the battle between landscape and picturesque gardens was raging in England, France, it seems, still had to leap the fence. In his book, *Description des nouveaux jardins de ma France...*, published as late as 1808, the elegant French count, Alexandre de Laborde, explained how to landscape the small gardens of modest households according to the principles of the now fully approved English style.

Like Krafft's contemporary publications, Laborde's book was also published in Paris in three languages, French, English, and German, during the period of the Napoleonic monarchies and while a fierce conflict was going on. While publishing works that drew implicitly or explicitly on the English garden, it was as if every European country wanted to recognize it as an achievement for the whole of mankind rather than as the triumph of a national style. Once the theoretical principle was acquired, the relative didactic activity could be launched with all its power of communication. Laborde borrowed from English ideological and practical experience the technique of before-and-after, which had proved so effective in winning the landscape garden's great battle against the formal one, and used it as an instrument of educa-

tion. (This technique was now being used in the new aesthetic struggle against the landscape garden by the supporters of the picturesque one.) It was a question only of ideology, aesthetic ideology, and not of reason. The difference between the bourgeois house and the pleasant home, which was the end result of following Laborde's rules, was one of taste and a few architectonic modifications (forms which could not be settled by a simple *maquillage*). In particular it implied a considerable transformation of the original estate, because the ideology of the landscape without a walled garden required a larger area, one big enough to establish a perfect system of ha-has. The way these scenes were designed and laid out expresses their semantically different approaches perfectly.

PLATE 152

Manoir antique change en un Château élegant.

Manoir antique change en un Château élegant.

Laborde did not analyse a bourgeois home here. This is an old château in the countryside that has a formal terraced garden in the Italian style with large formal *parterres de broderie* flanked by two rectangular pools and crossed by a walk on an axis with the castle. The diagnosis is implicit: the formal garden is an illness to be fought. The solution is the usual one: operate with the taste and techniques of the culture of the landscape garden.

In the author's own words, these prints proposed to transform the *manoir antique* into a *château élégant*. The second one, which represents the finished project, has eliminated every single straight line and even the castle has been softened by two pacific residential wings that mitigate the original military and defensive aspect. The two rectangular pools have been linked and form a curvy sheet of water in the foreground, the home of a little boat. A gentle grass slope (the naturalistic transformation of the former terraced changes in level) rises from the lakeside; it is marked by a serpentine walk leading up to the castle. The highly significant frame around this picture is made up of the mass of thickly planted trees that start from the waterside, surround the

lawn, and border the new castle. The shapes of the tall trees, planted in intricate groves where every now and then a poplar raises its head against the skyline, create real theatrical wings around a stage formed by the green parterre in the center and a natural or cultural backdrop (the castle in this case). This is the formal and semantic structure of the language of landscape design, which both characterizes the garden and is expressed in an unequivocable way. These two pictures and the former two reveal the widespread diffusion of the new, relatively complex aesthetic value that required an epistemological conception of the (also new) idea of the garden, and which could certainly not be placed in the limited and short-lived category of *fashion*.

PLATE 153

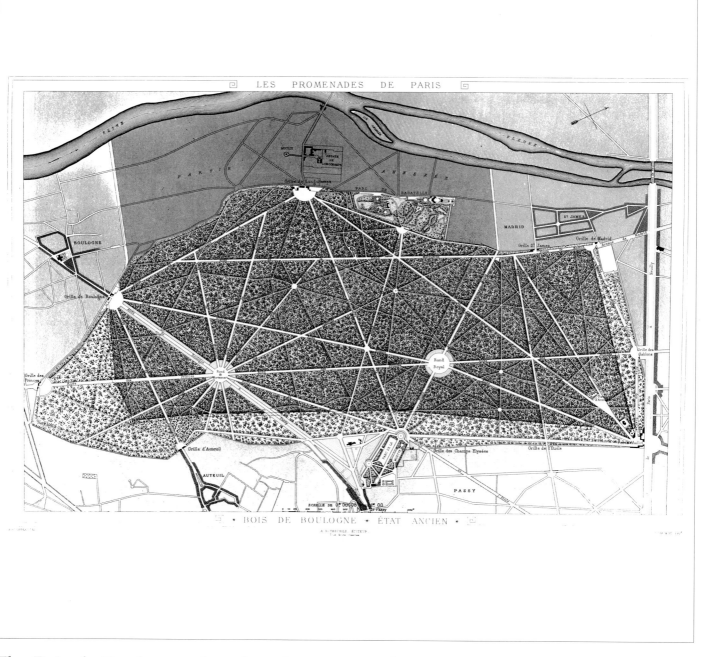

The Bois de Boulogne played an important role very early on in the life of Paris. The pilgrims' way from Paris crossed this enormous forest on its way to Nôtre Dame in Boulogne-sur-mer. A little church was built there in 1319 and was called Boulogne, and this is how the park got its name. The forest later became the hunting ground of the king. The old layout shown here was the work of Jean-Baptiste Colbert, one of Louis XIV's ministers. The park at that time was the setting for royal merrymaking and banquets as well as for poaching and highway robberies.

The two projects were presented together by Jean Charles-Adolphe-Alphand in his monumental work with the intention of comparing them. They show the situation before and after the romantic changes he introduced as director of the parks of Paris in the Second Empire. The meaning attached to a park before the consolidation of the new romantic and naturalistic aesthetic theory can be observed in the overall morphological plan of the first scene, which includes the new romantic park of Bagatelle laid out to the north at a tangent to the Bois de Boulogne. The *bois* was a thick woodland whose primary function was that of a game reserve full of wildlife for the kitchens of the king. This version was an ecosystem capable of guaranteeing the existence and reproduction of the game inside it. The landscape garden was meant to imitate another kind of nature, English pastureland, with its large meadows for cropping cattle and thick groves as wings where the pasture ended. In order to create a similar landscape in the heart of Paris the existing ecological system had to be destroyed, without introducing another. It was simply a question of satisfying the taste imposed by a new aesthetic theory. Obviously the best landscape solution for a *bois* of this kind was the old one. Straight roads cut through the forest taking travellers from one urban area to another. At the same time they could fully enjoy the inside of the conceptually infinite and physically enormous two thousand one hundred acre reserve.

*Adolphe Alphand, Les promenades de Paris, Paris 1867-1873.

PLATE 154

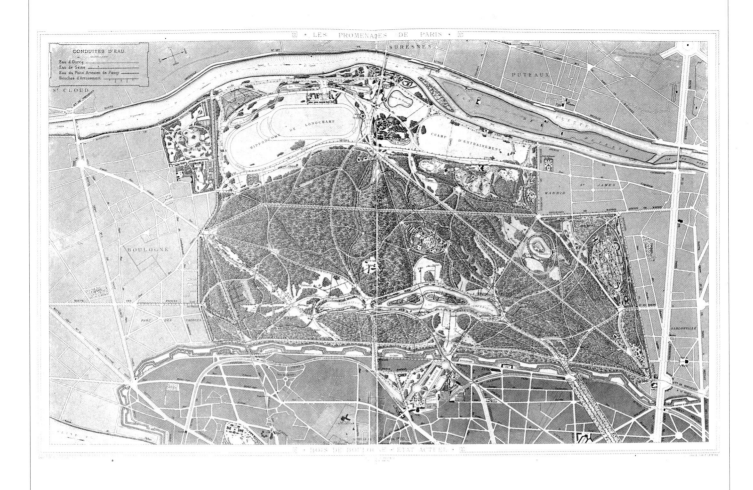

Jean-Charles-Adolphe Alphand, who considered himself the depository of the one and only truth, the high priest of the landscape garden and confident champion of its unquestionable beauty, turned the old forest into a pretty garden à la mode. In a certain sense it was incomprehensible because an overall view of the park could not be observed from anywhere. Order, which was possible thanks to the knowledge of the structure of the past *bois*, was replaced by chaotic disorder, even though there was a precise hierarchy in the various networks.

With all his stern convictions, arrogant Alphand certainly did not think that the old *bois*, whose original functions had been suppressed, had any particular aesthetic qualities. Neither did he consider that there was any objective reason, of a historical kind, behind its beauty as a natural artifact perennially governed by man. The fascination of an immeasurable mathematical geography that permitted the total and perfect knowledge of the whole eluded him. Alphand directed the projects before Varé, the architect, and Barillet-Deschamps, and through this project he became famous as the leader of a movement, later working alone on the modernization of the Bois de Vincennes and that of Bouttes-Chaumont. He wanted to transform the forest into something modern, worthy of the splendid botanical dreams (they were not to be such) established for Napoleon III's empire. The new Bois de Boulogne was not up to the aesthetic, typological, functional, and sociological standards of contemporary town planning based on the boulevards. Baron Georges-Eugéne Haussmann, the prefect of Paris, had recently invented and introduced this exceptional green contribution of tree-lined avenues into the urban landscape. The large park shown here has been diligently and perfectly drawn. But unlike typical landscape gardens, it is composed of a tangle of sinusoidal lines converging on two lakes and designed to concentrate the utilization of the park in an area smaller than the *bois*, near the built-up sector and parallel to the city walls. On the other side, along the banks of the Seine, there is the hippodrome and the area for recreational devices. Left more or less inanimate between the two is what remains of the original *bois*, stripped of the qualities and quantities that made it quite unique. The new design looks like the work of a virus (not necessarily negative in itself) which the great cultural and historical layout was unable to destroy completely.

PLATE 155

This minute and expressive engraving by Giovanni Battista Piranesi seems to be the showroom of all the ornaments that passed through the European garden from the the time of the humanist cult of antiquity to the commercial dealings of the eighteenth-century antique trade. Rarely were they romantically disturbing. More often they were vulgar eyesores in the botanical scenery of man-made landscapes.

This engraving dates back to the mid-eighteenth century and was titled, "Marble Urns, Cippi and Cinerary Urns in the Villa Corsini Outside the Gate of San Pancrazio." Its theme was the ornaments for the antiquarian decoration of a settecentesque Roman garden. Urns, and *cippi* and cinerary urns were full of symbolic values in all societies and in every age, so they were universal and widely usable in the garden, also because of their capacity to stimulate sentiments. Every manual produced at the time of the landscape or picturesque or generally romantic garden at the end of the eighteenth and beginning of the nineteenth century included, in the section on utensils for decorating and embellishing a garden, an enormous variety of urns, and *cippi* and cinerary urns. The strong visual communication of

Piranesi's engraving, which anticipated his frenetical publishing activity by a few decades, lies in its documenting in a powerful pictorial merger the types of ornaments and their necessary scenic setting. The objects are lined up in an exaggerated and imposing perspective which is proposed, implicitly, as an efficient example for any naturalistic project. Piranesi makes them emerge from an architectonic *rocaille* which expresses materially the relationship between nature and culture. At the beginning and at the end and in the cracks at ground level there are the inevitable plants used for ruins, which were indispensable for any scene that aimed to recall antiquity in either an ordered or tumbledown manner. This thorough scene is offered as a model for infinite, but perhaps less elegant and less erudite, repetition.

PLATE 156

The periodical publication of loose prints on the modern garden spread through Europe after Le Rouge's work. J. G. Grohmann, the German architect and professor of philosophy at Leipzig, began publishing his sixty albums, *Ideenmagazin für Liebhaber von Gärten, englischen Anlangen und für Besitzer von Landgärten*, in German and French in 1796. The last one came out in 1806. The encyclopedia was turned into a paper pattern for the reigning romantic Neoclassicism.

Grohmann's publishing venture came on the market a couple of decades after Le Rouge's and was apparently meant for more widespread consumption by various social classes. The models of vast gardens and costly ornaments could not be applied to the infinite suburban dwellings nestling in tiny gardens in all the future industrial cities. With their typical down-to-earth spirit, the English and Americans published treatises and guides for transforming a small space into a pleasant picturesque garden where the owner was also the gardener. Grohmann's intention seems to have been exactly this: to reach the market based on new quantities. The readers of his sheets were in fact more interested in the *idea of the garden* than in real gardens, and this was easily created by assembling a few simple elements, perhaps more ornaments than plants, which were highly signifcant from the symbolic point of view. The German architect's drawings were rather like a do-it-yourself kit. No matter which elements were taken out of it or which way they were put together, the result would always have been a romantic garden. This picture shows the exhaustive supply of all the romantic connotations of a garden that could be obtained in the field of seating. In a detached way the author invites the reader to choose according to his own personal taste. Local craftsmen will be able to build the objects whose symbolic significance is much more important than the craftsmanship.

PLATE 157

A Paduan architect, Giuseppe Jappelli (1783-1852) completed this Neoclassic structure inside the medieval Palazzo della Ragione in his home town on December 20, 1815. Jappelli first designed extraordinary Neoclassic and romantic buildings and then, after a grand tour of England in the 1830s, he built neo-gothic houses and exquisite English-style landscape gardens. According to many, his career took a stylistic step forward due to his conversion to the teachings of the new aesthetic theory.

On one side, Jappelli placed two rows of pine trees that seemed to rise out of rose bushes, and on the other side, a pattern of laurels, orange trees and exotic shrubs, while the covered and artificially lighted space was decorated everywhere with contrasting, brightly-colored flowers. This was the interpretation, in landscape terms as well, that Jappelli gave the city of Padua. The scenography of the layout was practically that of a large salon elegantly furnished with plants, as urban spaces had been for some time now as well as gardens that had not yet reached maturity. Similar ephemeral landscapes had, for years, been the setting allocated for experimenting with the skills of young architects, who presented a kind of preview so as to win commissions for designing the stable plant layouts of parks and gardens. If the plant scenery in a young garden, or in a free urban space, sug-

gested metaphorically the temporary continuity of the scene, then the establishment of real gardens, such as the one in this picture, inside a large covered hall for decorative purposes as well as naturalistic ones, was an attempt at portraying a *real* landscape. Behind settings of this kind there was the idea that a greenhouse could not only be designed, built, and organized for its explicit botanic purposes, but could also have naturalistic qualities: the study of the plant world could harmonize with its contemplation. The naturalistic greenhouse was to become the *jardin d'hiver*, whose main function was not the conservation of plants in a suitable microclimate, but the creation of a landscape that was out of the question for European winters, capable of carrying its guests away to warm and distant lands without the trouble and time of the journey to get there.

PLATE 158

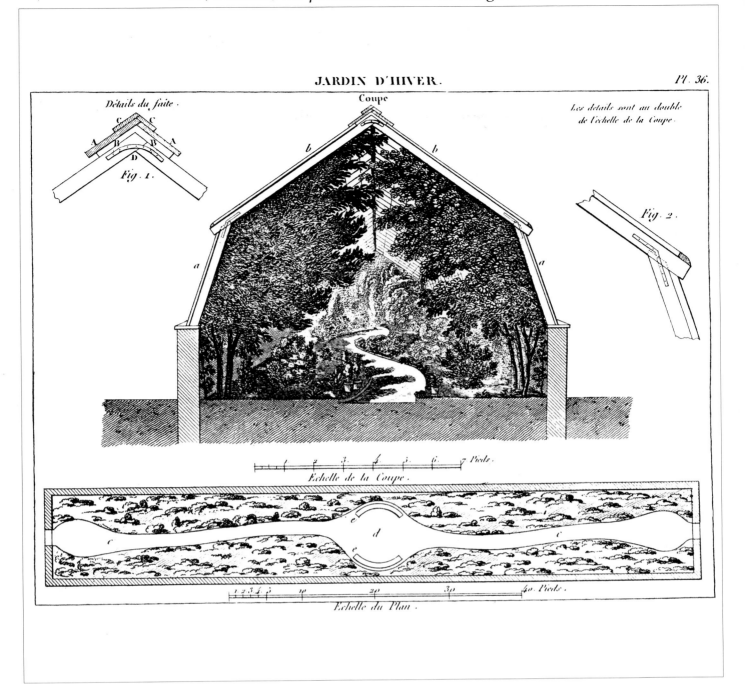

The naturalistic greenhouse, which was not necessarily tied to the role of a real *jardin d'hiver*, could also be a building of a size and cost within the means of everyone. This was proved by the drawing shown here from the sixth, and considerably enlarged, edition of 1859 (compared to the first one dated 1818) of *Traité de la composition et de l'ornement des jardins* written by Louis-Eustache Audot, which was a best-selling manual and late piece of propaganda in favor of the landscape garden.

If the naturalistic greenhouse was taken as a miniature that englobed a concentrated form of the whole plant world, anyone with the right sort of imagination could draw up a *Voyage au tour de mon jardin* similar to that of Alphonse Karr. This was of a poetical and geographical kind (rather than a naturalistic one) because it stimulated innumerable imaginary journeys through the most picturesque landscapes of the world. In the straight and narrow space of the little pavilion beseiged by trees, shrubs, and bushes (which are always overwhelmed by this particular form of cultivation), the short but carefully designed passage led from the two entrances to the tiny central circus furnished with curving seats that was a place for resting, meditating, or conversing. The symmetrical entrances were on a higher level than the middle sector. This gave the impression of standing between two hillocks from which the little winding pathway sloped gently down. Sunlight or moonlight penetrated the extensive glass roof and filtered down through the leaves. This rare nineteenth-century curiosity (and *folly* as well) that could be enjoyed by many given its modest cost, lay outside the European tradition of hothouses. These had always been designed for the conservation of exotic or Mediterranean species in a suitable artificial climate to satisfy the scientific curiosity of botanists and gardeners while also assuring the potentially everlasting cultivation of the plant world. In this scene the center of attention is not the plant to be carefully looked after; it is the stage where plants create the scenographic effects.

PLATE 159

Victorian England rose indignantly against the decision to organize the Great Exhibition of 1851 in Hyde Park, one of the most famous large open spaces in London, because it meant felling large trees to create the space for building the display halls. The architects were impotent before this inevitable catastrophe. The problem was solved by Joseph Paxton (1801-1861) an English gardener and engineer who proposed a non-architecture, a huge glass house, capable of conserving the trees while exhibiting the manufactures.

This 650-yard-long Crystal Palace was a monument inspired by the sensibility of the Victorians toward nature. Its gigantic glass vault not only made it possible to save the centuries-old trees, but also to nourish and cultivate them as if they were in a greenhouse. Paxton had had some experience in building large glass houses, but never as large as the Crystal Palace. He always experimented with new and ingenious technologies based on the utilization of iron and glass. The construction details of the Crystal Palace were studied so precisely that the whole building was prepared in a factory and then assembled in the park. It was the first example of prefabrication. This contemporary print reveals the elementary and essential construction techniques and the continuity of the walls and huge vaulted glass roof. The large trees in the foreground are the proof of the botanical effectiveness of this kind of construction, which was the pride of the nation for its bold productive techniques that confirmed Britain's position as the world's leading industrialized nation. Such a building as this would perhaps have been inconceivable with other materials and in other countries. The reason for national pride lay also in the respect (only to be found in England at that time) for the plant world cultivated in the parks that this particular technological ingeniousness had promoted. The Crystal Palace episode liberated glasshouses from every technical and dimensional fetter and established their constructional criteria: the metallic skeleton covered in glass was to become typical of all its European successors. The area inside could be big enough, as long as warm winter temperatures were maintained, to permit the cultivation of great exotic trees as if they were in their original habitat without any obstacles to their natural or environmental development.

PLATE 160

Among all the princes of the tiny nineteenth-century European states, King Ludwig II of Bavaria (1845-1886) was perhaps the one who delighted most in architecture. He experienced it as the necessary scene for a heroic life permanently immersed in a dream of the mythical and historical past. The first projects designed for his residence at Neuschwanstein were of a Neo-Gothic and sentimental kind. But his admiration for Richard Wagner and for the *Nibelungenleid* made him modify the original idea. In order to create an ambiance suited to a Wagnerian cast, the whole castle was decorated in a style resembling late antiquity.

His models for his other residences and their gardens were Versailles in its seventeenth-century guise for Herrenchiemsee, and the most sophisticated French Rococo style for Linderhof. A large *jardin d'hiver* was part of the king's dream for his Munich home, shown here in a photograph dated 1870. This became and remained a particularly important model for its passionately Romantic content, which was indispensable for a life full of emotions. Exotic trees, shrubs, and bushes were planted thickly around a luxuriant lawn that sloped down toward a pool where swans, Wagnerian symbols, sailed peacefully across the water. The panels without glass were painted realistically with dioramic landscapes. A little Moorish pavilion, a Turkish tent, and an Abyssinian hut of straw and matting were situated against these backdrops. Obviously, in such a *jardin d'hiver*, the consideration given plants was secondary if not inexistent. The great space was like a vast hall, unusually warm for the central European winter and decorated with bizarre floral motifs, some of which were permanent. It was suited to a restless lifestyle, as an escape from or contrast with everyday routine. But these gardens were not always built with this in mind. Sometimes space was dedicated to the requirements of botanical science, opting for a naturalistic arrangement that both gardeners and dilettantes could enjoy and contemplate. In this case the *jardin d'hiver* returned to its original role as a garden.

PLATE 161

Johann Wolfgang von Goethe drew these two curiosities as a sort of gigantic visual poem. The first, dated January 4, 1808, was an ironical project for creating the name Wilhelmine with a giant form of topiary applied to poplars along the drive to a villa. The second, in December of the same year, was a pseudo-project for a scenic aqueduct to be built in the mountains with a wooden structure that formed the name AMALIE.

The long word Wilhelmine was the poet's gallant and sentimental homage to Wilhelmine Herzlieb, his inspiration for Ottilia, who cultivated landscape gardening with all the passion of a novice while taking care of the elective affinities. The construction of AMALIE, which foreshadowed land art, was more ambiguous. It could have been an act of homage, but less gallant than the previous one, to the Grand Duchess Amalia, the mother of his friend, the young Duke of Weimar. But an esoteric communication could be hidden behind what is apparently an exoteric one: it could be a declaration of masonic faith, as the poet had recently become a member of a Weimarian masonic lodge called "Amalie." The correct historical context of these *follies* which here seem more like a kind of joke (and not really practicable projects) was the period between the end of the eighteenth and the beginning of the nineteenth century when the enormous quantity of publications on gardens, books of essays and treatises, pamphlets, loose printed sheets later published in volumes, had one central theme for all its readers, bizarreness. Ten years later, in 1817, Georg Wilhelm Friedrich Hegel began teaching aesthetics at the university of Heidelberg. He also discussed modern gardens and wrote that "a large park, instead, especially when it is garnished with Chinese temples, Turkish mosques, Swiss chalets, bridges, hermitages and who knows what other equally exotic things, needs to be and to mean something in itself. Nevertheless, this attraction, which is satisfied immediately, disappears quickly and one cannot look at such things twice."

Corpus der Goethezeichnungen, Band. IV a, Leipzig 1966.

PLATE 162

Like all great poets, Johann Wolfgang von Goethe (1749-1832) caught and expressed concisely, in a poetic form and not just from a purely literary point of view, a particular historical and cultural spirit. These two drawings of his dated 1787 reveal much better than the works of many famous and professional painters the romantic feelings of the time towards the landscape garden that imposed and expressed a new relationship between man and nature.

The young man under the tree transmits a series of unmistakable messages. First and foremost in Goethe's drawing the man and the tree, with its powerful trunk and tangled foliage, are conceptually two individuals on a par, and this is not just due to the realism of the presentation which is in fact only a simple sketch. The drawing seems to say that the two indiviuals have their own specific personalities. It is not a question of a man under a tree but *that* man under *that* tree. Moreover on a symbolic level it seems to announce the end of an epoch in which the garden was used chiefly as the setting for collective entertainment. Now is the time for the absorbing, perceptive activity of the individual contemplation of nature and the garden. Therefore, everyone was expected to become more of a gardener than a botanist, so as to practice that contemplation in a useful manner, in the same way that before being able to appreciate a poem written in a foreign language a person must absolutely be capable of *feeling* in that language. The morphology and syntax to which Goethe refers are expressed in the second drawing. This is in reality a didactic picture capable of illustrating even the grammatical moments of the theme, which is not simply nature here, but the garden (a villa in Frascati, perhaps the garden of Villa Aldobrandini). The lawn, the landscaping of the trees and shrubs, the rocks with the waterfall splashing into the pool, the bench and urns on pedestals: these are the constituent parts of every garden of the past, the present, and the future as well.

Corpus der Goethezeichnungen, Band. II, Leipzig 1960.

PLATE 163

The garden is the place of multiple methods of utilization by its owners. They can run it by themselves according to the English gardening tradition, or hand it over to competent and loving gardeners to contemplate the results of their efforts afterwards. The garden can be the stage for receptions and entertainment, or the place for solitary walks and various meditations. For those who can afford it, the garden is also the setting for family life.

Mario Praz has studied this aspect in a special kind of group portraiture, the *conversation pieces*, which were the secular and largely familiar reflection of the religious scenes of conversation to be found in all European painting. The conversation pieces were English in their origins and tended to register, especially in the eighteenth and nineteenth centuries, the whole essence of the relationships and feelings that formed a family unit. These were obviously portraits of the governing classes, and therefore the pictures always presented the symbols of the rank of the subjects, including the garden whose fundamental components offered an easy way of expressing that prestige. But apart from presenting its structural lexicon, the garden was always shown in its real scenic dimensions and portrayed as if it too was a person, a fundamental member of the family. This painting, ascribed either to Jean-François Garneray (1755-1837) or to Auguste Garneray (1785-1824) shows the Crown Prince of the Kingdom of the Two Sicilies, later Francesco I, and his family, overlooking the Gulf of Naples with Vesuvius as a backdrop on one side and a villa anchored to a rock covered with natural vegetation on the other. This essential and emblematic part of the garden represents the link between the inner part, which we can imagine, and the overall surrounding landscape. The median proscenium is an architectonic loggia in a classical style whose flat pergola is formed by a mass of grapevines. An agave to the left demonstrates the passion for exotic plants, and is treated as one of the main features of the scene. On the other side there is a bed of almost monochrome flowering plants. As a contrast, highly colorful flowers are being used to wreathe the elegant garlands that are wound around some of the family and around the decorative classical busts.

*Mario Praz, Scene di conversazione; Conversation Pieces, Italian and English co-edition, Rome, London, Philadelphia 1971.

PLATE 164

This family portrait of Theodor Joseph Ritter von Neuhaus, a diplomatic counselor, his wife, and children, was painted by Ferdinand Georg Waldmüller (1793-1865) in 1827 when the *Restaurazione* was safely consolidated. The elegance of the clothing of the four subjects is so affected that it gives the impression that this noble family is longing to be immortalized in its Sunday best. The garden, shown here in minute detail, does not need to be dressed up for the occasion; its daily appearance is sufficient.

A fundamental aspect of the picture is the relationship between the layout of the house and the garden. Placed on high ground, the garden spreads through the landscape to be seen behind the owner, with a large terrace for contemplating an *infinite* garden. This *belvedere* has stone paving and its balustrades and seats are embellished by architectonic ornaments enriched with Neoclassical bas-relifs that also serve as bases for free-standing sculptures. More sculptures can be observed in the architectonic structure on the balustrades of the terracing (behind the wife in this scene) which leads up to a little classical temple with a hemispherical cupola. A detail of this is enough to realize that the building is circular and that its entrance is a Corinthian *pronaos*. The garden is thus clearly announced as a costly work of culture where architecture, queen of the arts, is sovereign and is a symbol of the solid material and spiritual foundations of the family portrayed here. Just as the members of the family have been presented within a specific hierarchy, so the special and peculiar characteristics of the garden, and not just the architectonic ones, are treated in the same way. In the foreground there are flowers, picked by the little boy in the garden and offered in a straw hat to his mother. Behind them there is a large flowering shrub of a decorative scenic kind, then there is the irregular wild and complex shape of the great tree in front of other smaller ones forming a grove. This, together with our garden and its ornaments, is who we are, the diplomatic counselor seems to be saying.

PLATE 165

TABLEAU

DES GENRES, SECTIONS ET SORTES DE JARDINS.

Les Jardins se divisent en	Économiques ou Légumiers	Marais	De légumes rustiques.
			A couches, cloches ou chassis.
		Potagers	Privés ou ordinaires.
			Des grands jardins, avec serres à primeurs, bâches à ananas, orangerie.
	Fruitiers ou Vergers	Agrestes	En lignes.
			En quinconce.
		Soumis à la taille ..	En quenouilles.
			En vases ou buissons.
			En éventail et espaliers.
	Botanique	Médicinaux	Pharmaceutiques.
			D'étude.
		D'instruction.....	Ne contenant qu'une série de plantes.
			Générale.
			Pour la naturalisation.
	Plaisance ou d'Agrément	Symétriques	De ville.
			Public.
			De palais.
		De genre	Chinois.
			Anglais.
			Fantastiques.
		De la nature	Champêtres.
			Sylvestre.
			Pastoraux.
			Romantiques.
			Parcs ou carrières.

In 1820 Gabriel Thouin published, in his treatise on the garden, a concise *tableau* similar to those in eighteenth-century encyclopedias designed to reestablish knowledge and organize it entirely. In the same way that knowledge was expounded in the encyclopedias, Thouin intended to elaborate a classification capable of setting the universe in order while simultaneously revealing the interdependence of all its parts. At the same time this system would have formed a new kind of discipline for understanding the world.

The first theoretical works on the modern garden included typological identifications as well. Hirschfeld, for example, in his immense theoretical opus on the art of gardening, listed every possible and imaginable expression, in a literary way, chapter by chapter, not in the concise way shown here. More than a scientific arrangement of typological categories, Thouin's classification seems to be a declaration of war, because he claims that all the areas he discusses belong to the new aesthetics. There is nothing epistemological here. This is mere strategy designed for action. The list is what the author considers himself capable of carrying out at the time, in the continuity of the different components of the one same landscape culture. The designs for gardens published in his book are proof of this approach. This classification has pushed pleasant and agreeable gardens up the social ladder, because even though it was the last to arrive on the scene it has a large category to itself on a par with the other three scientific and botanical ones. For Hirschfeld the public urban garden could and had to be symmetrical (the German theoretician praised straight walks in public gardens) but all the rest had to be naturalistic. Thouin's classification includes, on the contrary, both specialistic gardens (including the English ones, together with Chinese and fantastic gardens, therefore considered as kinds of classical styles, while not being formal ones) and naturalistic ones. Curiously enough, Thouin safeguarded the possibility of having a symmetrical garden in a palace, which was something a real landscape gardener would never have accepted. This was not an early eclectic attitude, but rather the candid demonstration of a burning desire to do the new thing expressed by an old man who had worked for years in the formal gardens at Versailles, and nurtured rebellion in his old age.

PLATE 166

TABLEAU SYNOPTIQUE

DE LA CLASSIFICATION DES JARDINS

PARCS

privés
- paysagers.
- forestiers ou de chasse.
- agricoles.

publics
- de promenade et de jeux.
- des villes d'eaux.
- de lotissement des villes.
- funéraires (cimetières).

JARDINS

privés

d'agrément
- paysagers de 1 à 10 hectares.
- — de moins de 1 hectare.
- géométriques (parterres).
- urbains (cours, hôtels, terrasses).
- — au bord de la mer.
- couverts (serres, jardins d'hiver).

d'utilité
- fruitiers
  - vergers.
  - mixtes.
- potagers
  - maraîchers.
  - bourgeois.
- mixtes (potagers–fruitiers).

publics

d'agrément
- oasis (*squares*).
- places.
- promenades et voies plantées.
- de chemins de fer.

d'utilité
- botaniques.
- zoologiques.
- d'acclimatation.
- d'institutions, jardins–écoles, etc.
- d'hôpitaux, fondations, etc.
- gymnases.
- d'Expositions.

- anciens (à restaurer).
- des régions chaudes.

Another concise *tableau* for the scientific classification of all possible gardens was published in a different, now completely positivistic spirit by Edouard André in his treatise dated 1879. The desire to systematize everything was expressed in a historical period during which the identity of the very object to be classified, the garden, was neither certain nor incontrovertible. Cultural and artistic eclecticists and historicists thought instead that with the help of positivism all this was possible.

This classification of little more than a century ago is completely alien to readers today. Probably no modern landscape architect would ever use one of those terms that then seemed typologically indispensable. André's treatise, on the other hand, does not seem so distant. It contains structurally reasoned historical references, careful detail and love of the subject, thorough analyses and a description of every problem, diagnoses and consequent therapies, theoretical elements and technical discussions. It is still possible and worthwhile to find extremely interesting material in it, even without sharing the ideology of the garden that is implicit in it. This *tableau* was derived from the old English late Renaissance model, especially the orchard-cum-garden one characterized by the combination of pleasure and profit. The category of private, useful gardens was unquestionably a novelty for agrarian France and its small and medium estates at the end of the nineteenth century. During this period the publications of farmers' and good gardeners' almanacs blossomed as never before in France. The other typological classifications referring to modern taste were the traditional ones already seen in every treatise on the art of designing gardens. Here again, in relation to an increasingly widespread practice, the need to restore historical gardens is mentioned. This subject was intended as a special independent category, to be distinguished from the large fundamental types, and kept outside them, together with the unusual class of gardens from hot regions.

PLATE 167

LXIII. 1.

Pópulus monilifera.
The necklace-bearing, *Canadian,*
Black Italian, Poplar.

Full grown tree at Syon, 102 ft. high : diam. of the trunk, 4½ ft., and of the head, 96 ft.
[Scale 1 in. to 12 ft.]

John Claudius Loudon was a fundamental historical figure in the development of the idea of the European garden at the beginning of the nineteenth century. He made prolific contributions to cultural debates, to experimental activity, research, and the spreading of information, as well as facing the questions regarding the culture of a modern and knowledgeable gardener. The theme presented with this illustration is the relationship between botanical science and the art of gardening.

Loudon was endowed with great maieutic powers and an extraordinary capacity to communicate. He was a real innovator of the culture of the time. This is evident in his books and periodicals: he was the author of more than forty books and four magazines from 1803 to his death in 1843, without counting all the articles he wrote for other reviews and his unpublished works. In 1838 he published an enormous eight-volume book in London entitled *Arboretum et Fruticetum Britannicum; or, the Trees and Shrubs of Britain, Native and Foreign, Hardy and Half-Hardy, Pictorially and Botanically Delineated, and Scientifically and Popularly Described; with their Propagation, Culture, Management, and Uses in the Arts, in Useful and Ornamental Plantations, and in Landscape Gardening; preceded by a Historical and Geographical Outline of the Trees and Shrubs in Temperate Climates throughout the World.* This picture of the *Populus monilifera* comes from volume VII. As the title of the book announces, the relationship between botany and landscape gardening is complex and rejects hierarchies of dependence as the already centuries-old experience of Kew gardens had established. While being a scientific book which drew on and contributed to botanical science, its aims were not scientific in the traditional sense of the term. It was intended as an instrument for gardeners, to make them more knowledgeable about their work. The very wide range of possibilities it offered could be utilized to choose according to practical and aesthetic needs and with the aid of the most suitable technical information. This was one of the first encyclopedias of the enormous arboreal patrimony (which was quite amazing in comparison to the eighteenth-century *tableaux*), which had grown in England mainly for aesthetic and not for productive reasons, but which was now within everyone's reach in terms of knowledge and scientific study.

*Jacques Brosse, *Mythologie des arbres*, Paris 1989.

PLATE 168

Anton Kerner von Marilaun (1831-1896) was an Austrian botanist and professor at Innsbruck from 1860 and at Vienna from 1878 where he also became director of the botanical garden. He was famous all over Europe and the world for his treatise, *Das Pflanzenleben,* on the natural history of plants, published in two volumes in Vienna between 1887 and 1891. It was printed in many languages and became a frame of reference for everyone. It was a kind of state of the art of contemporary botanical science.

The popularity of scientific treatises and not the vulgarized versions of the same was linked in the age of positivism to the new significance of science, which was capable, optimistically, of meeting every requirement, of solving every problem. Kerner von Marilaun's authority on and general interest in the subject were the reasons for the success of his theories and the results of his research. In a botanical treatise of this type there were pictures like this one which offered readers the image of an oak tree without isolating it from its environment. In Loudon's eight volumes dedicated to gardeners, the trees were components of the landscape design and characterized the man-made environment and scenery. The presentation of a tree in its natural environment expresses first and foremost epistemological significance because it raises the ecological question, that is to say, the need to study the plant world by analyzing the natural context where it is to be found. George Perkins Marsh (1801-1882) was an American forerunner of such studies. He published his book, *Man and Nature; or Physical Geography as Modified by Human Action,* in New York in 1864, part of which had been written in Italy, in Turin. Perkins Marsh had in fact been ambassador of the United States to the newly founded Kingdom of Italy in 1860. The book was soon published in London and Florence and created a stir in international scientific circles. From the new world of ecology, other stimuli were to arise to disturb the minds of botanists, gardeners, the European garden, and the world. But anthropological and cultural conditions were reaching maturity for the creation of vast natural parks.

PLATE 169

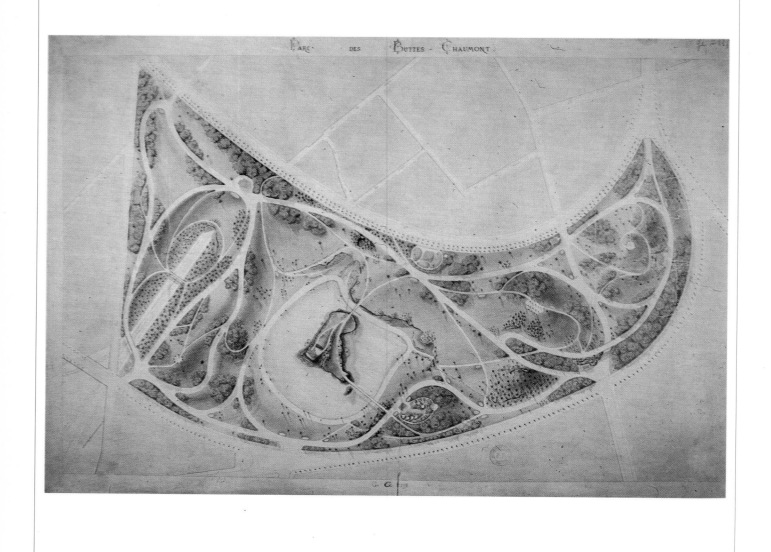

Pierre Barillett-Deschamps designed the park of Buttes-Chaumont at the time of the modernization of the city of Paris during the reign of Napoleon III. It was built on an area of sixty-two acres between 1864 and 1867, under the direction of Jean-Charles-Adolphe Alphand, who coordinated all the works of building the great parks and the tree-lined boulevards. The size and quality of this park make it a model of the public garden of the time. Formal and aesthetic commitment generated a new space for contemplation.

This public garden was the collective garden of the bourgeoisie in power. It was utilized by this class in the same way as the private gardens of the aristocracy were used in the past by their owners and guests. The interdependence of the formal models of the public and private *elegant French garden* can be seen in the homogeneity of the two pictures on these pages. The new public garden inserted in the relatively central parts of European cities was designed for embellishing the city, for walks, for the fun and games of children, and for the sentimental contemplation of the plant scenery, which created new and fascinating urban landscapes. The public garden was soon to become a symbol of prestige in town planning. When European cities became industrial, with new qualities and quantities, there was no parallel multiplication of public gardens to satisfy the

needs of new citizens. The landscape design of a public garden was composed of the elegance of the layout, where the pattern of curving walks was planned to offer vistas of carefully constructed picturesque scenes. The plant material was the main feature of these views. It was more complex than that in eighteenth-century parks and gardens thanks also to the ever-growing presence of exotic plants. The garden designer was aware of the fact that he was working with *biodegradable* material. The garden was created by the will of man. It grew and died like any living structure. The project was therefore the matrix upon which nature was to develop over time (for decades and centuries), to be contemplated as it matured. Following in the footsteps of private parks, the conclusion of the project would be observed only by future generations.

PLATE 170

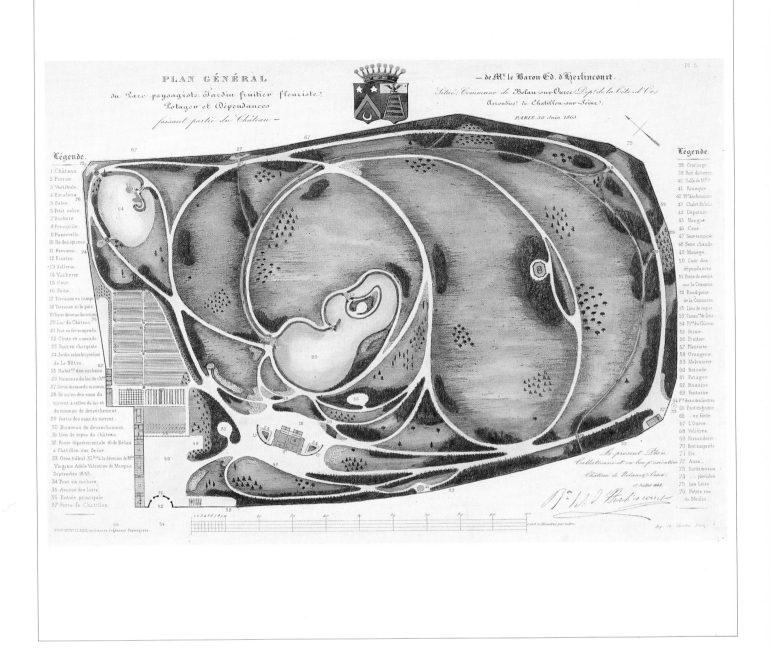

The new curved line, the elegant nineteenth-century French serpentine, no longer had the task of spreading the aesthetics of asymmetry like its eighteenth-century predecessor. The sinuous line slicing the ground into infinite large curves offered innumerable plant scenes to visitors along the complex centripetal walk. In 1871 François Duvillers collected his projects for the private gardens of princes and noblemen in his book, *Les parcs et jardins*, to show that the success of this taste in the Second Empire applied to public gardens as well.

The basic design is clear: the first walk borders on the external limits of the garden (the greatest perspective of the whole is to be seen from any point along this path). The others branch away from the first forming wide gentle curves in a potentially infinite sheaf, avoiding the inevitable repetition of views along a straight axis. The morphology of these innumerable views, expressed as a series of landscape paintings to be appreciated along the walk, is still quite straightforward, and based on the principles of landscape gardening. Each walk is flanked by groups of tall trees. The parterre in front of these is simply a vast, mown lawn. But the overall morphology and its components were to be upset by the spreading of the picturesque style to public gardens as well. The main features of this garden were flowers and *rocailles* capable of recreating artificially the most striking (picturesque) scenery offered by nature in its most hidden corners. From the French formal garden, to the landscaped, to the picturesque, the alternation of taste marked the use of private and later of public gardens. Behind all this there was a modification in the idea of nature, which was now viewed as separate from the world of agriculture, and in the relationship between man and nature, expressed in the necessity to feed the spirit and to contemplate the botanic composition through its specific seasonal development, linked to blossoming flowers and to its reaching maturity. These were parks designed like manufactures: now the life in them had to be carefully observed.

*François Duvillers, Les parcs et jardins, Paris 1871.

PLATE 171

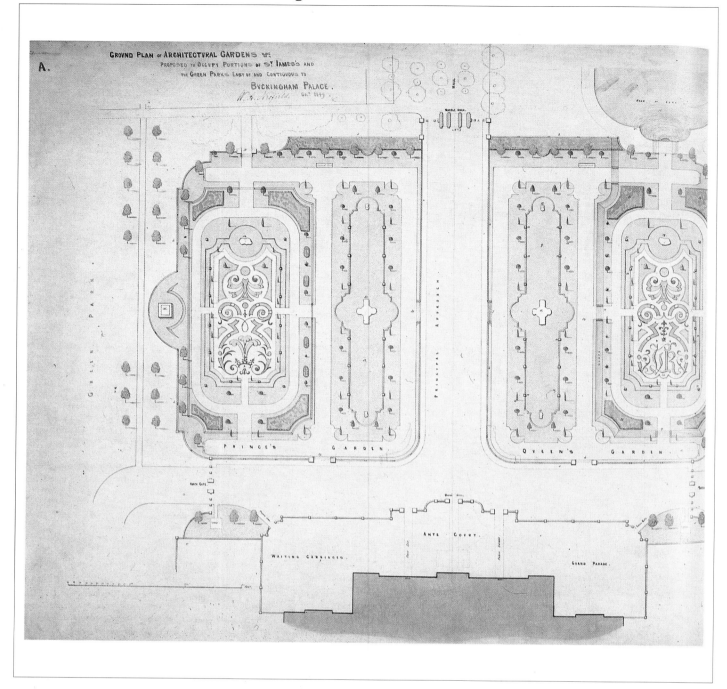

Historicism, which was extended culturally and operatively all over Europe in the second half of the nineteenth century, looked to the past with an archaeological and philological spirit that lacked the delicacy of the eighteenth-century and early nineteenth-century revivals. Reproductions could be taken from the infinite book of the history of man, each according to his own taste, as long as they were managed with responsibility. Why not gardens then? This was one way of justifying the exaggerations consequent upon the aesthetics of picturesque gardens.

The return to formality in the nineteenth-century garden had been conceptually anticipated by the work and theory of John Claudius Loudon, whose complex elaborations included the concept of *gardenesque*. But Loudon did not propose models for the calligraphic reconstruction of the past. This project, however, by William Andrews Nesfield (1793-1881) prepared in 1849 to complete the gardens of Buckingham Palace, was an eloquent example of historicist and calligraphic eclecticism applied to the design of a garden. Here the stylistic project was presented in the same manner, and repeated obsessively, like in Dézallier d'Argenville's eighteenth-century publications, which had certainly been long forgotten in England. The whole project, in its composite parts and in all its details, including the type of communication utilized (a plan with the trees drawn frontally), seems to be borrowed directly from the old prints. The design gives the impression of going back into a past where flowers had been

eliminated from the garden, when they had recently become an important feature. Their chromatic specialties were replaced by fine gravel carefully laid out in virtual beds which only had to satisfy fleeting glances and certainly not the requirements of plant life, which was no longer a subject of contemplation. It was also a disturbing semantic element for such a project in the late Victorian age. Loudon's *gardenesque* style (he had dedicated a whole book to suburban gardens) implied the possibility that anyone could garden, whatever the size of his property, overriding the old principle that gardens should merge with the surrounding landscape within an estate that embraced them both. Naturally all *little* gardens were banished from the new examples of the return to formal gardens.

*Frank J. Scott, *Victorian Gardens. The Art of Beautifying Suburban Home Grounds*, New York 1870; A.A. Tait, "Loudon and the Return to Formality", in *John Claudius Loudon and the Early Nineteenth Century in Great Britain*, Dumbarton Oaks Colloquium on the History of Landscape Architecture, Washington 1980; Brent Elliot, *Victorian Gardens*, London 1986; Jane Brown, *The Art and Architecture of English Gardens*, London 1989.

PLATE 172

Between the end of the ninteenth century and the first few decades of the twentieth century, Henri Duchêne and his son Achille worked systematically on the historical analysis of European and non-European gardens. They aimed to promote the restoration of historical gardens and, in line with their historicist culture, the design and construction of stylistic gardens corresponding to a concept of restoration that was so elastic as to include the reproduction of the formal sense of moments of the past.

Achille Duchêne became very famous in a Europe that turned to all kinds of histories to find nourishment and backing, and from France he ran projects in nearly every nation in Europe, including Great Britain. The water parterre at Blenheim Palace is an example of one of his works laid out at the start of this century. In the case in question, it is clear that this is neither the total nor the partial restoration of an existing monument, but enters into the realm of designing in the taste of a past epoch which is not even definable as a stylistic reconstruction. All this was possible because the contemporary cultural climate decreed that, more important than any philological and archaeological dimension, garden designers should be capable of mastering the *Zeitgeist*, which could thus be reproduced creatively, in any form whatever, and in a more faithful way than a project based on historical documents. From the historical point of view, even these curious gardens are a part of the history of the idea of the European garden, although the origins of their theory seem a long way off. But Jellicoe's recent exhibitive and educative projects for the Moody Gardens museum or the elegant return to the English eighteenth century in Quinlan Terry's contemporary gardens could raise doubts as to their irrevelance. Whatever the case, Duchêne's work as well as present-day activity have brought the question of restoration of historical gardens right back to the fore. Since the plant structures of these gardens are biological products and therefore biodegradable, conceptual and practical research is necessary both into the notion of restoration and into that of conservation.

PLATE 173

This watercolored lithograph showing a scene in St. James's Park, London, one of the most famous public parks, comes from the second and final edition (dated 1887) of Tour's reference book for adults, *Histoire des jardins anciens et modernes*, written by Arthur Mangin. The first smaller edition had come out in 1867 and was followed by another incomplete version in 1874. As proof of the interest in the subject, the book was reprinted in 1888.

Public gardens and parks in nineteenth-century Europe were one of the places designated for celebrating the power of the middle classes. The fact that not all the bourgeoisie had their own gardens, let alone a park, led to the idea of a public garden for the governing class in the same way that parks had been created in the eighteenth century for the aristocracy and upper classes in the more advanced cities on the Continent. Nowadays a city that does not have even a modest public garden (or a small natural science museum, a library, or art gallery) does not satisfy the expectations of decorous town planning of the day. What role did a public garden of this kind play? The abundant contemporary material on the subject illustrates this minutely. It was a place for husbands, wives, and children to walk in, like a private garden, on the weekend and to meet and enjoy the company of other families. Or it was the playground of a middle-class child and his nanny, who often indulged in sweet nothings with the odd soldier on leave. But there were also those who used the park in the traditional way, as a walk marked by vistas and alternate moments of meditation. This picture instead gives the impression that a bourgeois and nineteenth-century park was most of all a setting for courtship. The two figures sitting informally on the lawn are highly significant because they make it seem as if the whole park was intended for this specific use. Very soon, however, the park was to be opened to all, not just to the members of the governing classes, and not just for this purpose.

PLATE 174

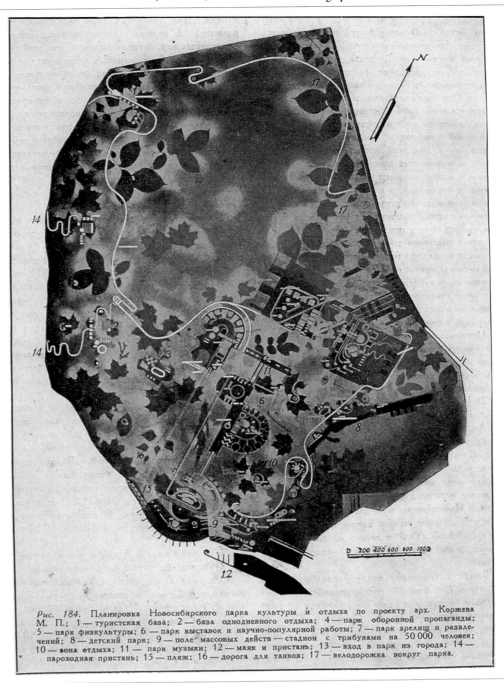

Рис. 184. Планировка Новосибирского парка культуры и отдыха по проекту арх. Коржева М. П.; 1 — туристская база; 2 — база однодневного отдыха; 4 — парк оборонной пропаганды; 5 — парк физкультуры; 6 — парк выставок и научно-популярной работы; 7 — парк зрелищ и развлечений; 8 — детский парк; 9 — поле массовых действ — стадион с трибунами на 50 000 человек; 10 — зона отдыха; 11 — парк музыки; 12 — маяк и пристань; 13 — вход в парк из города; 14 — пароходная пристань; 15 — пляж; 16 — дорога для танков; 17 — велодорожка вокруг парка.

It is enough to leaf through two photograph albums of Central Park, New York, one showing it at the end of the last century and the other at the beginning of this one, to note the *sociological revolution* that has taken place in the manner of using it. The urban public park in the time of the middle class's power turned firstly into the park for everyone and then acquired, in our time, all the characteristics of a place of *normal violence*, like any other area inside the great metropolises.

The epistemological debate on the meaning of an urban garden or park started in a programmatic way after the First World War thanks to the development of city planning and to the assessments concerning urbanistic standards. The public garden was regarded as a *social* goal that a city and a society had to consider so as to guarantee every citizen a sufficient quantity of public areas and services and not just spaces for housing, work, and study. Exclusions of a social kind were removed, at least conceptually. The ugly phrase *organized green space* came into being. It is obvious that every public service can be surrounded by greenery: this is both right and useful for the urban landscape. If, however, this phrase means that parks and gardens must be stuffed with equipment, then it is quite unacceptable. Because a park *is a park, is a park, is a park...* Certainly Gorki Park in Moscow or Central Park in New York are furnished with large numbers of various kinds of equipment available to the public, but their size is such as to guarantee the autonomy of the extensive internal part. The *socialist park* is in a certain sense the virtual model of public gardens for all progressive city planning. The park shown here, designed by V.P. Koriev, the architect, for the city of Novosibirsk at the beginning of the 1830s, is a clear example of this school. The key of this extraordinary constructivist and symbolic design is the following: 1) touristic base; 2) resting place for one day; 4) park for the propaganda of *defense*; 5) park for gymnastics; 6) park for scientific popular exhibitions and work; 7) park of theaters and entertainment; 8) children's park; 9) field for mass demonstrations; 10) resting area; 11) music park; 12) lighthouse and pier; 13) park entrance from the city; 14) quay for steamboats; 15) beach; 16) road for heavy and military vehicles; 17) bicycle track. But separated in a sense from and besides all the above complex functions, which are concentrated in one well-defined space, there is a vast park, which is wisely only a park, *a park, a park, a park...*

PLATE 175

Among the picture cards first published by the Liebig company during the last few decades of the nineteenth century for the education and amusement of the children of that positivistic bourgeoisie that could buy its products, six came out in 1906 on the history of gardens. In order to be a success, such a project had to be backed, from the didactic and cultural points of view, by a knowledge of the time. The contents of the picture cards therefore had their origins in current ideas.

The six pictures reconstruct from a precise cultural angle the development of the idea of the European garden. Those who studied gardens and garden history at the beginning of the twentieth century believed, implicitly, that this summary by Liebig was correct and useful for teaching. The division and concentration of a long history into six cards was a kind of abridgement that expounded contemporary ideas clearly. For example, the following observation was written on the back of the card on English gardens: "The affected style that had dominated French gardens provoked a reaction in England that led toward a return to nature." The garden evolved in an almost Darwinistic way with the self-assurance of the validity of the eclectic approach in both its historical and stylistic dimensions, and its sociological ones. After the English garden, shown romantically without any human presence, the series ended with an urban public garden which was useful and delightful for the very same children who collected the cards, the sons and daughters of the middle classes who are easily identifiable in the picture. The text on the back of this card is as follows: "While large gardens were once, so to speak, the exclusive privilege of a few people, today they are open to the public in big cities which compete with one another to create the most beautiful ones. Without adhering exclusively to any one Classical style, they take from them that which is most suited under the circumstances. Therefore by tastefully alternating various elements, such as fountains surrounded by flower beds, with myrtle or yew hedges, tall trees and thick groves forming elegant pavilions with magnificent sculptures, it is possible to produce very pleasant results in small spaces as well."

Formal, informal and dwarf hedges

Ever since the Renaissance, gardens in England were not just for contemplation. Everybody wanted to have one, no matter how small it was, and to take loving care of it. The ever-growing activity of gardening, which had even been adopted as an emblem of the national spirit, led to the decline of intellectual curiosity about theories concerning the art of garden design and a new pragmatic interest in the technical aspects essential for the daily creativity of all.

From the turn of the century onwards all British publications on gardens moved in this direction, starting from the popular columns published in newspapers and magazines. They proposed and promoted the practical application of knowledge derived from a refined material culture that made anyone who practiced it, on any level, a real and thorough gardener. An analysis of the media which for over a century has tried to establish contacts with the potential users of their message, always by means of famous authors, strongly confirms the validity of this thesis, which is even more well-founded with reference to the British. It is almost as if this demonstrates that a nation that is not privileged from the climatic point of view and that does not have a very large indigenous plant patrimony can make up for these deficiencies by itself. The picture, coming from a recent, highly successful manual (*The Small Garden*, London 1977) by John Brookes (b. 1930), a famous and highly qualified gardener, landscape designer, and teacher in important schools including Kew Gardens, proves this unequivocally. Hedging is one of the most coherent solutions of landscape design for enclosing an area (and today it is also considered an indispensable and irreplaceable habitat for avifauna and microfauna). Modern teaching methods reject the imposition of preconceived types such as those presented in eighteenth-century and early nineteenth-century publications. Today a subject must be explained and the correct use illustrated so as to form a responsible and knowledgeable gardener. Freedom of choice can then be grafted onto the branch of technical knowledge. *Hortus; a Gardening Journal*, founded in 1987 and edited by David Wheeler, has become the ideal medium of what is now a mass culture, and for essays of a more, and less, specialized nature.

PLATE 177

Claude Monet (1840-1926), the great master of Impressionist painting who brought it to a turning point, in programmatic terms as well, with his paintings of the shores of Normandy executed *en plein air* between 1867 and 1869, was also a gardener. In the second half of the nineteenth century Impressionism proposed a new relationship with nature and with the old dream of man's imitating it through art. From then onwards paintings of nature were done on the spot and no longer in the artists' studios.

Claude Monet's garden at Giverny, which was lovingly cared for by the artist from 1890 when he bought the property to the time of his death, is still alive today thanks to Claire Joyes and Jean-Marie Toulouat, who ensure the biological and scenic continuity of the original plant microcosm. "Perhaps flowers were the reason why I became a painter," Monet declared in 1924, and he certainly loved walking 'round his garden at all times of the day and in all seasons. Numerous discussions with the most famous French gardeners and botanists of the time contributed to the formation of the garden. In fact, the extraordinary garden at Giverny was possible due to a series of historical and cultural circumstances obviously linked to the artist and his specific *Kunstwollen*, and, in particular, to Impressionism or this painting *en plein air*, which intended to catch the mutability of nature and the even more complex mobility of light. Monet molded his garden every day as if it was a model whose body and soul he had to grasp in a special moment. The requirements of the artist made this garden a pictorial garden, one that was designed to be painted. Monet was a gardener, but he was also a painter. How, in the search for particular relationships and contrasts, could he separate the botanical elegance and tastefulness applied to the formation of the garden landscape (common plants mixed with very rare ones) from the pictorial requirements (with the typically Impressionist emphasis on the choice of the morphology of the plants and their chromatic qualities, where color was never an independent feature but related to those around it)? But all this also concerned a new fashion that Monet diligently followed: the vast layout of Giverny included a Japanese garden.

*Claire Joyes and Andrew Forge, Monet at Giverny, London 1975.

PLATE 178

This vase of irises painted by Vincent Van Gogh (1853-1890) in the final year of his life is an exhaustive example of Japanism, the last exoticism devoured passionately by the European world at the end of the ninteenth century. This terminal foreignism, which developed after the secluded Japanese civilization opened its doors to trade with the United States (1854) and Russia (1858), chose the Japanese iris as a symbol, bringing about, as a consequence, a revival of the old European *iris germanica*.

Japanism exploded in the second half of the century. One of the first paintings that included Japanese symbols is Edouard Manet's portrait of Emile Zola, dated 1868. Then Van Gogh (who reproduced in an expressive way entire systems of Japanese prints in his paintings) and many others followed, including Monet. The Japanese and German irises became the emblems of the ancient Orient and modern Europe, and Art Nouveau discovered the aesthetic point of reference of its qualifying symbol, the curved line, in the sinuosity of these flowers. The fashion of Japanism introduced the idea-image of some unknown or little-known plants, including bamboo. At the end of the eighteenth and at the beginning of the nineteenth century, a few botanists on rare visits to Japan had brought back rich scientific documentation. But Japanism was another thing; and its influence on Western gardens, while not being very apparent, was certainly not secondary. In London in 1893, for example, Josiah Conder published his book, *Landscape Gardening in Japan,* with dozens of illustrations. The treatise was of a positivistic and scientific nature, capable of analyzing that exoticism from a structural point of view. The history, the morphological elements, and the single components of the Japanese garden were presented exhaustively in all their interdependencies as well. It was no longer a question of approximate copies of distant forms transplanted into European gardens, as had been the case with the eighteenth-century fashion of chinoiserie. Now specific moments of that spirit had to be mastered in order to understand what it meant and to apply it in the original way. This was then expressed in the increasingly refined practice of using materials, and even tiny and simple ones such as gravel, bamboos and wood, to form banks and fences.

PLATE 179

During the Art Nouveau period, in the climate of the general renewal of the fine arts, the garden was not the subject of special research and experiments. The German *Jugendstil* and especially the Viennese *Sezession* with their more geometrical and Cartesian origins compared to those of Art Nouveau, introduced formal variations and expressed new sensibilities in the garden.

Franz Lebitsch, the Viennese architect, published these projects for new gardens in *Der Arkitekt* magazine in 1909. They reflected the sensibility more than the form of the poetics of the *Sezession*. Interest was centered on the possibility of creating small gardens due to the fact that when the new industrial cities grew and wealth was redistributed, the *petite bourgeoisie* and the lower classes wanted to have a garden too. Similar themes and problems had been observed, studied and elaborated by John Claudius Loudon in another cultural context. In the same issue of the Austrian magazine, Joseph August Lux, who examined the question of creating tiny gardens, wrote that "the art of garden design is the most evident and successful negation of nature as it is naturally. The naturalistic garden that imitates nature within a reduced enclosure can have a style only when it becomes a miniature, like a Japanese garden with dwarf trees. Art tends to create an antithesis of nature in the garden: it uses

plants according to architectonic principles, it fortifies the expression of human illusion." While there was a risk in these kinds of theses of a formalistic return to the mathematical vegetation as set forth by *ars topiaria*, in reality only a few sporadic cases occurred. On this subject, Lux went on to say that "art transforms trees and shrubs into spheres and cubes which in this way become architectonic elements; it creates walls and niches from live plants and it fills them with the laughter of fauns, the strength of heroes and the melody of fountains." The drawings of these four projects show, instead, that a garden designer endowed with sensibility will never automatically become a slave to dubious theories. Plants are not imprisoned here. The geometrical pattern of their containers tends, on the contrary, by means of a tasteful and elegant layout, to enhance the species and their colors even though the dimensions are those of a little garden.

PLATE 180

MASIERI MEMORIAL · CANAL GRANDE · VENICE
STUDENTS' LIBRARY AND DWELLING
FRANK LLOYD WRIGHT ARCHITE

Frank Lloyd Wright (1869-1959) found fame with his prairie houses whose real architectonic main feature was the landscape that embraced them, the North American grasslands. This aesthetic choice was typical of his concept of the relationship between architecture and nature. Later on the system of hanging flowering plants was to become a botanical connotation with specific semantic significance in all his works.

This picture illustrates a European project dated 1953 for the seat of the Masieri Memorial on the Grand Canal in Venice which was not built because of the foolish hostility of the Venetians. This project, too, includes multicolor plant elements that emerge and descend from the balconies, the enclosures, and the roof. These are cultivated plants, but at the same time they outline a setting of the future where spontaneous plants proliferate on a building. This is not a stale copy of the *Aesthetics of Ruins* which implies, in particular, a specific presence of plant life, because ruins were alien to the ideas of the great maestro who proposed the incessant transformation of the world through architectonic activity as well, and certainly not its decadence. Wright's project aimed at disturbing the solid static character of the building with the continual biological metamorphosis of the plant world. Wright never used flowers to decorate architecture nor, obviously, as a form of mitigation or camouflage. They were, instead, a decisive factor in the relationship between culture and nature, and important enough to guide and stimulate him in the search for and definition of an *organic* architecture serving the mutable requirements of life, whose forms and functions were not established in preconceptional terms. Greenery in Wright's architecture was certainly a metaphor, but it was also a solid vital presence capable of enlivening the stone. This is not therefore the same kind of integration of the plant world and architecture as that of the Classical and Neoclassic buildings and hanging gardens in the past. It is rather a means of democratically giving even weeds and the most humble of flowers the possibility of creating life in architecture and in its interstices, designed here exactly for this end.

PLATE 181

The great maestro of the Modern Movement, Charles-Edouard Jeanneret, the Swiss architect known as Le Corbusier (1887-1965), applied apodictically and rigorously functionalist and rationalistic principles to contemporary architecture. But he had a curious and ambiguous relationship with plants in urban contexts. His ideas established the instrumental utilization of greenery regardless of the specific characteristics of the case in question. The plant element was used as an integrative frame around architectonic or urbanistic scenes lacking in sensibility because they were always conceived as *machines*.

The absoluteness of his town planning projects for new cities in the 1920s made them so repulsive for the majority of their possible consumers that Le Corbusier soon began to frame them with the wavering foliage of trees. When he designed the mathematical system of Chandigarh, the capital of the new Punjab, in the 1950s, he distributed the green space mathematically thoughout the urban network as contemporary cultural standards required. This picture shows another of his variations on the plant theme. The place is Paris in the thirties; the scene is surrealistic, when referred to the context; and the idea behind it is that of creating hanging gardens on the roofs of buildings, a praiseworthy and always practicable program. The way of forming these hanging gardens, however, amazed and horrified every gardener. The aim was to force the plants into a state of non-growth, as any expansion would have upset the composition considered formally perfect.

The only plant elements, prisoners of the elemental forms of antinatural Euclidean geometry, are simple lawns, a few flowers and gross and unjustifiable revivals of late forms of topiary. While being included in the composition of the scenes of the terrace, the botanical arrangements for Le Corbusier were *"des aménagements techniques extrèmement délicats."* In India, Le Corbusier and an experimental botanist verified the possibility of constructing a huge pool on the roof of a building which was to be used to grow hydroponic monstrosities thanks to special concentrated fertilizers. During the 1930s, other architects influenced by the art deco style worked in the garden design field with geometrical rigor, yet on the basis of a different, understanding, responsive, and tolerant relationship with nature.

*Le Corbusier and Pierre Jeanneret, *Oeuvre complète 1929-1934*, Zurich 1964; Dominique Deshoulières, *Robert Mallet-Stevens*, Bruxelles 1980; Various authors, *Rob Mallet-Stevens*, Paris 1986; Elisabeth Vitou, *Gabriel Guévrékian*, Paris 1987.

PLATE 182

The subject of *land art* is the landscape and its artistic transformation by means of *eloquent signs* (in terms of size as well) inserted in the territory to be modified temporarily or permanently. The German art review *Kunstforum* published a monograph on the subject in number 42 dated February 1982. It was entitled *"Natur-Kunst"* and included these works created in Berlin and Bremen by a young artist called Gary Rieveschl.

The traditional expression of land art is the marking of a landscape with a powerful figure. The stable form could be a long trench, a circular hollow, or an infinite wall; the temporary one, a large colored spot on a rocky range or the wrapping not just of public buildings in cities but of portions of landscapes with sheeting, as Christo Javacheff proposes systematically. Rieveschl instead conceives projects that have roots in the past. His program is the re-proposal of what was done in cities on the Continent at the turn of the last century, when bedding plants due to blossom were taken from municipal nurseries and planted decoratively in flower beds which became one continual flower show thanks to the systematic seasonal organization of rhythmic and repetitive patterns. Flowers used as simple decoration and always in a repetitive manner have had very little significance and space in the history of the idea of European gardens. On the contrary, their return, after being excluded from French formal gardens and English landscape ones, coincided with a renewed respect for individual character and for freedom of biological growth. The use of plant material for calligraphy on the landscape on a large anomalous scale is felt today to be an unacceptable eccentricity, an abuse of nature by preconceived figuration, which seemed impossible at the beginning of the eighties. But the gratuitousness of these experiments by the artistic avant-garde weds with the possibility of a vast consumption of the Kitsch category that is implicit in it.

PLATE 183

In 1964 Leo Castelli presented "Flowers," a new work by Andy Warhol, in his gallery in New York. It soon became the subject of serial, multicolor, and multidimensional reproductions (from a miniature to a gigantic scale measuring 81" x 160"). "Flowers" is based on an image that maintains its matrix but is repeated conceptually and varied interminably in quality and quantity, because that was the great high priest of Pop Art's global project: the semantic pollution of the world by means of the multiplication of a figure.

The huge enlargement and the aggressive chromatic variations similar to the works of the Fauves transform the original sense of a modest European photograph. Andy Warhol took as a base the photo winning the second prize in a competition called "Photograph Your Garden" run by a French women's magazine. This picture by the American artist has a European origin therefore rooted in the banality of daily life that declares that the love of anyone for his or her garden (whatever it is and whatever are the species grown in it) is almost an updating of man's primordial love of flowers, of the sentiment that contains the gene of the impulse to form a garden. Andy Warhol treated this sentiment of simple souls ironically by working on the chosen flower material. He isolated four flowers in the grass, enlarged them, and threw them in the faces of observers in an extraordinarily effective poetic form. By means of the specific techniques of Pop Art, like the magic transformation of lead into gold, the flower plasters the walls of art galleries and homes, and fills the pages and covers of books and magazines obsessively, with the intrinsic capacity that a pop work has of being semantically self-perpetuating. This is how a simple floral portrait becomes a *form of communication* that, apart from the image itself, also includes everything else related to the social heritage, which means even the imaginary contents of every real and symbolic garden.

PLATE 184

The Scottish poet Hamilton Finlay is considered a *concrete poet* for his capacity to materialize his poetry but, in his own way, he is also an exponent of moving *visual poetry*. For example, he had his poem "Canal Stripe Series 4" written by a mass of British soldiers in the Nuremberg stadium as if they were living words that moved. These illustrations are significant fragments of the scene in his garden, Stonypath.

"See POUSSIN, Hear LORRAIN" is one of his typical forms of visual poetry, in this case referring to the two painters who generated with their works that new sensibility toward the plant world which was the origin, in England, of the garden in the early decades of the eighteenth century. Finlay wrote: "In my opinion the garden is a sacred place (the Romans had an idyllic-sacred concept of it) and the garden is influenced by ethics; and ethics (as Robespierre understood it) had to be founded on that which transcends the profane." The method used by the poet to express all this in his unusual garden is surprise caused by exceptional, erudite, and playful presences in an arrangement planned by a *gardener* capable of making even the most ordinary plant in a damp area seem precious.

From the landscape-design point of view, the two pictures in the middle express the desire to contrast the front of a garden, with its highly cultivated aspect, with the back, the part near the water where growth is apparently governed by nature alone. The signs that alternate with the plant landscape are moral communications (such as the pictorial and scenic criticism mentioned above) of a type that existed in gardens of the past, perhaps in the form of a presage of a future state of desolation. This is also true of Albrecht Dürer's monogram. But sometimes a figure is also an experiment of new and tiny material quantities to be included in a garden. The china mosaic writing is an example. The stone boats stuck on columns, or floating motionless in the water, are part of the playful category.

PLATE 185

In 1883 William Robinson published in London a book called *The English Flower Garden* which, apart from confirming his fame, made it possible for him (along with the income from his earlier publications) to buy a two hundred acre estate in 1884 where he created his unusual garden. *The English Flower Garden* was reprinted fifteen times before Robinson died, but he was also famous for the magazines he ran, in particular for *The Garden*, a weekly published from 1871 to 1919, for the periodical *Gardening Illustrated* published from 1879 to 1919, and for *Flora and Sylva* (1903-1905).

This picture comes from *The English Flower Garden*, which came out thirteen years after another book of Robinson's titled *Alpine Flowers for English Gardens*, which in a certain sense was its forerunner since it was about "all the plants best suited for its embellishment." In this illustration, flowers planted in the border and growing informally are the real stars of the garden. Robinson developed the thesis that both in the landscape of a large park and in that of a tiny garden, flowering plants with their cyclical development should be considered as the central part of the gardener's activity. The gardener was to select self-sufficient species that grew freely. On these grounds, any keenly conscious gardener could form and run a garden of the kind proposed by the current aesthetic and scenic revolution. This was the reason for Robinson's success and popularity and, consequently, for the almost clone-like spread of the principles and taste of his own garden, which the owners of gardens large and small looked to as a kind of model of perfection for their inspiration. Success brought Robinson, a man of lower class origins, the respect of high society, but he was never really accepted by it. Some touching photographs portray Robinson in his garden at Gravetye, which grew over time to more than one thousand acres, inside a pavilion near the house with his nurses, posing in a wheelchair with a rug over his legs, or sitting in his special caterpillar Citroên, which he used to travel round the park in his old age.

PLATE 186

William Robinson (1838-1935) was the leader of the renewal of the idea of the English garden after the inebriation of the historicist experience in the second half of the nineteenth century. His capacity to put the plant world and not the geometrical forms that imprisoned flowers back into center stage gave everyone in Britain who did not possess a castle as a backdrop to a *parterre de broderie* the chance to look after their own garden, however small it was.

William Robinson had been to France at the time of Napoleon III to study the organization of the urban public gardens recently introduced and run by Adolphe Alphand. The result of this journey was the publication of his first two books in 1868 and 1869 which were significant for the level of the analysis and critical approach. Immediately after these, in 1870 (the year he visited America), Robinson published *The Wild Garden*, a book which destroyed previous convictions and opened the way in English and, at a later date and in a different way, in European gardens to the aesthetics of the wild garden that was easily practicable for gardeners. Ten years later Robinson included some highly eloquent engravings in the book, which had been elaborated together with Alfred Parsons. This is one of them. Geometrical forms of human creation were excluded from the wild garden. The plant composition was artfully arranged and planted by man and then left to grow naturally in a wild state which would have brought about the desired landscape effects. Plant life, which appeared artificially but without any form of cultivation, and the emotion it transmitted were the features that characterized this new garden. It brought the theoretical and practical principles of the landscape and picturesque garden to their extreme consequences in the direction of a perceptive totality. In 1871 Robinson wrote two catalogs, *A Catalogue of Hardy Perennials* and *Hardy Flowers* which classified all the plants that could be used in British gardens. But there was nothing abstract or dispassionate about his method, as the plants were included with the aim of creating a wild garden.

Mea Allan, William Robinson, 1838-1935, Father of the English Flower Garden, London 1982.

PLATE 187

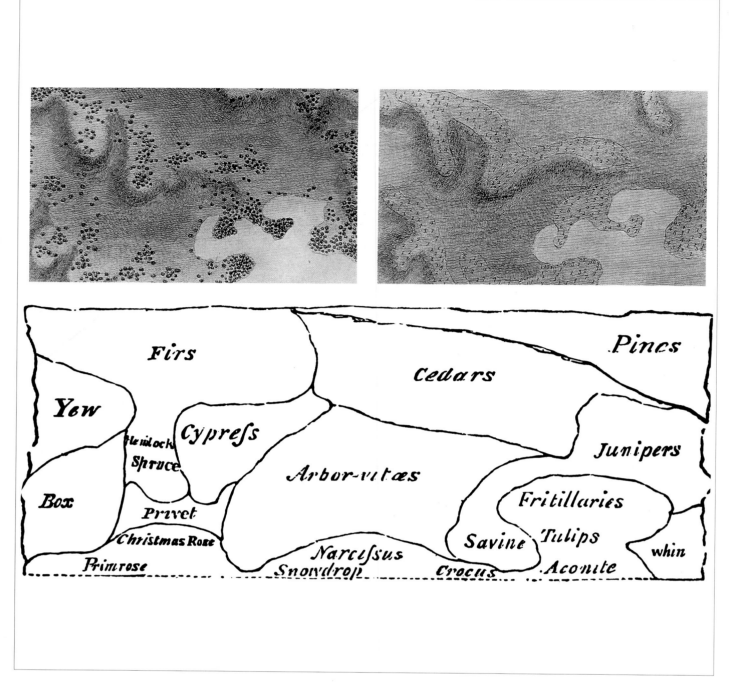

The two illustrations at the top of the page come from John Claudius Loudon's book, *A Treatise on Forming, Improving and Managing Country Residences...*, dated 1806. They prove that this conscientious and scientific botanical gardener was proposing for the elaboration of projects something radically different from the meager plans or perspective sketches that had been in fashion for nearly a century.

A mere plan or sketch for a project made the choice of a particular species, or of one plant compared to another of the same species, a simple consequence of the actual formation of a garden. On the contrary these two engravings, conversely, showing the same site, are complementary figures: both are necessary and indispensable for considering, elaborating, and setting out a project of a new garden. The top drawing is the landscape plan, the lower one gives the botanical outline where every number refers to a species. The designer of a project of this kind had to be a landscape gardener (and this could, to a certain extent, have been enough three-quarters of a century earlier, when the species used in English gardens were relatively few). But now the designer had to have a specific knowledge of botany with reference to the landscape (also because Loudon himself had calculated that more than thirteen thousand species were being used in Britain at the time). Loudon's drawing presents in a complete and legible way the whole conceptual and mental process that gives birth to a project. This was a cultural innovation for that period and foreshadowed future landscape design methods. The figure at the bottom of the page was also drawn by Loudon, but at a later date than the two above. It applied the same principle but utilized the method of the amoebic circumscription of areas to be planted with groups of plants to form a wood. In this case, the plan is not explicitly a landscape design but a technical and botanical one that could be understood by an ordinary gardener as well. The description of the species, their quantitative and qualitative composition, and their interdependencies helped a gardener grasp completely and immediately the idea of the project in the same way that a musician reads a score and instantly translates it into its musical performance.

PLATE 188

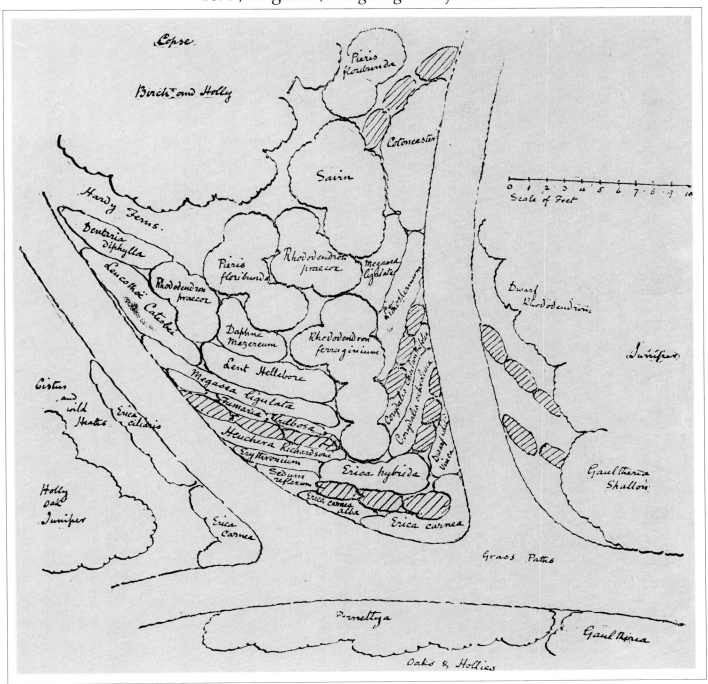

Gertrude Jekyll (1843-1932) was a gardener and a garden designer as well as an author of books steeped in the British tradition that were remarkably instructive and very useful for gardeners. While spreading her ideas on gardens, they also revealed her multiple activities. She came from an upper-middle-class Victorian family and developed the proposals made by William Robinson without ever explicitly declaring herself his pupil.

Gertrude Jekyll's ideas developed through the study of painting, decoration, the history of art, and the theory of colors, which were fundamental for her work as a gardener. She knew the most interesting intellectuals of the time, including Ruskin and Morris. When she bought Munstead Wood in 1899 she commissioned the then twenty-year-old Edwin Lutyens to build the house, and together they designed the garden. Up to 1914 this unofficial partnership (Jekyll & Lutyens) designed about one hundred gardens. Gertrude Jekyll became famous for this work, for the articles she wrote for influential and well-known magazines (Robinson's *The Garden*, and *Country Life*), and for her fifteen books. The first of these that contributed to her rise to fame was *Wood and Garden*, which was published in London in 1899. The book analyzed the relationship between garden and wood, and illustrated the continuity of the interaction of garden and landscape (a special characteristic of English history and culture) in a new way. *Wood and Garden* gave the impression of being difficult to understand, but in reality it contained operative and contemplative programs that everyone could grasp. It taught how to appreciate the garden and wood as they extended and merged together due to the landscape's changes month after month. A knowledgeable gardener could enjoy the seasonal alteration of the landscape even during the months when the habitual contemplation of the garden was usually neglected. Another book, which seemed easy to understand and which was instead very difficult to fully comprehend and to put into practice, was *Colour Schemes for the Flower Garden* which was published in London in 1914. This picture is an illustration from it. The theory of the color border expounded in the book was to bring the British flower garden to its conceptual and aesthetic peak.

*Ursula Buchan, *An Anthology of Garden Writing*, London 1986; Jane Brown, *The English Garden in Our Time, from Gertrude Jekyll to Geoffrey Jellicoe*, London 1986.

PLATE 189

Victoria (Vita) Sackville-West (1892-1962) and Christopher Lloyd (b. 1921) are the two extraordinary English gardeners who brought the idea of the modern garden to its highest and perhaps unsurpassable level with the formation and running of their mythical gardens. They saw the garden as a work of art. Their activity, their books, and their journalistic contributions won them enormous popularity based on undeniable authority.

Vita Sackville-West was of upper-class origins and spent her childhood in a large castle surrounded by gardens and woods. This refined literary friend of Virginia Woolf, whose novel *Orlando* (1930) was inspired by Vita, was a self-taught landscape gardener. When in later life she undertook the planting of Sissinghurst Castle, her home, she did it with great professionalism, cultivating the garden "as one cultivates life." From 1947 to 1961 she wrote a column every week in *The Observer* and no gardener since then has ignored her ideas. Her garden was donated to the National Trust and is still thriving. A posthumous collection of some of the articles from that exceptional column was published in London in 1968 under the title *Vita Sackville-West's Garden Book,* and it has already reached its thirteenth edition in Britain, as well as being translated into numerous foreign languages. Christopher Lloyd inherited his garden from his father, an architect. He had invited Edwin Lutyens to design the whole property so that the resulting refined model would

be a stimulus to his activity. Carrying forward Vita Sackville-West's idea of the garden as a unique work of art, Lloyd has cultivated his garden, just a few miles away from Sissinghurst, with rare sensibility and equal refinement. His garden soon became a point of reference for botanists and gardeners (including Vita Sackville-West) because of the new and creative relationship he expressed between botany and landscape. The garden cloned a multitude of figures consistent with the landscape in a vast area around it, almost as if its qualities had *formed their own cultural territory.* Lloyd's enormous popularity is due to his work as a gardener, a kind of magical great work, and to his best-selling books at home and abroad (*The Well-Tempered Garden* and *The Adventurous Gardener* published in London in 1970 and 1983; and *The Year at Great Dixter*, centered on the logic of seasonal contemplation, published in London in 1987). Christopher Lloyd has also written a famous column, *In My Garden*, in *Country Life* since 1963.

PLATE 190

Nobody ever thought that the independence of the British culture and practice of the garden could be affected by an impertinent foreign incursion. But in recent years it has been stirred by a Mediterranean and Italian influence. Ippolito Pizzetti (b. 1926) is a gardener and a landscape gardener, and his writings have made him well-known in Italy and Europe, and in Great Britain in particular, as an authoritative explorer and practitioner of an old lore of European origin.

Together with Henry Cocker (of the Kew Gardens school, honorable member of the Royal Horticultural Society, who was responsible from 1939 for the cultural management of the garden of Villa Taranto on Lake Maggiore created by the Scottish captain, Neil McEacharn), Ippolito Pizzetti wrote *The Book of Flowers*, published in Milan in 1968. This is perhaps the only book concerning the culture of gardening at least partially produced by an Italian author that has been published in Italy and translated for a British edition. In Italy there are no authoritative newspapers or periodicals ready to accept and guarantee the continuity of a gardener's column. In order to spread his ideas, Ippolito Pizzetti has had to rely on various weeklies (a collection of his articles has been published under the title *Pollice Verde*, Milan 1982), reviews, and publishing series. Pizzetti has written that "a garden is even more a garden when it is not crammed with various and rare plants and flowers and other ornaments, but is full of events... In my opinion a garden is not just made of trees and plants, or even by its design, it is made of the many things, the plant life and the animal life, that live in it." With similar logic he has criticized the recent, unfortunately widespread, practice tending to saturate urban green space with architectonic forms, by asserting that "a park is a park is a park is a park." His theory of urban plantation aims to widen the cultural outlook of a gardener to include the metropolitan dimension by using trees not just for simple decorative purposes, but as an organizational factor of the whole of the existing plant elements in their relationship with the city, its spaces, and its buildings. In an analysis of the state of the trees in Rome, Pizzetti wrote: "As we know, plants do not have legs or other organs of locomotion, and they cannot move if they want to; nor do they have a voice to say whether they like or dislike the place that we have chosen for them." Ippolito Pizzetti is shown here in a drawing from a book of portraits of European gardeners being prepared by Valentino Parmiani.

PLATE 191

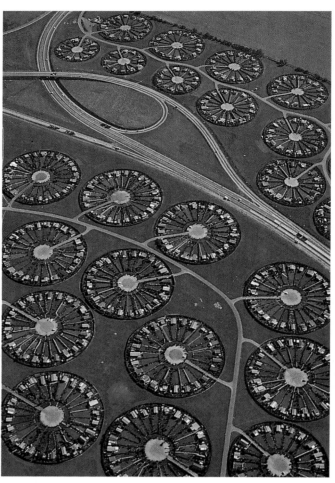

After the nineteenth-century experience of public gardens and tree-lined boulevards, and the debatable areas of *organized green space*, modern European cities are awaiting some new aesthetic and cultural developments in their gardens and parks. The time has come for parks and urban gardens in European cities to *leap their fence*. A great deal of the agricultural land around the metropolises is no longer economically and socially viable. It could become a landscape, turning the utopia of the never-ending garden into reality.

These two aerial pictures taken by Georg Gerster show two peripheral scenes: Swiss urban allotments and one-family homes in Denmark. One can optimistically believe that even the culture of the great European gardeners, and the British in particular, may somehow take root in these little plots of land and blossom in an original way. Unfortunately there is no guaranteeing it. The European version of the American park movement was a poor imitation: the garden-city theory was a provincial phenomenon and was unable to produce anything on a par with Central Park in New York. Contemporary gardeners seem to be rather hesitant in their outlook, whereas the emphatic way of considering a park as the site for merely architectonic design has taken great leaps forward. Today the garden must evidently compete in the historical centers and in the infinite suburbs with the urban environment of the great metropolises that have grown out of all proportion. Georges Perec discussed this (in *Espèces d'espace*, Paris 1974)

and quoted the banal comments of Bouvard and Pécuchet written in the sketches for Flaubert's unfinished novel: "Paris will become the winter garden; espaliers of fruit-trees in the boulevards. The Seine, filtered and warm..." The contribution that a park or garden can make to the improvement of a city is unlimited. This is the reason why European gardeners must succeed as soon as possible in founding and spreading a new culture with qualities capable of transforming and overcoming the ideological and technical narrow-mindedness that infests the municipal apparatus. The current, very complicated situation could give rise to a new idea of the garden for European cities, creating a strong and interactive relationship with wider landscapes.

*Georg Gerster, *La terre de l'homme*, Zurich 1975; *Geschichte des Stadtgrüns*, Band I, Dieter Hennebo, *Entwicklung des Stadtgrüns von der Antike bis in die zeit des Absolutismus*, Band II, Heinz Wiegand, *Entwicklung des Stadtgru/ns in Deutschland zwischen 1890 und 1925 am Beispiel der Arbeiten Fritz Enckes*, Band III, Dieter Hennebo - Erika Schmidt, *Entwicklung des Stadtgrüns in England*, Band IV, Dorothee Nehring, *Stadtparkanlagen in der ersten Hälfte des 19. Jahrhunderts. Ein Beitrag zur Kulturgeschichte des Landschaftsgartens*, Berlin 1979; Georg Gerster, *Le pain et le sel*, Zurich 1980.

PLATE 192

Bibliography

Paaw, P., *Hortus publicus Academiae Lugduno-Batavae...*, Leyden 1601

Marriot, John, *Knots for Gardens*, London 1623

Boyceau, Jacques, *Traité du jardinage, selon les raisons de la nature et de l'art*, Paris 1638

Mollet, André, *Les jardins de plaisir...*, Paris 1651

Austen, Ralph, *A Treatise of Fruit-Trees*, together with *The Spiritual Use of an Orchard*, Oxford 1653

Commelin, J., *The Belgick or Netherlandish Hesperides, that in the Management Ordering, and Use of the Limon and Orange Trees*, 1683

Hermann, P., *Paradisi Batavi prodromus sive plantarum exoticarum in Batavorum hortis observatarum index*, Leyden 1689

La Quintine, Jean de, *The Compleat Gard'ner*, London 1693

Van der Groen, J., *Der Nederlantsen Hovenier*, Amsterdam 1696, 1721

Nourse, Timothy, *Campania Foelix*, London 1700

Liger, Louis, *Le jardinier fleuriste*, Amsterdam 1706

Addison, Joseph, *An Essay on the Pleasures of the Garden*, in "The Spectator" n° 477, 1712

Pope, Alexander, *Essay on Verdant Sculpture*, in "The Guardian" n° 173, 1713

Temple, William, *Upon the Gardens of Epicurus, or of Gardening in the Year 1685*, 1720

Brouiers de Niedek, Mattheus, *Les délices de Water Graef on Diemer-Meer*, Amsterdam 1725

Morris, Robert, *An Essay upon Harmony*, London 1739

Halfpenny, William, *New Designs for Chinese Temples, Triumphal Arches, Garden Seats, Palings & C.*, London 1750

Mason, William, *An Heroic Epistle to Sir W. Chambers*, 1757

Mason, George, *An Essay on Design in Gardening*, 1768

Walpole, Horace, *Essay on Modern Gardening*, (1770), 1785

Whateley, Thomas, *Observations on Modern Gardening*, (1770), 1785

Addison, Joseph, *Description of a Garden in the Natural Style*, in "The Spectator" n° 477, 1711-1712

Whately, Thomas, *L'art de former les jardins modernes ou l'art des jardins anglais*, Paris 1771

Chambers, William, *A Dissertation on Oriental Gardening*, 1772

Mason, William, *The English Garden. A Poem*, 1772

Watelet, Claude-Henry, *Essai sur les jardins*, Paris 1774

Gerardin, René-Louis, *De la composition des paysages...*, Genève 1777

Charles, Le Prince de Lign, *Coup d'oeil sur Beloeil et sur une grande partie des jardins de l'Europe*, 1781

Cozens, Alexander, *A New Method of Assisting the Invention in Drawing Original Compositions of Landscape*, London 1785

Marulli, Vincenzo, *L'arte di ordinare i giardini*, Napoli 1804

Lalos, J., *De la composition des parcs et jardins pittoresques*, Paris 1817

Sckell, Friedrich Ludwig, *Beiträge zur Bildenden Gartenkunst*, München 1825

Johnson, George W., *A History of English Gardening*, London 1829

Dennis, J., *The Landscape Gardener*, London 1835

Ernouf, Alfred-Auguste, *L'art des jardins, histoire, théorie, pratique...*, Paris 1868

Hibberd, Shirley, *The Fern Garden*, London 1869

Lefèvre, André, *Les parcs et les jardins*, Paris, 1871

Hazlitt, W.C., *Gleanings in Old Garden Literature*, London 1887

Jäger, H., *Gartenkunst und Gärte sonst und jetzt*, Berlin 1888

Joret, C., *La rose dans l'antiquité et au moyen age*, Paris 1892

Amherst, Alicia, *A History of Gardening in England*, London 1895

Joret, C., *Les plantes dans l'antiquité et au moyen age*, Bouillon 1904

Triggs, H. Inigo, *The Art of Garden Design in Italy*, London, New York, Bombay 1906

Loisel, G., *Histoire des ménageries de l'antiquité à nos jours*, Paris 1912

Triggs, H. Inigo, *Garden Craft in Europe*, London 1913

Gothein, Marie Luise, *Geschichte der Gartenkunst*, Jena 1914

Dami, Luigi, *Il giardino italiano*, Milano 1924

Charageat, Marguerite, *L'art des jardins*, Paris 1930

Comune di Firenze, *Mostra del giardino italiano*, catalogue, Firenze 1931

Sinclair Rohde, Eleanour, *The Story of the Garden*, London 1932

Gromort, G., *L'art des jardins*, Paris 1934

Bienfait, Anna G., *Oude Hollandsche Tuinen*, 'S-Gravenhage 1943

Chase, Isabel W.U., *Horace Walpole: Gardenist*, Princeton 1943

Allinger, Gustav, *Der Deutsche Garten*, München 1950

Siren, O., *China and Gardens of Europe in the XVIIIth Century*, New York 1950

Hautecoeur, L., *Les jardins des dieux et des hommes*, Paris 1959

Masson, Georgina, *Italian Gardens*, London 1961

Berckenhagen, Ekhart, *Deutsche Gärten vor 1800*, Hannover, Berlin, Sarstedt 1962

Berrall, Julia, *The Garden*, London 1966

Clifford, Derek, *A History of Garden Design*, 1966

Fariello, Francesco, *Architettura dei giardini*, Roma 1967

Pevsner, Nikolaus, *Studies in Art, Architecture and Design*, London 1968

Woodbridge, Kenneth, *Landscape and Antiquity*, Oxford 1970

Assunto, Rosario, *Il paesaggio e l'estetica*, Napoli 1973

Casa Valdés, Marquesa de, *Jardines de España*, Madrid 1973

Morel, Jean-Marie, *Théorie des jardins*, Genève 1973

Grimal, Pierre, *L'art des jardins*, Paris 1974

Hunt, John Dixon; Willis, Peter, *The Genius of the Place. The English Landscape Garden 1620-1820*, London 1975

AA.VV., *Jardins et paysages: le style anglais*, Lille 1977

AA.VV., *Jardins en France*, Paris 1977

Brownell, M.R., *Alexander Pope and the Arts of Georgian England*, Oxford 1978

Comito, Terry, *The Idea of the Garden in the Renaissance*, New Brunswick 1978

Cowell, Frank Richard, *Gartenkunst. Von der Antike bis zur Gegenwart*, Stuttgart, Zürich 1978

Cowell, Frank Richard, *The Garden as a Fine Art*, London 1978

Huxley, Anthony, *An Illustrated History of Gardening*, New York & London 1978

Adams, William Howard, *The French Garden 1500-1800*, New York 1979

Harris, John, The Garden. *A Celebration of One Thousand Years of British Gardening*, London 1979

King, Ronald, *The Quest for Paradise*, Surrey 1979

Thacker, Christopher, *The History of Gardens*, London 1979

Adams, William Howard, *Les jardins en France*, Paris 1980

Buttlar, Adrian von, *Der Landschaftsgarten*, München 1980

Fleming, Laurence; Gore, Alan, *The English Garden*, London 1980

Hadfield, Miles; Harling, Robert; Highton, Leonie, *British Gardeners*, London 1980

Heyer, Hans-Rudolf, *Historische Gärten der Schweiz*, Bern 1980

Dennerlein, Ingrid, *Die Gartenkunst der Régence und des Rokoko in Frankreich*, Worms 1981

Grandes et petites heures du Parc Monceau, Paris 1981

Prest, John, *The Garden of Eden*, New Haven, London 1981

Watkin, David, *The English Vision*, London 1982

Baltrusaitis, Jurgis, *Aberrations: essai sur la légende des formes*, Paris 1983

Hansmann, Wilfried, *Gartenkunst der Reinaissance und des Barock*, Köln 1983

Thomas, Keith, *Man and the Natural World. Changing Attitudes in England 1500- 1800*, London 1983

Desmond, Ray, *Bibliography of British Gardens*, Dorchester 1984

Hunt, John Dixon, *Garden and Grove.. The Italian Renaissance Garden in the English Imagination 1600-1750*, London 1986

Shepherd, J.C.; Jellicoe, Geoffrey.A., *Italians Gardens of the Renaissance*, London 1986

Vercelloni, Matteo, *Il paradiso terrestre*, Milano 1986

Carita, Helder; Cardoso, Homen, *Jardins em Portugal*, 1987

Jellicoe, Geoffrey; Jellicoe, Susan, *The Landscape of Man*, London 1987

Mader, Günter; Neubert-Mader, Laila, *Italianische Gärten*, Fribourg 1987

Bazin, Germain, *L'art du jardin*, Bienne 1988

Hunt, John Dixon, *The Anglo-Dutch Garden in the Age of William and Mary*, London 1988

Jacques, David; Van der Horst, Arend Jan, *The Gardens of William and Mary*, Bromley 1988

Tagliolini, Alessandro, *Storia del giardino italiano*, Firenze 1988

Ganay, Ernest de, *Bibliographie de l'art des jardins*, Paris 1989

Index of names, places and themes